MY THESIS

STANDING ON THE
SHOULDERS OF GOD

JOSEPH DONNELLY

Inquiries and Book Orders should be addressed to:

Great Writers Media
Email: info@greatwritersmedia.com
Phone: (302) 918-5570

ISBN: 978-1-960605-85-6 (sc)
ISBN: 978-1-960605-99-3 (ebk)

CONTENTS

PART ONE

Chapter 1: Religions First - One..7

Chapter 2: Religions First - Two 11

Chapter 3: Religions First - Three...20

Chapter 4: Politics Second - One..27

Chapter 5: Politics Second - Two 33

Chapter 6: Politics Second - Three..43

Chapter 7: Science Third - One...45

Chapter 8: Science Third - Two 49

Chapter 9: Science Third - Three..54

Chapter 10: Science Third - Four 58

Chapter 11: Science Third - Five 63

PART TWO

Chapter 12: Introduction To The Future 71

Chapter 13: The Last Experiment..73

Chapter 14: The Second Reunion..77

Chapter 15: The Round Table 81

Chapter 16: In The Real Beginning 85

Chapter 17: Proving The God Particle Theory...............................90

Chapter 18: The God Particle Theory..94

Chapter 19: The Active God Particle Theory 99

PART THREE

Chapter 20: Standing On The Shoulders Of God.......................105

Chapter 21: God Is, So Let Him Know.....................................108

Chapter 22: Heaven 1 And Heaven 2.......................................114

Chapter 23: Hell, Heaven Two 121

Chapter 24: Behind The Door...129

Afterword 1 133

Afterword 2 (A)..152

Afterword 2 (B) 160

Afterword 2 (C) 162

Afterword 3..167

Epilogue...170

Synopsis...187

SECTION TWO

My Conclusions 209

Section 2 Afterword 285

SECTION THREE (A)

Our Conclusions Post 14/04/2022, Real Time. 295

SECTION THREE (B)

The Silent Enemy..307

SECTION THREE (C)

The Penultimate Corner..317

My Lead To Revilations...324

My Book Of Revilations..328

PART ONE

CHAPTER 1

Religions First - One

THERE ARE BUT TWO GODS, humanity and God. So why might we of humanity in our true name species, hold and maintain ten thousand different world religions. Which by tone, most refer to be in the service of God.

Bar mistakes, in this our work, I will set all records strait. For I have gained the insight to know God better than he. By then to show understanding of how we all begin to belong together on Gods terms set by us of humanity first, even first religiously.

Not least because it must come from the likes of us in our true species form to set God to task. For his sake then ours, for which I will give chapter and verse how this can be done, as to the why it must be so. Based on the tiny principle, every single living human being ever, at one time stood shoulder to shoulder with God.

From when we realised God was indeed an entity, we formed our religious groups in serious intention these past four or five thousand years. With other substantial godly links pre those time marks.

By the simplest of realisations, I came to understand nothing begot nothing. Leading me to think in terms of the how and why we of humanity broke all the assumed codes of conduct. By how we managed to associate time passing in ways no other creature species gave signs of.

Therefore, it must be us, you and me, to set all standards. So, God in form can measure his own intentions, of which he is not yet self-aware of. Not least because some of humanity have been almost foolhardy to deny God in concept. Therefore, in repair, it is for all of us, that means all of us, no matter how we self classify, to set God in task. Which means but one thing generally.

We of humanity are to form in rational time and of rational mind. A style of approach to thwart God by stimulating him in no small way or of no serious cost to him or us. How stands on a realisation, which can only enliven God to our project. But in caution, we must be aware while still practicing all our daily traits. Our intention is not to draw God to or sway God in our personal plans.

All we must do for another first in all histories, is present God with the apex fate accompli. Whereby we impose our achievements on God as the ultimate end product of his hoped-for outcome of time passing.

We of humanity without any formal attempt, are to ready our conduct and thinking to astound God without effort. Which will stand on one factor only, bound by God's own time line. After all, he set the clock running.

Without demand I allow for no abstaining to my offering, but in case of. I will have to ungraciously charge such people who do not follow this ultimate plan for humanity. Bearing in mind we will each hold the same input to our final offering before we set God's task.

Plus, to remember, we are not officially testing God, all we are doing is helping God relax and take things a little easier. For at long last his only possible aim is closer to realisation. Which is not a statement of completion or acceptance.

My lean stands on the premiss, we of humanity will be the first lifeform to release Gods own genie. For there has always been more to God than we ever knew. Even though we tried to get his ear some ten thousand times religiously. More seriously we can now update to suit our time to imagination, meaning for all time.

Although for the past four or five thousand years, which tells its own story, when we first rigidly came to God above theory. It is only in the modernity of now we can set new horizons.

Having already cleared many hurdles on our behalf, at last we are prepared to accept God as God. Even under our own prompt, we can now go on and justify why and how I came to such conclusions.

I have titled myself I, not for aggrandisement. Simply to limit the reflection of I not to be taken as me over we if by others, who may think I am in competition with them. About how God should be viewed by any of us who believe in God for our separate sakes as if we are not of the one species humanity.

I follow no channels except those to be created by others if for their own ends. My total claim of excellence is in the name species, our human species. For when I set standards, they are not just mine. All have been suffered into place by the stalwart of humanity.

In far too many cases, those who have and still suffer at the hands of fellow human beings. Never to give up the concept of God, who when counted are my foundation to be able and progress. They allowed people such as me and you continue. Even if not to have helped them, we try to limit or alleviate the cause of their/our misery. Alas on their behalf I hold check for a moment. There is much to do before we can improve nationally, let alone before we can task God.

For us to help all the disadvantaged people of our species throughout the world. We must at first pivot all religions to this one task, not least because we are going to bring God to life on our terms, which means his terms.

So not to be lost in logical semantics, when I set our human species to my plan. My statement can be realised when to include all members of all nation states to be the same species. Those same people who hold ten thousand different world religions, most built around the/a God supremacy theme.

Although we are each wise and cleaver enough to give our God credit for our situation. All we must do in this case, my case, is accept the real supremacy of God for his sake. Which will show a class of generosity to bewilder God.

For in any state of mind, God did not heed all religious philosophies, only some maybe. Which becomes a human tribal point of reference, whereby some of us separated God to our desires or did we.

Historically by whatever means and how. God did contact and indicate to various individuals in the past in seeming, his interest in some of them/us. Never to be fully explained even by God. He was never sure why he was interested in any group if represented by the individual that caught his eye. So why did he leave motive for some individuals or groups to enjoy and display his shown interest, even over ten thousand times.

Fortunately, we can give real living insights if we set in comfort to the realisation of why and how the universe is 13.8 billion years old. Then what is our single role per the individual, the clan, tribe, group, national, different skin coloured people. Who all may only average a national lifespan of less than one hundred years. Against the known length of time owed to the universe as it developed.

With God already having shown and expressed his interest to some of us historically, hence we were able and create some of our world religions. Though not all were set by God, with many following the good example of other core religious setups.

Unfortunately, in or from that huge conglomerate of pious fortitude. Some groups sought, even if in God's name. To limit the expansion if forced, of how some religious doctrine. In order to expand or to defend their standing with God, action was needed.

Battle could be entered so no infringement to their/our doctrine was encountered. Although claimed to protect God's sanctity. Sometimes if to increase their/our standing faith, by destroying those who would destroy us in God's name. By our victory we might force some of the vanquished to boost our faith numbers as an alternative to death by murder or sacrifice which might now seem to be ungodly.

All to do from today post the year 2020, to curtail or fully ban such unconnected reasoning. Is set here and now a new primary religious standard. Which returns the emphasis of how and why we must now set God his second/first role since time began.

CHAPTER 2

Religions First - Two

I T CAN NEVER BE ARGUED God did not make his presence known at various times throughout human history. To deny God in concept is not an argument. It is an open presentation of those who are blind ignorant. For which I enter into second and third place the importance we of humanity will now set for how our politics works. Along with how the study of the sciences proceeds', both open to improvement.

By all modern essentials those factors of science and politics. Have contributed more to our personal self-destruct mode to deny God in our name. So, in quick and positive reply, I set this our first order for all religions to send to God in representation. We of religious persuasions, admit and now subscribe to the one and only religious role, to maintain and increase God's interest in us of humanity, all.

Whereby above all the efforts and or how the medium of science is now being presented to us for her own ends. I take in our species name to set before God the one formula. Which can only be read from the human emotional perspective. Enough so to enhance the standard of God.

For we of humanity are the only species or event ever to have occurred, to be able and rationalise God to us. But far more importantly, God to God, for we dare now, while standing on God's shoulders, to take him by the hand and set his task.

Which I set from a human perspective only. Bestowed upon us in our species form by us alone and never God. It was we who discovered God and never the reverse, except by interest. My claim by number stands in part to the fact we have created ten thousand world religions, with many of no consequence. How I can justify such an outrageous statement stands on one religious principle only, which is nearly this.

I give no quarter to any named or claimed group who set to deny even query my next fixed uttering. Set to be a statement of all future political directives. For in class my religious standard is post haste to be adopted by all political regimes active throughout the world today.

I cede to politics only one part of self-control of my plan, but on terms that any counter measures must include my symbol of, open bracket, question mark, close bracket (?). As an ultimate benchmark we are all to be religiously inclined from now on. which means we are all to stand on the shoulders of God.

For our ten thousand religions to take on the study of God and enhance the reality of God. All to do is for all groups to follow one ruling. So, to become the cornerstone of how we can now better face the future futuristically. Because in all realities, most of our ten thousand world religions had almost got things right. By entering the/our/their conceptual idea of types of afterlife owed to all of humanity ongoing.

My plan of to add, (?) my symbol representing God, can only enhance the same formula when written so. Formula + (?) or (?) + formula, to become a fixed narrative. Which is counterbalanced by the obvious. God will attend to us after life, now he has been given licence by us to draw up his plan.

Endorsed by us of the species humanity, contained by the smallest of our differences with all other creature species. Ably expressed by how we aspired to create ten thousand different reasons of why we are here, at least self-representing.

Pre the necessary examination I will present to make our case. My, to be our first standard to lay before God and hold his interest. Plus, to set all political systems on the same path we have pursued these past four or five thousand years religiously. Almost begins in our normal life parameters, already set relative to us individually. Who all have the approximate 80 plus years of living to contend with, plus to act and react in.

So, if religions really attend to God as we say, he can bear further interest in us all by our term species of the human genre. Which will be the first from all other creature species ever included evolutionary. To be able and express an emotion outside of their own capacity to understand its intent even reason, which will eventually unlock all dreams.

If and I assert again, I have demanded we all take on the hazard of accepting the concept of God. Then for us to chime God to our collective interest over that shown before to some individuals, plus to sanitise any claim to God from any quarter. We must use our collective religious platform to begin my/our plea.

To avoid claim and counter claim by the disheartened from any religious or political camps. My first new religious standard will for now determine the very status of how religions can be defined in the future. Also, my adage will have a huge bearing on how politics can be set.

Our/my primary new religious code stands as a maxim. Holding so much force and power to be able and redefine how we can determine the sincerity of any religion in the future. For my maxim is designed to draw God's interest to all who follow my religious version of it.

Not least for the first time in real history, we will have set God to work in tandem with something we found out thousands of years ago. Even though we only have our individual lifespan to experience life so far, my new up to the minuet maxim draws us together from the past and into the future.

My simple maxim is this, to be set in stone. Whereby the defining doctrine of any true religion in God's name. Is that all religions, based on the main principle they are led by doctrine. Therefore, they carry the first order of conduct individually religiously under review but contained by doctrine.

Hence from now, their first new primary standing order for each religion is to bring all adherents and followers in name. to "Natural

Body Death from old age", now, displaying equal doctrine only. Plus, to run on the understanding, no single person within our/my religion will have suffered the indignity of being enslaved, of being used, intimidated, tortured or of being bullied even discounted or worse. Making the true statement to lay before God a unique plan.

Whereby, we religiously set a standard worthy of the most advanced species in the universe. Big and bold enough to now lead God in how he can meet the challenge of dealing with the full product of his time in waiting, we the ultimate species of/in the. Who at last first, might have cut a trail for God to use again if we are wrong?

With God being God and taking 13.8 billion years to aimlessly gather the information of how the universe formed. With no one to tell the why, how or because of, what can I/God do, but never interfere on your own account. For that would delude 13.8 billion years of time by another name.

So what now if we hinted God at his own intention, we the only species who can now set God's rational. Not least because for four or five thousand years, we of humanity had been trying to link our religions some way or the other to God's reality. Never to what I have so far realised now, to the cause and matter of why we came to religion in the first place.

Plus, blindingly, never to realise we as the one species we are, even then ago, had already really come to God just like now. For then ago by coming to God in the guise of any religion we followed, even if to have created the phenomena spread among many religions of like structure. Whereby if and when we die or when dead, God on our say so could finish our story at Gods behest in heaven.

Which is the true wrong accolade all or most religions deserve. For we through the idea of or with how we set their philosophy. Broke from the normalities of how other species seemed to operate, open to later examination if required.

With other creature species seeming only to operate on the one premiss, to propagate as a means to a new beginning, compared to our aspirational footprint, which meant more than to renew. It is for us only to set the why.

Our great trick even unknown, was formed if through our basic religious codes of following the life conduct concept, leading to a post life result. Necessitating the need for a better mediator than we knew of, to tidy all the loose ends up. Bound with the great plus, our human species began to recognise how other creature species were tied to bland instinct. Being the foundation procreation was built on.

So, in essence, our split or separate courses could be balanced in equality. By fitting all other creature species into one cup named procreation and natural instinct. With us, humanity, in the other cup still carrying instinct, but with our breakaway religious aspirations aspired.

Not to overemphasise, to aspire means of God. If we aspire and other creature species do not. Only means they are not on the same wavelength about God as we are. Because we endorse their standing of natural instinct, then they in all cases can also aspire. But not on the same scale instinct applies to us. Which by good cause keeps us with them to also be a part of God's plan when we show God, but on different lines than us.

Which is a freedom clause for God, if he becomes confused about how he has waited to be made aware by one species only. He can count time in its proper role to have been an event with an aim he created 13.8 billion years ago. Even if to not understand why or what for. Because as of then even until now, he had no role model nor so a form, shape or size from which to start.

If God never had or knew of how to set a standard about anything, it has now been set by me. Who by definition is us, because of our true common ground set by our species make up. Exemplified by one small factor, which when reviewed, shows the measure of our true excellence. Displayed again and again on all levels of our makeup, further endorsing our high quality of differences to other creatures in the same timeline.

By giving those or this single example, will be shown why I on our behalf have been able and differentiate on how we came to God and others did not. Further, so my standard stands for every other creature living or dead. Who could have formed their own genre of being a specified species type.

Specified already defined, but for aesthetics and to set a standard, even to be unique. Our human singularity is profound, we unlike those of pure instinct. Have the open ability to apply our single lifespan experiences to include our own ancestors' trails or footprint, to be our own if needed.

When other species propagate to a single lifespan plan. We reproduce to extend our original form of how we first aspired four or five thousand years ago. By updating those uncalled for aspirations, whereby we were to become the only event of 13.8 billion years. To be able and account for that single timespan over and above the cause of it.

Being an event beyond description until the year of twenty twelve, highlighted by this same human species. Although the event of twenty twelve carries a lot of weight, it is not the full amount of support we will need to show God was in fact an element in his own right.

What the event insured was to endorse our, my, your proof of God. Could be achieved by the only other element to hold sway in the universe. Even when to consider we the human species we are. Were formed in form through the unrelated event of active evolution.

A process we could use in name to account for all changes since day one. At least on the same plain we began to think of God pre and post day one. Which in both cases could be and now were entered into reality. By the only species able to fill our diary.

If to consider and we must, God is the entity to have set evolution in motion unknowingly, then we must round that theory. Even if to consider God did not trigger any event in any Case. So how then are we here and directing God to his new role gained from our self enlightenment.

Unless we are the eventual key to the wonder of all things. Not by our superiority if ever, but from our ability to overrule all the complications owed to all the other creature species of evolution. Who developed on the very same scale as we, by starting in some cases, eight hundred million years earlier.

Perhaps laying the proving ground the same for us, except we did not know how to agree to the same standards evolution applied for others. Although the same product, our human type species evolved from only about three million years ago. Except to our condition, we added our ability to survive differently under the same conditions as others in range.

Unmatched until from about 250.000 years ago more so about 60.000 years ago. We stretched evolution beyond its own unknown limits. We began to make her overplay her own hand, so much so we began to break ties with her from about four or five thousand years ago if not earlier.

Not that we made any plan to that effect or result. But from that those near timescales, we set evolution to have its own master and creator in the name God, the primary creator of all events.

Even if God was waiting to be told of his role in all things. Well before we could consider God's relationship to be with us or we with him. Now in the same field and mind of thought. We stretched further from evolution but moved closer to God in concept and reality. Noted when we at best began to realise God was a certainty as we are a certainty. Which gives no credence to either unless we come together.

Under clear circumstances, we so far are the first instigators of finding God through our religious endeavours. Which becomes deserving of its own status of being the founding reason of why and how humanity. Forced our separation from the nature of all other creature species who are still led by evolution and pure instinct.

They in turn have no seen opportunity to change their status. Not least because they are fulfilled in a way not known to us of humanity in general. Not by example, for their individual life range in being, tied to their mentor and creator evolution.

Which has no known new setting, especially when to consider. Created or evolved species life cycles, run in time to be from about 24 hours long for various types if insects and others. Who nevertheless have to reach their evolved purpose of procreating by various odds in any case.

Along with other creature species, some set in ocean environments, who may have lifespans in double numbers of years. Who also procreate, by which some species will simply follow their developed rules of instinct howsoever. With some sea creature species to have existed in the same form generationally for as much as 500 million years.

We might read the story nothing is set to really change evolutionary, unless from the outside. Maybe when assuming to have found God in cause without understanding the reason for or the cause of so far, we will near understanding.

Not to compare the standard of instructive procreation practiced by all other lifeforms. Our human skill to have created our own God concept, has set a standard unquantified by any scale. Even beyond our human reasoning capabilities. Which is a sign well below our now proved ability to equal God in verse.

We are the only species now and never to have been appointed so. But nevertheless, it is for us starting today to set God's standards for his sake more than ours. Simply because God has been waiting in the wings for 13.8 billion years to be named. Then much further, the same waiting span was also spent so he could relate to all the aspects of development we in the name creation, which only means time, set our tone for God.

We have already shown God in the past a measure of our difference to all the chemical elements, then to all other lifeform creature species. So, from that alone without guessing, we can now put God to role. Plus, we can show God the door to his path of reconciliation with us for our errors of judgement. All of which will be totally new to God.

Not least because we the single species we are. Can show God in task from where he can start to build bridges between our guessing and reality. But only for his sake, why his sake and not ours might not do as a standard. It might set God in error if we get it wrong.

To not even avoid such a possibility but realise it. We, humanity, must make it obviously clear. Although we are assisting God, we offer ourselves to his examination in proof there are no alternatives. Simply because there aren't.

If God can mull in the dark for another 100 billion years before he hears us again. He will not receive a better plan than the one we began to offer. When we first created any religion pointed to the aspect of there being a head God.

We can begin again by reminding every single person alive today. We are the total and full result of what time meant. For we, humanity in our species form, were/are the only species to have come to the idea of a creator or instigator. All we have so far missed is the why.

Which is now an open door, because although we can never match God, except in one field. We can turn his dead pan wait into his own enlightenment. By bringing him to the fore, simply by letting him know. It is now time for him to show his hand, albeit under our instructions.

But never to spoil or interrupt other aspects of what evolution might yet produce. For that feature is still the hand God dealt himself pre the Big Bang or when time was set to begin, but not by God.

One feature we must lay before God in open honesty is owed to our genuine religious fortitude. Although not fully set, for me they are the key to how humanity was able to progress.

Which I now give due credit before our religions confuse reason and cause. They still are the true masters of how we came to God. Providing we do not make any of our religions God.

CHAPTER 3

Religions First - Three

OUR MOST COMMON ERROR IN coming to God religiously, was made almost ten thousand times over. Most missing the point delicately and in vanity. Which is an ongoing statement when to consider. We of the one species who did not recognise that fact. Realised in open harmony and debate, God was for us, because we were for God. Alas at such times four or five thousand years ago, that mixture was easy to upset.

Because when we drew those conclusions; the God part of our findings was always diluted to be our finding. Almost as if we each were to copywrite God. Then in the assumed case of open infringement, instead of God harmony, we had God division dressed in ten thousand different masks.

Unfortunately, or perhaps the reverse, this conundrum became apparent almost at once four or five thousand years ago. Whereby if God was for us, he could not be for them. Almost as quick as we found God even if only tribally at the time.

We set God in conflict over harmony in the name of group vanity. A trait we continue with today, alas under different headings, which will carry their own attentive following. But just in case, not least to protect our vanity, even if in copywrite, often pertaining to some or all, even to be one of our tribal traits. We began to give God different roles to maintain our self- image.

Often not realising what that meant, even if we were to have slipped the leash of sound and fair religious obligations, God's name was compromised. Which when done we could only follow our own choices expressed by a lax form of how we run things politically. Which is due its own explanation.

Until I make that clear, the only defence I can offer for our religious conduct up to now. Stands to the matter of how virtually all religions have set the foundation. Whereby God is the overall judge of our lives conduct when we die, now sanctified religiously, by me, to die naturally from old age only.

Which most religions cover by setting God to be involved in his other apartment we call heaven of paradise. While still involved one way or another in his holiday villa here on Earth. Where he had seriously visited on various occasions over the past four or five thousand years at least.

Prompted by how some of this newish species humanity, tried to plan a course for their/our existence. Strange but then ago our self query was delivered from different tribal angles. But fortunately, God saw us as the one group.

Which by return needs to be reciprocated by us in our single species form, by endorsing a single religious concept species orientated. For God's sake, not ours. That matter can be attended to if we set/put one of my plans already mentioned into place.

Whereby we all openly submit in true deference to God or all God's or no God if that is your forte. But we all must keep to cause and reason in all senses, which is one of our separation clauses from all other creature species.

But to maintain our historical image of what religions should really deliver, we now must set the standard for all religions with God in mind. So that we, others, even God, can follow the one image now created by the only species to be able and recognise God and his needs.

How we might define any and all religious will stand on our next move backed up by the recognition. We owe our religions more than any other aspect of how we interact. Now that we have set the one core base requirement to any aspect of their makeup or intention.

Perhaps the best way we can justify or correct any religious standard set any time over the past four or five thousand years. Is to use our learning ability of now and project it back in time. To set the standards we should have made any time when we first came to religion and God or God and religion,

By accepting the obvious of now, whereby we can follow in ease we are the one species ever to hold separate religions. Plus, in the name of species our religions must now be aligned to bear how modern thinking must work, except for small realignment.

For good case results, we must mix on the same ground, which in all cases stands when we die. But not how we die, which is the hand needed to force some of us to both commit our standard religious beliefs to suit Gods unknown intention for us.

A solid statement when to consider we have proof God did visit various individuals any time over the past 60.000 years. But more directly over the past four or five thousand years. Because some of us in the guise of our tribal or clan background somehow stimulated God.

Only to disappoint him by not being able to relate to God properly, except tribally and religiously. For when God stood on our shoulders at any time of his interest in us, all he ever heard was the cry me before we.

Which was more natural for us to transmit at various times than for him to receive. For in all cases much was going on among all the other creature species to offer God other forms of interest. But because of historical backgrounds. We are the only form of matter to have drawn God's attention, because we can reply.

From which without knowing until now, our stimulus needs to continue for more reasons than gaining moral ammo or money. Allowed so by how modern reasoning can now set God in task. By applying the/our human logical plan of what was instead of what we thought what is.

So, if our religions are the bridge to God in all senses by acclimation. We must pay them all the same grace to be still called religions. Which is a real cause in God's name, for we cannot allow a group or series of religious beliefs call to kill each of the same flock in

God's name. While at the same time avowing those same religions to love God in both deed and faith.

In order to quash any anxiety, I might bring to any person locked in faith to their particular understanding of God. All I submit now is not to or for them, but God on all accounts. For in all senses my representation can only be yours/ours also. In that I have no wit or skill beyond you or others. My whole makeup is from your or previous efforts of mankind in general.

My projections and wishes are yours except now mine better suit God, not for my sake but his. Because we in the one name humanity, set by our species parameters are the one and only people of God.

We are the one and only species to be able and advise God, after only four or five thousand years in partnership with him. Compressed to be of our individual lifespan in excess of eighty plus years we hope.

Against all other lifeforms who existed over the past 800 million years. Against all other chemical and astronomical actions or events over the past 13.8 billion years, that could not equate to God any way or by any style.

In order to help some of us reach the heights required to dare and set God in task. I propose on our behalf, not as a lone figure, but as a single member of the one and same species humanity. I reassert my/our standing about how our religions were and are the key to how a single self-defined species. Can now stimulate God to think on our lines, which might be the key to God's new understanding.

Plus, by laying my/our plan in good faith, we will be setting a standard for God. He could only ever wish to have found for himself. For if he was to have been given title to murder and kill in his own name. Who could later judge the conduct of their own actions if called to. While picking through the smashed and broken bones of their own command.

Even if from now on I add firm ideas of how humanity in the same form of how we manage our religions. Manage our politics and additionally of how that feature led us to follow scientific roads. Sometimes expressed as main thoroughfares.

We must acknowledge my observations, all of our religious acceptances, far outreach those new and old other advantages.

Meaning in light relief, I state it was and still is our religious historical cores that were, are the first best and greatest stimulus mankind
ever had. But were self challenging, not least because of the number
we accumulated.

Many often showing disparity, which offered no clues to the
authenticity of one over or set against the other. Even if one said we
could kill humans in God's name, when another said we must accept
and respect each other in God's name. Why is not a question when all
claimed to hold the same ground in their own eyes and in God's name.

Opening the open wound, whereby if we now profess to set
God a new base standard concept. He is over and above all else, but
in line to comment on their, some religions behaviour.

Because they through us, are the only signs in God's timespan of
13'8 billion years. Capable to take God into areas of vision he never
could have contemplated. For until then/now, he never really experienced anything. Except when we, one in the same species. Drew his
interest in less time than it takes to blink, over watching galaxy grow.

Our 20 20 vision from about the year twenty twenty, can now
set the/a religion or all religious practices. To be the fulcrum on
which all human understanding pivots. But in deference to God first
and our species somewhat after.

We must mark the standard for any religion to remain a religion.
Which becomes very important, when we realise all religions of any
type are automatically aligned to God. So much so, even without any
form of known God contact on a purely religious basis, many stand.

We of the species humanity, are species aware enough to set
their standing. It is/was our religions in formation, that were responsible for our first break from how other creature species only followed
pure, natural instinct. Shown by how we dared aspire even when
un-driven or un-guided. Leading us to set new standards.

In order to determine the standard base line for all religions
numbered in the ten thousand range. All can still remain in their
original form, but now sometimes not as a religion, set now in task
by how I feel how God might like religions to be seen as. But never
for me only us, humanity.

To qualify in name to remain a religion, for the baton has been passed on. All future doctrine or verse alluding to any specific religion from any timeframe. Must from now/then adopt in clause, tenet or creed, this my/our new extended prospect.

Henceforth, all wishing to remain in the religious band accepted, agree and accept this newish rendition. All adherents in of my/our religious group. Can only expect under our religious code to be brought to "Natural Body Death from old age". Endorsed now from the very core of all religions.

Further enhanced with the fixed extension, no person should have suffered the indignity of being enslaved. Of being intimidated or bullied, tortured or abused to their detriment. Being refinements, which are ours to muse while in free debate rather than a free for all.

Which now as a core code written into all religious perceptions by me first in all names. Not in the singular, but me of species, me of humanity. Me to become the fixation I, so in plain language from now on all of us can state in open harmony,

If any claimed religion contravenes the above intention, then I as the individual we all are. Can for moments of stability, declassify some religions if they do not follow in good heart our intentions to bring humanity together at first religiously. Which in fact is a burden of intention taken on by all religions if they call to God to be their mentor.

No religion is entitled to assume from within the structure of any religion, there is a select band of people who can operate as God on his terms. Now that we have determined what we would like to bring to God in his name by our own judgement. None therefore can order the destruction of human life on or by their human terms. Using the illusion, they were instructed by God to murder in his name.

So not to compromise the true sanctity of all God bound religious philosophies, plus to savour the moment. At the same time and in step. All religions in their own name will pass the same maxim to our other medium of control now known as our political systems.

Who in turn to show no bias, they in the collective of the United Nations. Can determine the correct level, to declassify or reclassify a religion or not, but by name.

How we might handle this new understanding, although set from our political perspective through the United Nations religiously. We will have to vary the standard politically. Because ultimately, our political systems in second place. Will be the other true medium to give all our religions their deserved first place standing in our associations with God then humanity.

CHAPTER 4

Politics Second - One

H AVING CREDITED OUR RELIGIOUS COUNTENANCE to have been the primary mover of how humanity has developed. Not least because of how they/we gave us a purposeful aim of study about our existence.

We now have to realise first hand but second tier; the influence all our political systems have had on us so for, by acquitting ourselves to set them to their station. Which is not to be an exercise of reading history. Though we must acknowledge some historical events or attitudes.

Before and during such new studies, day one of our reasoning can be dated from today. By which we can cure all political systems of their ills. By introducing in repetitive post haste. My same maxim to be the cornerstone of all political institutions from now on.

In name the maxim is still one of my prospects. Although of the same standing and standard when used previously on religious lines. This time on political grounds only, scope can be taken to adjust the core of the maxim if required but under strict guidelines,

What cannot be done to either application of how the maxim is meant, be it for religious or political interpretation. Is for any not to agree. Which is why we need a neutral force like the U N to be adjudicator.

Starting again at the front on political terms. All political systems, styles and energies are now disposed to set the one and same standard for all adherents, followers and electorate. On such political terms, each person can also expect to die a "Natural Body Death from old age" as the one standard only.

Plus, not to have suffered slavery, intimidation, brutality or bullying or torture or any abuse even as murder, from the same source of self. Belonging to the one and same species of humanity. With that one maxim/prospect spread over two of our main human influences, our religions and our political systems. We will have another first in human history, by setting new proactive standards, whereby we state officially in group. We are not to kill one another for any reason without exception.

Which is a fixed standard in both cases, except if it is decided politically only. The term Natural Body Death can be made fit into a well meant legal plan if to defend the individual by the community of the individual.

Knowing full well we are now backed up by God under all circumstances. But by just having set different standards on some political lines if assumed needed. None can use God's name in murder while we live. Until "Natural Body Death from old age". How can we differentiate between how we hold our new political and religious contracts never to kill while we live.

Our biggest effort must be spent to understand how such rules can be broken or changed. Without setting different direction to either our political or religious standards. Which is a task, for we are walking on old ground with new shoes. Never to have been available as little as ten years ago, even internationally.

By setting in stone our religious aspect never to kill even in God's name pre "Natural Body Death from old age". So not to impinge the maxim concept, because I stretched it to cover all political aspects only. I now give licence, but not in order of how some of us might have to kill politically.

Which must always remain a political levy only. For when we refer not to kill in God's name, we clear all grounds to set the society God might have wished to be involved with eventually.

A species, born of God Particles, a new scientific medium. Who at last dared set before God his own imagination of what his wait and see could deliver. A selfless species lifeform, able and happy enough to set God their plan of what God was waiting for.

So much so to be clever enough to show God how he might further improve their outlook post "Natural Body Death from old age". Wise enough to admit to God their/our single life span of 80 plus years is not long enough for God's company.

Smart enough to then hand the steerage of the next future to God alone. So, he can use our wisdom properly. Even if to extend God's realm of Earth heaven, to be a proper part of the universe.

But before then, soon. We must show God by sign. We really are smart enough politically, to set human killing standards restricted to the absolute minimum. Until we can dispense with the crude fact of the necessity to kill. Which is a must, for it is almost the last page we might need to turn, to prove our integrity in God's name.

Many of our greatest human assets are given off by our emotional ranges. Which as known, features can be extremely strong or less so. If to define where the line falls, we must draw two pictures. Both with the same relevance even if motives are similar.

If I have set to create utopia. Then we must protect all rights politically to that declaration. Balanced by two standards, one of me the other of we. For if we have attempted to set a society never to kill each other from now on, we must be prepared to defend that prospect. Which can now only be done under political direction.

If others do not agree with the form of any political society, we have so far formed. Wishing to change our efforts by the force of logic or arms. Prepared to kill in the name of their political plan alone. For in their logic, God may not be in their political frame to divert their thinking.

Then also we in us must preserve the right to defend our political philosophy even if to kill. But now never like before, not only by style or execution. But if to kill politically as I seem to indicate. Can only be done on historical grounds which is a false currency.

When to encounter the depth of our emotions we must take care not to lead ourselves into the corner of pointed reaction. But we all can wear our emotion in open view, providing they are not used to intimidate, bully or waylay the clean fresh thinking offered by our younger generations.

Who can show us the best opportunity we might need to see the error of our ways right up to now. But only if we heed their new advice at the right time of their deliver of it to us. Now under their generational terms. Which can be fully transmitted any time while they and we mix at the same point of reference, within our 80 plus year lifespan.

Though to be so obvious we do not see the consequences of how we might promote our best standard of now never to kill each other in God's name or in the name of any new certified religion as a religion. Who are now charged never to kill in God's name if to maintain their religious status.

How best can we set our young to kill for us politically when we and they intermix in the very generations we are each involved in at this moment of time. What signals do we give to them in reality and us in reflection.

Dear son or grandson, could you please remove by legal killing, on political ground only. Such people who might use their human right to oppose our/my obtained standards as I/we see them. Whereby under collected circumstances or from various influences or imaginations. We are threatened with death by or from their judgement and standards from whatever source except proper defined religions.

The next page we may have to turn on such a request to our young, by good grace will come from them. For before we know it, they in the same generational mix we are in now. Will be better able and rationalise our joint standing of to accept we are indeed the one species. Leaning from how we have shown them the importance to keep God online.

One of their best assets of now about our young, stands on the solid ground they are not phased about the past as we are, so their new enlightenment to us comes from a better outlook than we ever knew. Not least because they are developing the rational to bring us all forward at the same rate. By at first not to always listen to what we say.

To allow all societies grow in the active standard of being able and present to God. A single species who now pledge not to kill each other politically or religiously in God's name or for Fatherland or

Mother County. Even if murder was done to get there, only sanctioned politically.

For by U. N. charter, no religious subject of any persuasion can kill of humanity in God's name, even if to protect their faith vows. For if death or murder is caused by any claim to be in God's vision of such acts. Our U.N. will have already set the rules of such standards. Not to have come from any religious source.

By imposing again, the open statement, any human murder or death outside of "Natural Body Death from old age". Even in God's name, could not have been carried out on religious grounds.

For mankind has no mandate to kill one another on any grounds. Unless only politically, which is always to preserve the idea. We the only species to aspire beyond the understanding of that concept. Are in honest preparation to present God with a plan he might have devised while waiting to see what was offered to him about any aspect of reality. So it might be.

Where we can outrun God. Is by how we have now recognised our successful range of understanding to set God's own plan of how it might be. Stems from within our 80 plus year life range.

Eighty plus years includes at least three full bore generations. One of my age, born in 1945, younger as middle aged, then younger but more vital. Because almost before their life has really begun. We might ask some of them to kill in our name but only ever politically.

How so works on one main factor. We will be asking them to kill to preserve our best ideals of to be able and present to God our plan not to kill in any name. But once done by them, they can sit at our right hand to wait God's pleasure. Which has always been our plan if only we knew it, but God might.

If as I half suggested, we might only kill on political terms to protect and defend our set lifespan until natural body death. That of course is one very serious matter of concern. Unless we now have set inbuilt securities which are there when to realise our 80 plus years of living now is the most crucial of all time.

Not least because it is while we live our activities are paramount to be able and set the realisation of standards that are already there but need to be released. To our understanding at first, then for God's enlightenment. Not least because God is still waiting, so in order to improve his interest in us again. We can reintroduce him to the sheer power of our collective emotional ranges,

Which have always been most stirred about how or why some of us can and do kill and some of us do not. Then some of us are never sure, until we are involved by circumstances beyond our control. Like for instance in the era of now, if murder was done against a younger family member to be a child. What then.

Under such a deep shock situation I dare not make my own observations count. Even though I have set rules and codes of conduct to suit all political and religious situations. By setting my reactive kill ratio to be only workable in the political field.

Apart to not allow murder retribution under any true religious code now endorsed by the U. N. My open aim is to ask families and friends of such frail and innocent victims. Not to react in kind to whom so ever or why so ever the life of our young was lost or taken.

On this one basis only, by using your/our full emotional range. For in all circumstances however read. I will not be crude and suggest retribution will not bring them back. Nor will I suggest we are bigger than that. I can indicate the law or political legality is there to take control of such situations under their punishment portfolio.

My emotional line of thought must follow the point of all religious sufferance. Which must rely on emotional ranges some of us will never fully arrive at even while living our 80 plus year cycle until "Natural Body Death from old age".

Which is a backup of why I only offer we can never now kill for any religious reason. Especially when God will eventually show his hand under our enlightenment. Which beyond a dream, sets a broader standard than how politics works when ordering our young to kill on our behalf. If only to defend or protect any styled political system if they feel to be under attack from any quarter.

Knowing under all circumstances our politics as a force is more forthright than our religions. Helps us providing we do not bend to its will at the expense of how we conduct ourselves emotionally over any topic that might affect any of us at any level.

CHAPTER 5

Politics Second - Two

I N ORDER TO AT FIRST release our U. N. then to improve it, not departmentally. But as the primary United Nations voice. I now set before her and all political regimes she represents. Our one standard for her to embrace a new acceptance. Which will enhance and invigorate her. For in all realities, she has more failures to count on than successes.

In having set my "Natural Body Death from old age" prospect to be upon all religious and political ideologies. Naturally means the same standard applies to the United Nations. So, in effect the primary aim of the U. N. is to get all of her/our species to natural body death. But her burden starts now.

In essence, she, even if by indifference, is unable to put her own house, the world, in order. By not working the best end of my prospect "Natural Body Death from old age". Plus, with no person to have suffered slavery, brutality, torture, intimidation, exploitation and worse and more. She has no right to comment in kind under the frail foundations she stands on, unless she asserts to be positive and proactive.

By her first chance to be so I give her now the biggest reason to be a feature of morality. For if she is bound to help and aid her subjects in the millions locked into the misery of living in refugee camps. When classed to be homeless and stateless.

Much worse to be forced and put there by member states of the United Nations in part. Which is not a matter of blame but is a moral disaster. For if a nation state is disposed to live with the crude and disgusting situation. Whereby for no other reason than self aggrandisement. Some and or group individuals. Take charter from the understanding they have been appointed politically and religiously to play their hand as they see fit.

Often added to in complication by the misunderstanding, ethnicity is scaled from the top down. Sometimes on tribal terms, sometimes taken to be endorsed by the United Nations. Because of her open standing to comply with the needs and wishes of the despot and democrat alike. The godly and the ungodly alike. The rich and the poor alike, which is not of her making.

Except in all modern situations, all enterprises need funding. More ably done from a rich base than poor. From which without being a standard, could lead to the situation whereby. Some groups might take to gain benefits from their own generosity.

On her own account, our United Nations has already created a weakness. For by copycatting the old human rights mandate. By copycatting the deadly political standard of self serving on party political lines. But far bigger, by ever mentioning the word religion in any context to then re-endorse religious tolerance, she compromises her own case.

Although she carries all those faults, her biggest comes from how she outshines any other form of nationalism to be internationally racist. Planted from her own conduct above charter.

Stirred because she has made almost the same mistakes all politicians continually make. By automatically following the/my steps taken syndrome observation.

A tiny lucid expression, which when run, can display the shortcomings of all political decisions. The expression works to be in the negative mostly. Whereby if a decision is made about any aspect of promoting or instigating a project on party political lines only. Even if later when shown the project does not deliver.

Like minded promoters of the deal, still support the original plan, not for its worth. Simply to continue per my suggested steps taken syndrome maxim on party political lines, for that was its source.

Effectively self-serving, even though the route style of the maxim is carried over by all political systems nationally and internationally. Which on that level means more or less. If the phenomena is run, even without realising it. International standards need to be recognised above following our steps taken syndrome attitude.

If my steps taken syndrome operates within an appointed rather than a specifically elected organisation. Then its constitution must be held to override other base influences. Even if they were to come from the mix of organisations or nations who set my/our standards first.

Without being repetitive, when the U N was set up post the second world war ending in 1945. Although based on the lines of how the failed league of nations didn't work. This new concept was almost overstated at the off. Not least by how she had to give cause never to repeat the mistakes recently made.

From which as a unit, without ever realising the why or the how, by readopting the now fated and dated concept of human rights. She endorsed my insight of finding failure via the fated steps taken syndrome standard.

Although not in true form, the representative human rights readoption, was indeed a steps taken exercise. Where was the unrealised alternative to it. Having taken to old habits, all to do was support them. So, in effect, human rights as a/the main concept of differentiated unity. In balance, that standing was to become a human right.

It was open to misinterpretation, if the idea had to be laid down as an equal standard for all. Presented as a human right, all directions of it were set for the individual beyond expectation. For it told the verse of me over or separate to the plural of we.

Therefore, on the two main levels of our best expectations religiously and politically. Our human right for the individual was cast to be discretional. Whereby a person could apply their desire to be of any religion or name, of any political persuasion or name. When yes or no could not be questioned.

Unfortunately, such efforts of broad benevolence introduced to alleviate far reaching problems, which only grew over time. Plus, nothing done by our United Nations at instigation did anything proper to improve our human division already there.

When to offer the individual the human right to be self-obsessed religiously and or politically. To later enter other human traits of how we individually felt about sexism and gender on the same basis also. Which perhaps more than any other emotion can draw us as we are to interact better without aggression.

Alas with human rights to the fore, plus to have had the League of Nations approve its structure, meaning and intention. Although when the League died, it was not noticed or evaluated, when the League did operate human rights. It did not necessarily apply it in the same way it was made fit through the United Nations.

My remarks are retrospective not least because I tend two different standards to have been drawn from the one concept. By the term and conduct of accepting the idea of human rights within the League of Nations, who underplayed it. Then later through the United Nations, who overplayed it.

We find ourselves encumbered because we could not mix metaphors. Never to realise, although our League of Nations rendition starting in 1919. It only and directly applied to generations of people no longer alive. Therefore, conditions and standards and acceptances of now, per those alive today differ.

Sometimes for the best of reasons, sometimes lost to ineptitude, which I have cast to be of political cause only. But now in line to improve, because all political systems are to offer and bring all their constituents to natural body death. Beyond the limits of party politics or land mass national boundaries.

As stated, human rights under the league post 1919, had its own conditions of how it was operated. Not least because of Empire and Imperialism, which carried their own clause of being racist and or to be superior.

Although human rights was thought to transcend all skin tone references. It could not and did not work politically. Which as a source, even under how and why skin colour tone was an imagined racial feature. Too often expressed in negative styles historically or since. Not even to be connected when the U. N. updated its own rational of what human rights should mean.

Never to blame in the cause of putting things right. But if we have a cause, motive or structure regarding how humanity is endemically racist. Politics alone fits the bill. She ideologically does not yet know how to follow the wind of change. Even if to reflect upon any God based religious theory, where all are equal in Gods eyes.

Politics cannot split hairs if religions are ethnic by degree. But does if she needs to express her own ethnic reproaches on skin colour tones. Which is a matter under review by myself of this generation. Trying to rationalise into shape previous generations and our/their legacy.

My findings irrespective of other opinions, not least because in note, some of my ideas are unique. Therefore, they have the resonance to tackle imagined fables we suppose about how or why we are different because of our skin colour. Which so far, even the collective of all political attitudes our United Nations. Still do not know how to deal with wrongly imagined race issues.

Which run unabated, because in allowing the human right for us all to choose our standard and ruling about personal choice of whatever ilk. More so on or of religious subjects and or our politics one way or the other. Even when to allow us to choose neither, which is tantamount to providing chaos. Especially when the matter of being opted no choice, means my choice.

By having already set our U. N. on the correct path. By getting them/us to manage the ethics of all religious and most political regimes. Never now to wantonly kill. For my prospect of applying "Natural Body Death from old age" with acceptances, is our new benchmark. Plus, and in extra addition, with our not to kill each other clause, because essentially, we are the one species given simple details.

Except when we excite ourselves, not over our now neutral attitudes about religions and politics. But other matters like ethnicity and skin colour. Never to have been tackled properly in scale. When we gave up or were forced to give up Imperial control over other nationals.

A good pointer I use myself about skin colour, because attitudes about it can be more extreme. Comes from how I personally reconcile my belief in God on any and all religious scales. For in practice God is skin colour blind.

But also, by my understanding, I feel he so far has no reference to any colour, except those to have called his name. Or the only to have called God in their name. which when he hears or indeed heard. It was in the one sound called species, in the one name of our human species.

For God in his time scale, has seen the coming and going of thousands of species over the past 800 million years. Even if to have lasted as long as the dinosaurs set for about 150 million years. They never came to God, so God never drew interest from in them.

Whereas we of the species humanity, drew interest from God at various times over the past four or five thousand years and still hold his interest. Not least because we in our species condition so far, are only of interest to God vocally.

There is no visionary realisation of us to God in his state of mind except in our species network form. How could there be when all we do is get old and die generationally. Which means over the past four or five thousand years. Hundreds upon hundreds of new generations in keeping with the one standard. Attempted to approach God in each other's name, but always vocally.

When God did show forms of interest in some of our ancestors as he did. That too was always done on the same vocal plane; for God in his form was open to be approached by any existing creature species like the dinosaurs for instance. But never declared himself back. For if he did, even to us. the game was over. Wait and see would not have been needed.

There would have been no realistic situation whereby if God had been exposed by such creature species before us. There would have been no possibility for us to post develop, for God would have been revealed. Which meant his motive would also have been reached. Even that he did not know of it then, but only now, when humanity came along.

So, in my half conclusion, if as we did enhance God from the measure of our species inquiry being the only so far to include the future in our reasoning. His only outlook was to be interested in the one species to do so.

When we all evolved "Out of Africa", being a genetic fact. We ancestrally would all have been black of skin. So, in effect on God's own time scale. When a single species some four or five thousand years ago came to him. It was the same colourless species it always was/is.

Which is why God in seeing no defined skin colour, gauged over our genetic lifespan of less than three million years. But in hearing the sound of the first species to show interest in him in 13.8 billion years. Set our species as it should and will be in the future, colourless of skin.

Without setting his plan, for it was for him to always learn. The same colourless species we are, drew better pictures for God than he could imagine. It was we who bridged the gap between our ancestors of any age. But under terms God did not even know about. For in concept, we created the post human death area where we could combine with God on his terms shown by us.

Without my full study in front of our United Nations, fed by other sources except from God's religion. I fail us/them by not being able and support the true concept of species. By promoting the undriven ideal we are still only and always were tribal. Often described by our yellow, black, brown or white skin colour, being living features.

For in being allowed to choose our own religions. They become divisive if our skin colouring is to take part as a definition. Which is allowed politically and nationally. Though it can be matched as a distinct medium. Therefore, it can be made carry values decided in either case by peoples of different skin colours. But never religiously, for God is skin colour blind and only human species aware.

So, to give our U. N. her sea legs, they in we for all political ends can restate their charter. So, when we, any nation state declares to be ethnically different. Such matters can only be accepted politically. For in line, political ethnicity seems to be wrongly wired to highlight our differences before our likeness.

Such matters must be given ground historically, leaving the door to be open for genial and general discourse. About thoughts of historical conditions as they were thought to have been or were.

Only carried by the one aspect of control now administered by the United Nations proper. Who at last can take licence on her/our account. For she can restructure her own aspect to update our tired and jaded attitude of how we think we should let it run anew.

By already suggesting the U, N. can now determine a basic religious standard. Whereby no person within any religion can kill another human being for any reason whatsoever. Especially in God's name. Our U, N, in us will have structured tomorrow by expectation. For by adopting that standard in moral law beholding to our U. N. she in we will have created a united platform for all our worlds 10.000 religions, no less.

To increase her form, our U. N. on more religious terms only at first. Can lay down the in- house law. If and or people in group form. Do kill in God's name under their own seen religious code. That as a matter ends forthwith.

For even if not to take God's side, which is an open writ for any nation state in the U. N. because of their existing standing, unless but. As any member of the conglomerate, they/we must show to try and comply. Providing we do not openly challenge her core directives which run anew.

Like for her to state if a person or persons who would claim to kill or maim in God's name, in God's religious name. Are not agents or messengers of God religiously or politically. Therefore, if in claim to do so, murder, even in retribution is no longer an act of God.

It is a criminal act motivated on political grounds only. For in most national constitutions. To defend the nation state rites. It is allowed defence of, can be carried out in the extreme. But in theory must carry justifiable mitigation. Which comes only from political imagination, if no command can be given of how to defend national morality.

Religiously this cannot stand, for if God was/is or could have been the appointee of any or all religions. He never knew nor does he ever understand why his, this human species would need or want to kill if they are to direct him in his true role.

One of my better fixations about how to conference our U. N. stands in what we can deliver to its/her/our overall wellbeing. For it can guide itself onwards and upwards again and again by associating our religious and political aspirations to the interest of the one species, humanity.

I give now into the hands of the U. N. charter. A means to disassociate from previous failure. For as she carried the past of how the League of Nations failed into the twenty first century. All she could do was tread water to preserve her impotency.

Our U. N. now already empowered by me to determine the exactitude of all religious standards. Who must now apply my "Natural Body Death from old age" maxim. From which I round the circle in the same way by uplifting the human rights offering of over one hundred years ago.

Although a great benefit to millions of people; the 1919 maxim even with all its updates and trimmings. Delivered less and less by intent as time went by. For she had no hand to hold as modernity kicked in.

Without any prompt, if a person even from the League days, took demand to express their human right. Portrayed as an object of use by the individual. Which allowed all sorts of despotic political leaders blight the rest of the twentieth century. Because they the individual, brandished their human right in the singular,

Even today the singular use of its initiative, can destroy the human rights of the singular. In practical terms, often misbalanced in courts of law. Shown by who could pay to have their human right upheld against a losing defendant for lack of funds. Which only enters the human rights saga ungraciously.

At all its worst levels of abuse or misuse, if and it does occur. A singular political despot. Chose for the good of all their willing subjects. God by religion from now on, has no political bearing in my/ our human rights regime.

With the religious restraint not to kill in God's name on any account now removed. Our leader could then direct his vassals to kill at random, if necessary, to ensure the integrity of the state, just in case; and it did and does happen.

Not to be the last word on that theme, but if I have directed the term human rights to have been taken on as the human right. Therefore, open to types of abuse. Because in class my human right was to the singular in connotation. Why not, for when first introduced, it was a great step for mankind to the good.

By the fact, even if only by my example given on my say so. When I now suggest we/our United Nations, underwrites my term aimed in the plural. To be the update as "The Rights of Humanity". I give the term to be used in the collective form only.

So, if our United Nations was to now downgrade a claimed religion who allowed its members kill in God's name. Not now to carry the term religion of God to its name anymore. They, our U. N. could underpin their observation of to withdraw true religious status to a body of murderers in God's name. for being an affront to God in our name.

By signing off with the new maxim "The Rights of Humanity". Backed up with another of my prospects of expecting "Natural Body Death from old age" under all religious and political headings.

Our base has been set so we can begin to refocus into the twenty first century, where one of our ways forward is now carried as "The Rights of Humanity". Which is a defined political adage. Highlighting the means to improve using our best means to do so, our United Nations, applying their role as we before me.

CHAPTER 6

Politics Second - Three

B Y ANY FORM OF PRESENTATION, we must strive under all political banners to enhance all political regimes. Even to re-educate all involved in the standing of all existing systems. Now when driven by real determination, we will set the world strait. If we use our U. N. properly.

Which can only ever be achieved politically. For that medium is our only hands-on example whereby we are self reliant in form of running our own methods of self control. Even with the embodiment of all religions still holding first place regarding our real welfare. Politics is still our best tool for the task I propose in this modern era.

Providing we do not lose sight it was mainly our religions which were our innovators. When unbeknown to their own mix in vast numbers. They brought us from the restraints of pure instinct by how they unknowingly closed us to aspire.

In essence, by my accounting, I set all standards to be so. religions first, politics second. For she eventually began by feeding off how religions began to structure the reason for our existence.

That is until the new nemesis of science, in all her given forms. Came to reverse role with my two stalwarts of our earlier human advancing.

Science in all its guises, began to lead under the most honest of pure circumstances at first.

For she in form was the only true supplier in explanation of our conditions of life.

Even if to wrongly interpret the cause of our existence to have other reasons than we had already worked out. First by religions, secondly politically. Then now first scientifically. Nemesis yes, mentor no.

CHAPTER 7

Science Third - One

WE CAN NEVER ESCAPE THE obvious which it is. But even so, human beings have for ever been trying to do this. If not avidly over the past four or five thousand years. Then over the past one hundred and fifty years under the terms of enlightened denial.

Religiously we had it made, certainly over ten thousand different ways. Politically nearly, until she began to overreach her own capabilities, when to challenge some aspects of some religions, at first without the ability to do so. Politics stumbled along until she found an ally.

Until science, a social medium for both religion and politics. Began to question such aspects of our control features, by applying a proof or deny synopsis. Whereby if one or the other ideal had offered or claimed a standard was applied from the depths of the society, they/we moved in.

Like if the leading form of our/any religious countenance gave reasons for how the sun and moon worked. Even of what caused the weather in God's name when it rained thunder and lightning. We politically accepted all we were led to believe.

Until the practical terms of science really found meaning. For in essence, when she, even under our religious wing. Began to give chapter and verse for how the sun and moon did what they did.

Why when it rained thunder and lightning. Such events were more down to the atmosphere of the weather, set by humidity and air pressure. Rather than by God or God losing his temper.

Never to be a slight on any deal we by tribe had made over ten thousand different times religiously. But now some scientific trends began to help politics aim for the number one spot over religion.

Science in discovery was more suited to gain a political ear over a religious one. Her legacy suited the concept. Not least, for in time, science presented to be finite. Which alone is no claim, but in the context of expecting to be told by God as his charges. We were given godly facts from scientific insights, delivered by political reasoning.

Effectively science gave us answers we always thought were in the scope of God only. Thence over time, when we were given to examine what God delivered and science could and did in any case. Especially if our head was turned politically.

It became easier to accept a bird in the hand, rather than hold great expectations of what was in the burning bush. Fortunately, science in her new fusion of energy, managed to turn her own standard of presentation. Even if not to be able and account for the future as religions can.

A true and indisputable fact of science is it has recognised the species humanity. After all she coated every single person with the powder of DNA (Deoxyribonucleic Acid), Which is an anode by way of definition in the case of humanity.

It determines the fact we are a separate living species to all other creature species, because they are also dressed in the same underlying feature, we have on the same DNA scale. But applied by different paint brushes. Which represents the proper way to think DNA if it is seriously used to prove worthy differentials, between species,

To always have been a record of how all lifeforms are almost shown to have formed or evolved. Certainly, over the past 800 million years. Never to close the matter, but from when our DNA was first found of classified on the scientific scale. So grew the concept of God factually.

Only now we do not know how to read the verse our DNA code revealed or could uncover. For although ranged within her own boundaries. Whereby she can associate other creature species likenesses with us. But cannot set why only one species, humanity, are the only to bring God into the equation.

Therefore, it can only be by illuminating the true science of experimentation, all of which will be revealed in its glorious context. By setting the start point of our new experimental theories to belong to the lifespan of the individual. Which is where all study and learning is directed, and always will be.

Thus making every person alive today, to be the most important factor of all histories. For we will now be the first, but never the last. To lay the foundations of purpose beyond the imagination of all political systems.

Because when our ancestors set the first path to our standard of any religion. It was in God's cause without him being aware. In this instant, let it be clear, it is I who make this statement leading to create our final acceptance of God. Which is said in good God faith, not to claim any accolade or praise.

My standard is set for all good and true people already in God's eye. To step back from their fine position and give each of their charges in each other the same chances they/we already have. Of coming to God by standard in their own lifespan of time. Until "Natural Body Death from old age" calls at their/our door.

Plus, while we/they wait our future. We will not have suffered on any scale to have been a slave, intimidated. Nor to have been bullied, nor exploited, nor to have been murdered or to murder in any name religiously. For in religions is where the one God dwells.

On the plus or minus of any scientific scale from now on. But in line with how our ancestors laid our plan in the hope and faith field. It will not be necessary to value the progress of science day by day, but only in modern type. Simply because science is loaded to fail rather than aid us in these modern times about God, even religion.

Making it more than vital for this generation alive today. To be the one to credit science with the true discovery of God without knowing it. For when science runs her experiment clauses. She can do nothing less than prove of God.

Thus, helping this generation make God aware of his only aim beyond his own understanding. For in aim, it will be for us to direct God what to do when we meet with him in heaven.

CHAPTER 8

Science Third - Two

SCIENCE IN ALL REALITIES CAN only prove things, never the reverse. That is how she set her stall from day one, which is a coincidence of fact. But in any case, proof or no proof is still proof.

No person can disservice science in any way except to accuse her of attempting to deny any of our concepts of God. Under the false prophet, some scientists no longer or only half believe in the idea of God. Often based on the supposed malfunctions of some religions.

But latterly more so because of induced personal feelings to the effect. As they know and their species peers do not, even about God, they then can decide. When by the projection of any planned experiment, God cannot be found, therefore God does not exist. Plus, on the scale of individual scientists. Feeling they are important enough to have God reveal himself to them. So, if not, God is not there.

Which highlights my conceptual idea, this our present generations, those alive today. Are so far, the best to lead God into his required role post life. That is human life only of our species type. For by sign we are the only to have come to God and must play out our hand at God's table.

It is well to understand, for the past four or five thousand years. Science as a growing force of understanding, accounted for and educated us about the factors of our environment. Like when to show us how to improve farming and animal husbandry, science was truly born. She gave us something like reason and purpose to be our mentors for a time.

From then ago right up to today, many thousands of great scientists walked with God by their side. In the innocence of honesty, many earlier studies felt they were led to their scientific conclusions in good God faith.

By reading the script right, they gave credit to forces they did not understand. Not physical or elementary force. But those they had to assume were spiritual, not least because all human societies carried a God clause religiously.

Even though many scientists were aware of our mass international religious outlooks. Which did not suit the standard of experimentation, whereby results were generally in the singular. They still accepted God was the final experiment, until their generation was done.

Although as stated, great scientists still walk with God in this generation we are also alive in. Others if by projection saw no possibility of ever fitting God into a test tube or of being spun in a centrifuge to be separated out. Still accept God, though not necessarily by religious terms.

Perhaps because they have read the page where it states when all experiments have been done and proved in the positive or not. How and why do we think God begot that reality, unless something is there in the name cause and reason.

Which must be a good and fair rational if used. Whereas not to accept such a possibility, apart to be a denial of science, for she has no cause without reason. Therefore, if some very great modern-day scientists deny God, they deny themselves.

Which rounds on how some scientists have set or read the handbook. Science for beginners. A dated lively account of how science ultimately began 13.8 billion years ago. When God lit the fuse for the scientific firework display of the Big Bang.

As a very modern study, our concepts of how the universe was made/began, started just a few generations ago. Fed at first religiously then endorsed scientifically.

Whereby a good soul tied to full religious orders, worked on the imagined principle. Now knowing the universe was expanding with galaxy per galaxy moving away from each other.

An image was formed, naturally to comply with what that meant for the universe to expand and where into. By the matter of where it/they, galaxy per galaxy came from. If by dint of having a clerical/religious background, our scientist of a few generations ago. Sought a true mathematical rational for how the existing universe began.

Instead of using the expanding ratio, which in theory is futuristic. By mathematical extrapolation, the plan chosen was to look backwards to see where galaxy per galaxy came from. To such an extent, when he/we came to reduce each by shrinking and getting closer together. A singularity would be eventually reached.

A time of total empathy, when everything in being nothing, still had to be able and account for the expanding matter of now to then ago assumed. It was genuinely worked out mathematically the singularity was a static state, if of matter only, some 13.8 billion years old. But under an unknown set of circumstances.

However, in pure scientific terms, the singularity was given to be a timeline where all matter in the form of what all galaxy were actually made of. Through extrapolation, had reduced and reduced to such an extent. All matter on block, was now, then. Given to have shrunk and compressed to be the size of a pea or at best the size of an orange.

All left to assume even now, is if the singularity was set. It needed to be titled post singularity. Which was given to be in the form of an explosion, like a big bang. In consequence when the Big Bang Banged, it was given to have been detonated like a bomb.

Spewing the dust of energy in all directions equally. But with such force the effect of that upheaval, still continues today, whereby the universe is still expanding.

The only diagnosis that could have been set to the Big Bang happening in any case. Not least because of the timeline supposition, was that God started the whole process. Who else or how else even scientifically. Which had no force or form 13.8 billion years ago, but God did.

Before science was born, she had already blotted her copybook. Not 13.8 billion years ago but yesterday. For when she referred back pre and post big bang, she had overstepped her own rating. For the result of her observations were always unsound about the content of the big bang situation.

It was never down to concept to set parameters. She is simply a recorder of data on our behalf. Which are elements to be used to prove of God in reality, and not to experiment to his doubt.

Science must constantly remind herself; she is a product of humanity and not the reverse.

Which works on one main context only, based on how humanity uses its products.

By taking science in her own view to have set the standard of time. We must accept by record; it was her call about the state of the universe at its outset. So, in line with the common ground God set the big bang off. We scientifically must correlate such ideas to follow acceptances.

Which must have standards or in the case of science a ratio. So, when God said go, off went the Big Bang regularly in the one form of expansion.

Even though the time spent for the universe to develop as it had over 13.8 billion years so far. Post the big bang, instantaneously, science which had to have been expressed mathematically.

Set the realisation, one billionth of a second post the Big Bang. The new expanding form of matter had already set distance ratios outside the limit of mathematics. Which in turn compromised her ability to doubt God.

For at that time by my standards, being equal to any example expressed. The billionth of a second does not fit into the projected scale of any scientific statement even mathematically. For if the instant expanse of how matter in no form was supposed to work, we learnt nothing.

To understand light or the reflection of energy is given to travel at 300.000 km per second. Where is the standard to set time movement to be at a level one billion times smaller than a second.

Which on the same scale if used, meant when the big bang occurred, matter regressed. For if a billionth of a second is ever mentioned it must be there to represent expansion. Unless of course if God's terms were counted over science and mathematics both.

Which simply means it is not in the range of any scientist in the form of a single personality to ever deny the concept of God in any way shape or form. For to do so is to deny the reality of how the Big Bang never did occur. But something did.

Therefor if God did not set the big bang, what else did he do to set the clock ticking. But only in considerations to his own standards. So far, he knew nothing, unless time was set by God to wait and see what might occur from any event yet to come.

CHAPTER 9

Science Third - Three

B Y NO COINCIDENCE BUT SHEER luck. Science in the name of some very prominent scientists working in various fields. Including on solid ground studies like of DNA, Chemistry, astrology and much more, have grown so smart and intelligent.

Enough so to include the fields of guesswork to now be their stalwart. For when they can theorise in the name of mathematics, what will fit and what can't fit. Led in part by the new black of supposing theoretical physics will supply all the answers in the future. Through the shining example of their wisdom. So much so. I say again many prominent scientists today deny the concept of God wholeheartedly.

Perhaps for no other reason than they personally do not receive God's acknowledgement for their felt contribution to science and us all. If God does not see me, I do not see God even though I can study in the theory of tomorrow off piste. To supply answers God can't give me, because I don't follow his design plans for all the ignorant people unlike me.

My mild condemnation is set as a metaphor in comparative from. For if very intelligent people do not believe in God. That statement is the very same as if a despot political leader did not believe in God.

In consequence both parties condemn those they are set to help and aid in all ways. For to spite the efforts of the political despot and or high grade intelligent scientists. Even if they claim their choice not to believe in God is their human right. Because they govern or educate. They do not have any right to determine for us.

Which is raised more when we introduce my "The Rights of Humanity" maxim. Which by good fortune will be made work by the solid, sometimes not so well educated citizen. Who still carry the baton in God's name, in such a clever way to spite what might be laid against us/them in the form of political hardship.

We can hold fast by keeping our minds active in what we can expect from God. But only at his silent behest, for we are the only species so far to draw God's interest. By making sounds over the past four or five thousand years, unique in the universe. Noises of inquiry with a sting in its/the tail.

Our triumph on moral social terms is how we of common and ignorant beginnings have outmanoeuvred our despotic leaders and leading scientists, who each might not believe in God. Stands on the fact of however we are downtrodden by whom so ever.

We have managed to squeeze our maintenance of our God belief back into the full round of human influences. Which in curious ways has been followed up by the best end of media sources. Even though many individuals in those fields might not believe in God for their own reasons.

Nevertheless, on a win, win scenario, from keeping to follow a God concept yes or no. God still lives. Which we all need to understand for our sake. Which can be settled here and now by the smallest of acknowledgement set by accepting my "The Rights of Humanity" now more so.

All to do without attestation, is for a single person. In combined effort from our worlds 10.000 religions. Plus, from all of our political systems pretending to represent us fairly. Can be balanced if we as individuals accept God in concept, a reality in being, leaving little to be added.

Because we are already living the crude consequences of not having a combined plan, which is God in concept. When we did practice that ideal differently. We had no alternative but to set God to have instigated the Big Bang 13.8 billion years ago, which in part has now been accepted but when and why and how.

Of course, we were led to such vast conclusions about God's involvement in anything, sometimes leading to everything. It was no error of judgement most old hand scientists included God if as a medium or at least a catalyst.

It is only in seeming when we get a higher class of modern scientist if. Who are vain enough to stifle God for bland reasons beyond their own admission. But sometimes set on the lines of them being a celebrity subject, when it is trendier to deny than accept an unprovable object like God under celebrity contract dealings set in the hand of now.

Which can make our task easier to accept God in concept than ridicule those who have no God ideals. All both camps have to do is realise the importance of how and why God followers still follow God with no expectation.

While other God followers who believe in God, have already set God's intentions one way, often for themselves. Which as an option can never be solved religiously or scientifically, if part of both factions do not believe in God for everybody.

For not to believe God or of God, does not give others the option one way or the other. As I do not believe in God politically or scientifically. From that very position simply means in high court. There is no God, therefore I/we are not obliged to follow Gods religious or political indicators about itemised conduct.

Fortunately, we by setting the U. N. to adopt my "Natural Body Death from old age" maxim on all religious and political fronts. We can stop the banality of those in any camp self determined, from claiming immunity to believe. Which is tantamount for us in this case me, to hark on about the waste of time it is for some scientists in particular, to deny God in concept.

When originally, they could do nothing but accept God as their saviour, God was the chalk board they could write their speculation upon, nothing has changed.

Fortunately, science in scientists has been her own saviour and ours since time began. For when they set the standard God was there pre the Big Bang, he was. Only now we can prove it scientifically.

Which is not to be a deserved accolade for scientists. But is for us grafters who kept faith in the God concept. Not least because we recognised the aspect of God had to be. To make sense of science first and himself now.

For God was motivated to be motivated, for while I will give reason and cause. Four or five thousand years after we first came to God religiously stated. Which is a situation never now to be reversed. Because without knowing it, God lent his hand to aid him for his sake first then ours first. For when God made us, we made he.

CHAPTER 10

Science Third - Four

FORTUNATELY FOR US ALL, SCIENCE at best did deliver us God. Even under the extraordinary circumstances of some modern day scientists, who may at some times have dealt God also. To then change their minds later. Which should never be the trait of true worthy and fair-minded scientists, who's mantra is to try, try and try again.

Be it so, in order to evaluate the standard of experimentation. Which when done will always produce a result, even to the negative. Which in scientific terms is never to be discarded. For by adjusting the experimental criteria, differences produced may also be negative to intention. Which is a positive result.

That is why all scientists could fit God to have set the Big Bang to activity. What happened later was beyond the capability for science to corollate. Where were her markers. What were God's intentions, being two small thoughts entered in the past twenty five years only.

Perhaps brought on because we per scientific study, were beginning to see the sequence of chemical reactions. From one billionth of a second after the Big Bang to yesterday, 13.8 billion years later, which by anecdote is the night sky.

What our great and good did not realise, was to the effect, nothing is new in the universe. Each and every galaxy, then solar system within, share all the same features in repetitive regularity. An entire galaxy will form, then blow up, to reform and do the same old stuff again and again.

For in all cases, they/we share common ground. We each are made up of the same elements constantly repeating, except perhaps by timed age. Whereby if we form or find more elements than the 118, we have identified in our solar system and galaxy. We will also find the same number even with those yet to be discovered in other galaxy.

Which can only be a hit and hope scientific strategy. For although science knows about other galaxy, it is only by count and assumption. For there is no living chance any scientific enterprise, can begin to imagine. We will ever become familiar with other galaxy outside our own milky way.

Which draws God into frame having never lost the image. Which has always been bigger than the individual human being of whatever creed, colour or claim. Which makes our task easier if we are as fair minded to all levels and grades of scientist, even top grade ones.

Even if some moved to be negative while being positive about God earlier. Plus, even if some scientists were always negative. Sometimes not only for or from scientific perspectives, perhaps under prevailing circumstances.

Not to wave my or our religious banner in self praise, nor to belittle or chastise. But we in God, do know more of God than we know, and God knows this, but not the why. Being our greatest asset in universal form these past four or five thousand years.

Stated before, but now in greater depth. My open suggestion our religions were, are in fact the main source of human energy. To be the leading form of communication any medium of interaction can use. Is reinforced by the following, which remains in parity, but at their own levels.

Politics, although a leader, is the weakest form of human inter-action. Because whole banks of political systems. Take it upon them-selves to deny God in context or block individual self choice about such matters. Yet are to become beholding to some new religious ideals often expressed politically.

Whereby some groups even within our U. N. carry religious tolerance of old and human rights of old times also, to be the norm.

Even when knowing the limit of such standards, have not served us well so far. Perhaps expecting science to lay a better platform for us to deliver from.

For in part, she sometimes does not differentiate between how religion or politics run. By confusing some issues in relationship to her style of setting proof by experiment. Yet is unable to fit the idea or concept of God to any specific religion or political outlook.

Returning to the fact of God before the why, but of separate significance. Although thought to be a better servant to us all. Science who gained its charter from the efforts of religion one, then politics two. Became science three on her own merit. Providing she kept within certain boundaries more so religiously.

Which she did well by keeping in touch with all aspects of how God was revered and acclaimed generally.

Her greatest plan was to maintain, if not only to set the real criteria. God in a sense was the creator of everything if at times indirectly. But he was/is the source of all. Which is why when needed, it was right and proper, science set God where they did without opposition.

Unfortunately, science along with all other of our influences had different perspectives not unconnected. Her outlook and general study area involved the total time span of time. Therefore, accepting God was the instigator of time, was a formula setting. Like God set the big bang to go.

Whereas through religions first and politics second, we had to rationalise the not so obvious as stated before. Although religions and politics are well dated and were in the hands of our species historically.

If and when any aspect referred to us four or five thousand years ago, even until now. Which should not apply now. For if we are of today, we are to live our lives until "Natural Body Death from old age". Our lifespan of now is linking only the 20th and 21st centuries. Which will set its own ruling.

Our links with our ancestors, although very real, had no valid time set connection except religiously. Determined by the medium of God 10,000 different ways, but God,

So, in effort without the need to fully compare, the only thing we carried forward in equality, was our perception of God. Producing a curious crossover. Whereby in human terms God found relevance to the thinking of the day as it was held four or five thousand years ago again and now.

Changing without altering until science had procured God and denied him at different times in crossover timescales. Leading to the proof of God before any religion could. Even though this did not happen until less than ten short years ago. Creating its own problems yet to be resolved without harm or favour, just imagination.

If I had assumed in error, science is to be our nemesis. It stands on her ability to change tack about a subject she is unqualified to comment on. For she has no charge to include God experimentally. In order to only assume God was positive before being now negative.

Without pattern, when science in any guise set God to have started creation. After his assumed initial input, a core standard was there to include God in everything. Which worked until my reading of a hinted at post 20th century revelation.

If God started the Big Bang and we later proved him not to have existed because of the frailty of human doubt. Plus, shown by how God now seemed to act by directing some of his religious charges to kill in his name, plus when after thousands of years of experiments. At no time was God's input required to influence anything. Plus, God did not serve the neediest with help. Therefore, in an experimental mode, God was negative.

Translated to read God was not now active nor was he ever. Although not a general declaration, but in case, my reference here, is it was a senior scientist(s). Who had previously supported the God concept under all plans. Who now turned twice, in stating through the agency of science. He/I did not now believe in God, a full human right.

Would he/they/we have followed such a shallow trail if my/our United Nations new maxim of to share "The Rights of Humanity". Had been introduced earlier than my timeline of now.

Alas when a senior scientist(s) now deceased. Turned his mind from God after once holding God's hand. He/they had to complete his own circle mind wise. For if there is no God in the 21st century, there was none 13.8 billion years ago.

Therefore, when the Big Bang activated, it being a scientific assertion, was a spontaneous act. Something just happened, so in effect what did happen spontaneously. Was the unappointed forming of the universe including you and me.

Features we do not have to account for, except on behalf of science or the ranting of some great scientists, not to be an issue for science. For by her hand alone. She brought God back to us a short ten years ago. When the God Particle was rediscovered via the LHC, under CERN control.

Which when done displayed in dramatic form of how unsure science is of herself. So much so almost not to be trusted by her own innards. Which other great scientists highlighted on two counts.

One set about in the year 1944, then one in about the year 2012. Both of huge significance, for in name, both put science fully in the negative. Yet when recorded did not display science to be spontaneous.

CHAPTER 11

Science Third - Five

ABOUT IN THE YEAR 1944 with science on the brink to bring us into the atomic age. Unfortunately, under the first example of trying to create an atomic bomb, even if to end a cruel war.

On her own account without limit, science when working on this great project, designed or designated to aid mankind. Also offered great peril to us. Alas the expected limit of how new experiments in nuclear fusion was expected to work caused doubt.

Some scientists working on the project in expectation of its potential. Queried the outcome of what might happen when nuclear fusion was first released by mankind.

Counting from when the bomb went off or was set off or ignited or when dropped. Science through some scientists simply did not know the limits of their own invention.

In order to trial all theories and alleviate all doubt. They set to test by experiment the limits and effect of this new technology. Not to waste time, merely to examine if some worse guessed at outcomes would be realised.

Doubt expressed by some scientists, led to their theory, as they were creating an atom, atomic chain reaction. Whereby matter in form, was now man made to disintegrate very quickly. Almost in the billionth of a second time range.

Therefore, where was the limit of such activity once the process had been released. Sometimes lampooned now, but then ago circa

1944; the main concern expressed by many scientists. Related to the obvious in connection with what they were doing.

When to explode such a device and create a chain reaction of matter deteriorating very fast. What were the limits of such calculations. Could the chain reaction continue unabated. Would the chain reaction we were creating, run beyond our control. By miscalculating the effect of how we were releasing atomic fusion or nuclear fusion.

A curious situation to the extent. Overall science then ago was not sure. Almost proved in paradox, when she tested the new form of atomic destruction in/on her own homeland. If to evaluate the bombs integrity. Plus, to see if the chain reaction could be contained when the new atomic bomb was dropped on enemy territory. Which it was in 1945.

By the act of testing first, which was an experiment, they/we in the name of science stated in the positive, we do not know, we are not sure. Yet by a strange mix of emotions on another level, practically all the senior scientists involved in the atomic bomb project. Were tied to the positive about God in being, that is circa 1944.

Scientific doubt was double endorsed circa 2012, when another great experimental milestone was to be undertaken. But not before a similar scenario to the bomb testing uncertainty of 1944 was offered.

Our new experiment in 2011, which involved the search for the smallest assumed piece of matter in the sub-atomic range. Now that we, science understood if partly from the 1945 atomic bomb testing. The building bricks of matter, atoms, had also been made up from their own smaller components, hence sub-atomic matter. Hence to find proof.

From 2011 with the ability to attempt and find the smallest size of matter to set a standard, which is always a scientific requirement. Already knowing of some of the component parts of how atoms were constructed. All we were hoping to prove in general was how small could matter in particle form be,

Although valued work was done to set us in the boson range of study about size. Plus, if boson matter was identified, it might already be in scope to be lattice field formed. Which had been proposed by the best end of how science should work. By setting a viable cause, reason, for events to occur rationally.

By good chance and under fair connection. Without claim some of our media sources in valid use. Connected the boson name in term to be the smallest, therefore the first in size. Had to be involved around or in or from the Big Bang period of time in a scientific timeline.

Therefore, as God was involved by media timing then ago. The smallest or the first size of matter could only have been set to God's standard. So was born the God particle. For who else or from what source could matter in any definition be called if ever to be the first or smallest.

Before the switch was set in the Large Hadron Collider. Heed had to be considered from various angles about what was expected. By knowing the standard needed to search for results. Whereby forms of matter or anti-matter involved, were to be accelerated to as close to the speed of light, we mankind could achieve, a monumental task.

Some senior scientists in being aware of possibilities offered, plus, even by our/their forms of experimentation. They knew we were to enter new ground. Whereby at such speeds we might induce a living phenomenon we already knew about.

We might here on earth, create a black hole, a regional area of space so dense in gravity. It sucks in all forms of matter in its vicinity never to be seen again. Turning a new corner for scientists to worry about again, what next or what now. Almost like how some worried about creating an uncontrollable chain reaction a few short decades ago.

By good fortune and planning, when the LHC experiment was first run in 2012. Its main objective was achieved. We were able and identify the smallest of matter ever to be.

So, in effect we now had a new start point consideration for time in God's name, who did not set the Big Bang. For time never started in the fashion we assumed 13.8 billion years ago.

Time only started four or five thousand years ago by us, but on God's plain. It was we and only us, humanity, who levelled God on all counts. But who have yet to convince God, which calls for more than experimenting.

Because with God now involved, we must make a case for us to be interesting enough to God. For him to maintain his already shown interest in some of our ideas over the past four or five thousand years, when he had less to go on than he has now.

With that in mind, let us begin again to nurture science off her slow blundering committed around 1944 and 2011. When she let self doubt creep into her psyche, because she was not fully aware of her own capabilities. Not least because some scientists acted like ordinary people and drew human emotions into the equations.

With those two dates above of the modern era, we are drawn closer to science for the good. Apart to our good fortune of being alive today. From which all of us when involved as we can be, will eventually know of God. Not least because unknown to self, we discovered God for his sake. For until then he knew not what to do.

Beyond sincerity, when we endorsed God the singular, which in all cases means the head God, we did the most incredible things scientifically. Which becomes a comparable ratio, never to be measured except by experiment. But not by science nor by politics, only religions God associated.

But in deference, not to a religion, but the concept of religion, just like the concept of God. Being a provable fact before we have to consider we will create a chain reaction or a black hole here on earth. For as far as God is concerned, we can prove the concept of God. Over and above how we can prove our 10.000 world religions are all correct.

Which finds root scientifically before it can be seen politically. For although both features have run with religions and God these past four or five thousand years. Our weaker force politics, in part abandoned God when she came to compare how science was shown to work.

Not that politics is out of the picture yet. If from now she sets her stall on my new and invigorated religious terms. She will grow better to fit her promissory commitment long overdue.

At first by not attending to the steps taken syndrome party politics induces. From now, like from all religions, she will run on the main principle of fitting "Natural Body Death from old age" to be a fixation.

Though science does not enter that range yet, because she has not seen how to, which is forthcoming. She did unwittingly serve to us the greatest motive to begin and understand the real concept of God in the making by reason.

Whatever science or particular scientists, made of the idea of God now, then or yesterday. Tomorrow only began in the year 2012 scientifically. When science releases by revelation, the fact of the matter, matter had a diminutive size.

Before we connect with that example of our experimental prowess. In good faith though tenuously, we must acknowledge in full form. From about sixty years ago, when a renowned scientist working in the field of splattered atoms. Examining the finer and smaller make up pattern of how atoms were formed.

A fair realisation came to mind, whereby in atom study, it was now considered there was a series of smaller and smaller particles arranged to make up the whole. Which is a single atom.

Though to be a matter of scientific conduct study. Beyond what was realised in guessed study so far. A place was made for where the boson might fit into ideal formula. Science in its own good name set the plan. This imagined small piece of boson matter, could even be dispersed in lattice field formations.

Perhaps to fill what was thought to be the empty space among other atom debris, within the area of single atoms at first.

Plus, by inclusion of a religious input to be suggested regarding motive, for at that time of only yesterday. God was still responsible for setting the Big Bang off.

A consensus was mixed, generally stimulated from the best end of media sources. Who directed the search for the boson, next in line or to be the smallest size of matter. If/when found, could be called the God particle.

Not to be whimsical, but in press jargon the God particle is a better and more active connection to make than the boson lattice field. God makes better headlines. But more, some of our fair minded press hacks. Could write an emotional storyline about God rather than small matter.

Which might be used to bring some of our religions into better view if they all now had the same starting place, like from the God particle.

Above all expectations on scientific terms, by having been funded politically at a cost of billions of money. When science found the boson range of matter or now the God particle; the air was cleared. For here in proved photographic proof, was seen the God particle.

Meaning but one thing only, even if unseen at the time. God did not start or open the big bang. He attended the start of how we marked the start of time instead. He committed his hand to the advent of time without knowing why. Until he was revealed in the Large Hadron Collider under sponsorship of the CERN organisation.

A cold hard political enterprise allied with the guise of scientific wonder. Who in kind were more prone to offer politics a return on her investment. For when the God particle was found; the lead was not for or towards God.

It was more suited to look for forms of dividend, which might still be the case for science and politics. Playing you scratch my back and I'll scratch yours.

Whereas yours truly, born of political and scientific ignorance. Supports God more now that I have him at inception. Which puts him to be at the start of time 13.8 billion years ago and now. Which cannot be denied for the fact of his position in terms of reality is not in doubt.

For who in the political world can now argue a case for no God or God does not matter. When he/it is the substance of real matter. Then who in the political world can argue, God does not matter or count. For he has no bearing or form to be realised.

Even when connected to scientific knowledge, which tries to explain the matter of the universe but cannot explain the how or more so the why.

Who can explain the matter of the God particle but cannot explain the how or why. All of which must be read in new chapters under a new perspective of the same title, so be it. But now from the year 2012 we all can stand on the shoulders of God to view the lattice field of God particles already in place.

PART TWO

CHAPTER 12

Introduction To The Future

A FTER JUST INVITING ALL TO stand on God's shoulders on their account. I can offer no great stimulus due to any individual for doing so. In a sense we, practically all, have been doing that over the past five thousand years 10.000 different ways.

Though no new plans can be made from such an effort. Post such an option, perhaps under less commitment. I can offer all interested parties to sit at the table with God as I now do. I warn without threat, I will do all the talking. Your verse will come when you set your hand to condemn me first and God next.

In the meantime, no sound is to be heard from any quarter to phase me on our behalf. All my efforts, ideas, thoughts, reasons and hopes have only come from my life experiences. Which were gained by you good people as your life experiences also.

To discuss or challenge them later will bring no real consequence. Because in counting or checking them, amid the real heartache and sorrow. Were moments of unsurmountable joy and happiness tinged with fear and regret. Issued by no more than reaching maturity of age and character.

From which I drive my original observation of me to be the talker only. Giving you the chance to lick your wounds and sit in silence to learn at first. Which will bring us all to emotional levels for the benefit we all will achieve in the near future.

If we all sit to face God at the table as I suggest. Do not be alarmed if I interrupt God which must be done. For it is we who will set God's path from now on. Which can only work one way. For which I will set his direction, unless he or any of you our species, can do better. Which can only follow from 'in the beginning'.

Which occurred not 13.8 billion years ago but only yesterday. In the year 2012 when the LHC of CERN direction did not produce a black hole to swallow time or chain react.

CHAPTER 13

The Last Experiment

I LIKE BILLIONS OF PEOPLE HAVE and do maintain a God concept. Although self challenged by how we gathered 10.000 religions about us in all uses. Self challenged by how we have watched some political systems. Ignore the concept of God to distraction.

A mixture often copied by how some of our religions then ago and now. Deem to operate themselves on Gods terms. Whereby they kill religious people in God's name, directed without presenting the why. To become an experiment in human interaction that cannot be made fit.

For where is the scientific or political ethics of such actions. If no experiment can be met or no direction obeyed, were we directed not to kill politically also.

How then, even in these modern times, can any group or individual be directed to kill those who are claimed not to follow God on or by our terms. When the people sometimes killed do not follow or believe of God on any terms. Or in any case.

For killers so inclined, come with us all and sit at Gods table, but still with only one spokesperson present, yours truly. All may sit at God's right hand in comfort, but even then. God will not answer now no matter how I vex him, which can never be our aim.

All I am to do is make God aware we all are God aware. Which is now drawn from the year 2012 on two counts.

One, half stated already. When a very renowned scientist(s), who under unknown circumstances. A person who at one time. found more notoriety after he wrote a world bestselling book. When done. amid the acclaim he got for his theorising about everything. Misquoted by me now, he is reputed to have said. "Now that is done, we can begin to look for God".

Not to be sure of all personal details, but later on, such an esteemed scientist seemed to fall into doubt about the need or reason or why to look for God.

To such an extent he or high grade scientists of like mind. Seemed to withdraw their support for the theory of God. Naturally open to speculation. But if God now had no standing, what was his/ its replacement.

Although God was well used in the Big Bang theory. Even if the hint was, he lit the fuse or turned the wheel or flicked the switch to set the whole thing off. As galaxy are part of the result of the Big Bang if it occurred.

Then if God was not. How was the Big Bang banged. Unless it was to have been set by a new scientific study without to call on the un-existing God. So, when the night sky was set to form, the original first act without God involved. Was titled to have been spontaneous.

So much for the exactitude of experimentation. Meaning as a product of time, evolution humanity style, eventually was spontaneous. Plus, as most of our earlier great scientists walked with God. Often bestowing credit for their greatest of discovery to be of God's influence.

Where in the sand could the line be drawn to separate previous great men of science and the new breed of greats. Who seem to practice more in the fields of virtual science. But do not now include God in any play station.

Of course, credit must always be given to those who genuinely expose knowledge and learning too all. Providing all doors are kept open. At least to the extent that if I don't know you might.

Which even now must be a written in stone scientific maxim on the bare grounds if I do not know or understand, we might. Which can be made spin on a half truth or be denied on the same half truth.

Because some great scientists did not see what other very great scientists were working on or looking at, even to be out of focus.

All such imaginings can be realised by noting the similarity of two human events. One which occurred 13.8 billion years ago; the other to have occurred less than ten years ago. Although pure scientific phenomenon, they both belong to God then ago and now. For he is the only common feature of time in time.

Not to confuse the issue, science in capital letters is of less consequence than any single person alive today. For she is not a noble gas or any other defined element. Nor is she an answer, nor can she propagate on the set terms to reproduce herself to maintain the status quo of following pure instinct.

Nor can she determine or decide upon how those in us who broke the bonds of what instinct allowed occur. To be able and replace our human mistakes by offering her solutions, when she is only a reflection of us all whether we like it or not.

In other words, if science or scientists, wish to interrupt me when I representatively suggest to God his real purpose. It is not I who keep her quite it is we. For science has no voice of her own, she is a complete product of mankind, in the pursuit of our study and not sciences.

She is not entitled to string two sentences together about God or of God if they hint negative. That is not a scientific topic, the whys and wherefore of God are not in her domain. They belong to us alone, the single species of humanity.

But what we can allow is for science to reproach herself, but as ever now reinforced on our terms alone. Which by reflection it will be seen why I take on the challenge to set our stall in place.

Whereby I stand alone to convene with God in our dignity, but never in direct contact. We should never have allowed science cause doubt to our expressed integrity already done 10.000 different times.

Again, to focus our minds without enhancing our natural instinctive ability to be hostile. Plus, to square science away. We must heed her errors without bearing malice or animosity to any aspect of science or those who operate her various departments.

Even if some of them have been sponsored from political funds, often in the expectation such enterprises by returning positive dividends. Plus, they have managed to quash in part the surety of God in concept, which is a chalk and cheese situation.

Especially crucially now, when politics and science have performed combined acts separately over the past one hundred and fifty years. To limit how the ethics of religion should work or were expected to work.

From which as I remind myself, it was our religious outlooks at best to have been the prime movers for science through politics. To be our mentors, because unless through them, we were never really disposed to take direction for God.

For we did not then know God did not have any idea what to do with us. How could he have, we only showed up about four or five thousand years ago, while he was in his own presence a very long time before that.

So, to help us better understand why and how God was only entered these few short years ago. I will start again. In the beginning, when I close one door on God's behalf and open the only other available to reconnect him. Is done by me in our name we.

CHAPTER 14

The Second Reunion

Without changing direction only emphasis. Within the same meagre period of time, these past one hundred and fifty years. When we were able and credit God to have started everything in the name creation. We missed a beat on several levels.

For when we were able and contemplate God was the creator and all around us was from his hand. We lost sight of three things in no particular order. All relating to tribal humanity. Which is still the bridge we need to build to cement God's interest in us more than before.

Though no blame can be attached to our condition. We enhanced our errors because we did not know the how of any situation we opted for. Even when we populated every continent throughout the world.

Where there is full evidence on all lands but held in check by tribal laws at first then by religious overtures. Which meant we all carried God with us tribally. To be a small matter of little consequence.

Until we came to sequence God, our tribal God's into either our surround or by imagination. However done, and in whatever cause, some we got right, some we got wrong. But all were correct.

For in definition, all procured for us, even by tribal associations, a place to be eventually with God. Formed from two imagined situations of how and why.

How could have been led on a no time frame basis. Whereby tribal existence was a constant. Our ancestors brought us into life, taught us, then died. We in turn brought our children into life, taught them and likewise died.

Except, because of what we could accept to be a constant. If through our learning and teaching patterns, we were satisfied, not much more was needed tribally. Then for self comfort and in deference to our existence, plus to round the circle and complete the cycle.

Why not follow as we were in the environment we were in, with the flora and fauna replicating us in a sense. Was there not a hand or an influence to be responsible for all we experienced. Even to be strong and powerful enough to bring the images and sounds our ancestors made while teaching us.

If we could remember them while they are now dead. Will our children remember us when we die also. Who or what is responsible for how I think. Might it not be the same that brings daylight and rain, which seem to be a need for all things. Yet is also capable to mix life and death in ways we do not understand.

So might stand the Great Spirit, who also teaches, but only to our needs and desires as we think we understand them.

Applying the why to other situations could have created its own standard on the same lines, but with more complicated factors. Not least driven by different circumstances on similar lines to what did happen elsewhere, but unrelated religiously and tribally.

For if on other lines a tribe also settled for the same format except. Several tribes already interacted with us and we they because of conditions. We to our advantage formed our historical even ancestral connections to be of significance.

To the extent we could trace an ancestral link to our equal parents to have been a male and female. Then before to have been master and creator of all we saw, including how the sun was to rise and why it rained. Plus, in equal style we created the first concept of religion by name to associate God with us and we with him.

For before we knew his shape or style in being our one true God, who was our ancestor, which meant creator, so we imagined. Even if to be more specific, which formed reality.

By tracing our most recent to their most recent ancestor by pure memory only. Our story in unwritten form set a direct link between us of now to us of then ago. But who were we.

Without distinction we were tribal, who in good faith and high ignorance. Formulated our own history unlike how other creature species could not. With our history set on one plain, whereby all circumstances were to our tribal existence. So, when we followed our ancestral links, we eventually came to a point of time known as our singularity.

A point of reference when we met our original ancestor, we called God, but in line with our splendid and masterful ignorance. By a dead person year count, our meeting time with God our father was about five, thousand years ago. Which was not a bland guess, only a tidy one.

For in no time at all, being about four or five thousand years long we came to God tribally and still. Without having to enter the understanding of God's wait of 13.8 billion years. Until he responded to, not a tribal realisation. But a species sound, made by the only group class of species, to have broken the bonds of natural chemical instinct, and natural creature species instinct.

Here at last stood a group in the species name humanity, finally to begin and understand. Although already well established in our God culture analysis. We need to set that issue in stone. Which can occur if and when we sit at God's round table, at first on our terms. Then we shall see.

Not set against how God reacts. But how we act tribally against our better judgement. Which is a matter of no consequence when I set the tone of further conduct to be only proactive. Which can only be established by us all under the one suggestion when in contact with God.

But is open to all to further debate within the parameters now set on God's behalf. For so far, we have not given God credit for the present state of the wonderful universe we can admire in the night sky.

By which without blame, we might blame our initial scientific approach. When we started to run scientifically before we could run.

By not being able to realise science and all her wonderful tentacles are of no consequence, unless. If/they are brought to understand everything yet to learn. Is already known by God in any case, even if he is not yet sure of his ability.

So how and why can an insignificant creature species dare suppose, they/we can educate God first for our sake then his. Which follows.

CHAPTER 15

The Round Table

S IT US ALL IN COMFORT, rest all our worries to set one task only. To realise it is for us alive today to be the first to reach the one and only God proactively. Which is a forward move with the future in mind.

It does not matter who sits with God at our table. For in all instances, they will be of this spread of generations, counted to be alive and living now, but much better we each will carry the best efforts of all our ancestors.

Plus, we have the extra ability to take what they taught us further, for in all cases we are of the moment. Plus, we are encased in new and better conditions of existence they never knew of.

We are the true collective, encapsulated by how we can now think under our new adaptation of "The Rights of Humanity". The plural collective of we over me for better human harmony.

A perfect solution to belay the old fashioned idea of expecting in the singular. When now we can realise it is vital to consider in the whole. Because we can now guide ourselves to consider past personal insights.

Like following tribal or racial or ethnic trends by continuing in the singular of species. Which we already know of, but were not sure of how to express that image until we found "The Rights of Humanity"

Other insights I have offered to introduce. Come with as much force and better insight. For when I intoned, religiously at first, we must gather another maxim to be one of my prospects. Whereby on religious terms we must adapt to set a common standard for all, but more relative to God.

For the idea opens doors, in that on religious terms, each person of all religions. Under my maxim to read, "Natural Body Death from old age", is to be our only expectation of how to die. Plans to include, no person should expect to have suffered slavery, intimidation, bullying, torture, indifference or exploitation or worse, until "NBDfoa" releases them/us.

My separation between religions and politics at this juncture, is set in time because we are all closer to God than we have ever been. So much so to have set the above maxim religiously first. Means we are not to kill of each other religiously again.

On the first level of concern, such acts like murder in God's name is an affront to God and a direct denial of natural history. Yet natural history in most cases, plus from some political outlooks. Allows certain kinds of killing if to survive or for survival work.

With the final twist in the tail set by me, held in the tail of most political regimes. Though in tandem with our religions, I set the same idea of "Natural Body Death from old age" only. At some stage might not fit all political systems per.

Although to be aligned with the same extra conditions "NBDfoa" offer. Because some countries do or do not follow God religiously, only holding political values.

Some activities in the name of state first, may create situations whereby if in their claim a crime syndicate oppose a state directive good or bad. In the name to steal or rob even to kill. For they carry no religious code to be controlled by.

Under such situations, some state directives in counter, might destroy by death such forces. On the grounds they are anti state, which is tantamount to be anti social by terms of having little regard to life or death by any reading.

Therefore, they forfeit the standard of obtaining "NBDfoa" for themselves. Which remains undecided. But remains a political core, wrongly addressed.

Because all states on political lines only, need to be able and defend their "The Rights of Humanity", in terms of defending the rights of the collective over the singular.

If the few in singular form display standards not to comply with all independent state directives. Directed by our United Nations, who still expects compliance of her secondary political directive. For all state nationals to expect "Natural Body Death from old age" plus extras.

If ever and because the U. N. has to standby and allow small internal political actions take place to defend the integrity of a political regime first. So be it on political terms, but the U. N. can and must set limits or restraint applied. Only when pressing her directive of applying my "NBDfoa" prospect over any state directive to wrongly apply "The Rights of Humanity".

Also, for the best of reasons though of more intensity, over the good or bad. Our U. N. must stand square shouldered with all religions. For she will have set their standard to be called of who can claim to be a religion.

Based on the main principle to be maintained on all religious terms. Whereby no person of any religion who would use God's name to kill others of any religion or not, just to kill. Under our U. N. directive, are not to be classed as a religion. Until at least they can get God to countersign our U. N. charter, which is not a fable.

Having just recognised the surety of all religions and systems by U. N. certification. Plus, all political systems and attachments provisionally. Before we can sit at God's round table in self representation.

We must rest science on her ample laurels. When we read the following account of how science eventually brought God to us all while in self denial of the concept.

Simply because she as a topic has now displayed her very fine and very good limitations. All in the wrong context. For when she put her hand on God, she denied what she could not see or feel. Yet now spends her split time in two vectors only.

One, whereby she wants to or tries to account for in understanding, how every past event occurred and in what cause. Two, she then projects into the future the impossibility of events that will never be seen or experienced except on paper. Simply because she does not know who she is in the name reason. Yet denies reason.

Even so, for our total benefit. I will set her to be fulfilled as far as she can. When she too can sit at the one table, we all venture to, with God at its head.

CHAPTER 16

In The Real Beginning

With clear eyes we can all accept in 2012 the Large Hadron Collider by processes of accelerating matter to splatter other matter. Hit its goal. For in an instant of time a photograph was taken. Indicating to all and sundry the object of the experimental exercise was met.

For here was proof, we of humanity had at first found evidence of the smallest matter form imagined. By other factors, when it was given the name in mention to be the God particle, even before the experiment was set up.

Nevertheless, but in evidence, when the photograph was taken. Science got a new name to be the prover of God let alone the God particle. Where better to start than at the beginning. Except by reflection.

Although science keeps showing her petticoat without realising it. She almost spoilt her self image within these meagre one hundred and fifty years I have mentioned before.

When she brought to us the Big Bang Theory, she wasn't always happy with such a scenario. After all, how unsure to say all that we see in the night sky, was at one time compressed in size to be as small as a single pea or at best to be as large as an orange.

But in good order and in good time, such a being was released to grow under the only key possible, deity. Which by the thinking of one hundred years ago was all that could have happened.

Because then ago there was no other way to explain our existence, unless we were created, hence deity was the creator of the Big Bang, but science made it a theory.

Not to labour on about the battle of the sciences modern term. But as voiced in the past few years by senior scientists. the Big Bang did not happen, it was just a theory.

Therefore, God did not set in motion the advent of time, it was all spontaneous, which works until the time is done for any of our 118 plus elements to give reason and cause for their/our existence. Which is still in the balance.

So far there would seem to be lots going on with no answers except to deny cause. But how to deny reason. When the very source of doubt is literally a figment of our imagination. As it must be, for science in all its forms is only subservient to mankind alone. She is our exhaled breath.

Fortunately, almost against the personality of some, even many great and eminent scientists. it will be from us, her status is restored, but from now on, on our lines.

In double note to recheck why we experimented to try and find the God particle, comes from good scientific sources. Whereby a series of scientists by following and tracking the makeup of what at one time was thought to be the original God particle: the atom.

They traced it beyond its limit of size to contain in part the guessed at boson range of matter, even if to be set in lattice field form or not. If the atom was the smallest form of matter. Then smaller forms were found, so on to the search for the atom's atom.

Which realised to be our/the God particle. So, in 2012, began God scientifically by our religious head. Which cannot now be denied.

When to bear in full mind, science is not an element, nor is she a factor of fact. She is only a means whereby we of humanity can bring God to realise his own task. Which he can hear while at the table of reconciliation we are all entitled to sit at.

At first, as we live now before "Natural Body Death from old age". Then post God's acceptance of what is said. For believe you me, God will hop skip and jump when he hears what we have to say in order of preference.

Which begins now post 2012, but a little bit because of 2012. Which is a reverse of 150 years of doubt carried by growing forces.

Not to credit or dispel the idea of power science has claimed for herself. But they are the very reasons of how and why we have reached God at last. For when science moved her own goal posts in pure vanity.

Experimentally and scientifically, she missed the beat of how and where and why, we of religion and God. Would be able and weigh her efforts against ours for God.

Which is a no contest reality, because we had found the 'fifth dimension', our religions. Before science reached the fourth dimension of time. Which was far better than our original adaptations of how we viewed time.

Relative more to the conduct of our ancestors before our own conduct. Which oversteps our limit and understanding of what time was or could deliver. Whereas our new big brother science, had all time at her disposal. Even if at first to include God as the instigator of the Big Bang Theory, to start it in activity.

What science missed open end, was she is of no consequence at first without humanity, then secondly without a God inclusion. Even if to explain how the far reaches of the universe work. Is of no consequence unless to be interesting to people who are not scientists.

For when science began to display her wares, like the intricacies of how galaxy worked. Even to invent new friends like quantum physics, like wave structures, like wormholes. With additions of mixing parallel universe or multi universe into any imagined equations. Plus, to think and operate theoretically about all else.

Plus, to claim extra to the four dimensions we know of. To the extent we need a further seven dimensions before we will be able and explain the real nature of the universe above what we can see in the night sky.

Plus, in more chaos, we seem to have lost a lot of matter and cannot account for the supposed mass of the universe in full flow. So, in consequence we delve with dark matter on its own account, which is not on hand to justify itself.

From which by reflection we can maintain all aspects of reality when we successfully present our case for God. Graciously supplied to us in all aspects in the year 2012. Which not only revealed the God particle, but the only case for God ever.

Which when now realised will allow us all sit more comfortably at God's table. Even if only one voice is used on all our behalf now.

I speculate as most of our great living scientists already do. But on our account, I mention God in his reality context. In the exact same way, all aspects of known scientific interaction are already stretched beyond the limit just mentioned.

I do not draw a picture of God from any of the imagining some scientists have already come up with to promote science only. For that edge creates a fantasy that science is its/her own entity, which is a falsity. She has no fuse to light except those attended to by mankind.

So, in due consequence, because of her indifference about God. I set this fantasy right. For when a photograph was taken of a single God particle. Apart from defending the vast cost in political terms only. To find something that was always there in any case (just proved in 2012).

A flood of doors was opened without any chance to stop the torrent of new appreciations owed to the devout of good old fashioned God. For now, we could see him for the first time.

So there goes my parallel universe, my quantum and or theoretical physics, my extra dimensions, my wormholes. Which all in turn already bow to God, none are outside his own range even if not fully understood by us first then he.

If and only one or several thousand great scientists, settled there was indeed a start point for everything. Only it was spontaneous, that is cause but not reason, which again is cause unsubstantiated.

Under such circumstances, what we must first do about the time, timing of the Big Bang. Is recognise how it energised without intent and from all matter compressed the size of pea. Which is simply not tangible.

Even if science through some of her greatest mathematicians, try to quantify the nature of matter pre the Big Bang. By inventing scientific subterfuge to round the corners. Like pretending dark matter must exist, because light matter might have gone astray.

Until we can lay the dinner table, so all the portions are the same, which sets new standards.

Meaning we only ever needed one scientific constant, which is the God particle.

All to do from now on is fill all the gaps not left in the past. But made in the past because we set our scale from the wrong perspective Big Bang wise. Regarding the original way the concept of the Big Bang Theory helped us make a start in how we could visualise the nature and development of the universe.

I will now present my version of how events did occur from about 13.8 billion years ago. With when we were able and realise. All histories were/are only of significance to us of humanity.

Science from now on can only aid and assist on our terms. For now, we deal the cards in exactly the same way science had to suit her ideas and ideals. But now God sits at our table.

CHAPTER 17

Proving The God Particle Theory

IN 2012 WHEN SHOWN THE supposed identity of the sought, God particle. We saw a volume of study open ended. Yes, there was photographic proof of an event. With defined support of it or part of the same. Which was a true sign of there being a new or separate piece of matter to be now the smallest in size plus forever.

Who in the name of science from now, then in 2012, would never need to try and prove the existence of the/a God particle, God particle. Which aids us to set standards for in case. We now have a start point of reference to cover all theories ever or at least from now on.

Therefore, in essence now that we have a defined size of matter. Recognised by separating from its host, we can scientifically say, in the beginning was the God particle.

Plus, to accommodate it or the fact of it being able to be split from a conjoined circumstance.

Gives light to the incredible, a recovered God particle was also a Mother God particle.

For if it was part of either an accelerated proton or neutron aimed at a target proton or neutron or parts thereof. To be separated howsoever meant but one thing. The remaining bits of, minus the God particle. Were not what they had now become, for they were less by a limb.

Which means leftovers was the other result of the experiment. Although taken from part of the atom. Whether it was an electron a proton a neutron or sister small bits, now minus its boson or God particle.

We had something, from which when I detail my idea now. It stands in mathematical proof. For that very agent of science through the reasoning of some very great scientists. Even or more so, over the past 150 years or more poignant. From the concurrent lifetime with all of us alive today.

By simply not accepting any God standard if on religious terms or not to believe in the fantasy of God in any case. I have offered a reasonable service to all scientists so their/our future studies could hold their own ground. If more outrageous theories arise about our existence from other scientific theories.

Humanity who must be able and live through any new proposal, can use my symbol of, open bracket, question mark, close bracket, (?).

Plus, when seen attached to all future equations or formula. My representative symbol for God (?). will allow for further projections even in theory. Bearing in mind science is often only theory.

In double reference, it should be added to all existing formulated expressions set to explain how history activated itself and how history must now lead us to behave. Leastways from as long ago as the year 2012 in this modern era.

In serious reflection, I set the allowance for all great men of letters, who now must use my suggested symbol. They by self choice when setting their definitive formula base. Can self determine where to add my new symbol.

It can prefix any suggestion, like with a plus or minus symbol before or after. So, formula can be entered so, (?) + XYZ, or XYX − (?). Which is intended to offer a greater measure of understanding to layman like yours truly.

People who should not feel their ideals are always under attack. By better informed people who play their own hand of solitaire without regard to others. Simply because they think they know they are right or can create their own answers.

Now at least by including my symbol they can still be right, but at least they now offer by show. We have an opinion also.

Under my new regime, no new or old formula needs to be ridiculed or overstated or overcompensated if better mathematics, though incomplete, comes along.

When I now continue, I cannot enter the symbol (?) even if for God. For in my case, I have to include ideas that may not belong to science, nor can I prove they are of God.

Especially when I have led, I can fixate God at the table we are all gathered at. But here goes. As a group my last bit of scientific ammunition to prove we have all been more right than wrong about God's existence in the past and for the future especially, but now under different terms than before.

The properties of the God particle shown to us all in 2012 are immense in application if not in size. For when it was separated from its host mother form, enough so to be declared by name. It displayed a unique aspect of its form, it was recoverable. Which means little until it is claimed by any scientist down to people like me and us. It has properties so far unimagined or not.

The photograph produced by the LHC displayed a piece of matter and anti-matter at the same time. It left an energy trail shown also. Even though it had been imprisoned, it was self sufficient, just in case.

Without the need to build bigger LHC's. we can all hold our breath and live with the wonderful effect the existing LHC brought us. For instead of debate and worry about who did what and when. Science gave us a better idea of where to dig. Not for all the answers, but for our proper beginning.

Which was directed and occurred about 13.8 billion years ago under the silence of magic. Set by the master magician, who when he opened his magic box, let the magic flow. Not least because he did not know how to do anything else. He did not even know how and when the/his trick(s) would be realised.

Therefore, in the beginning, at the cost of the Big Bang Theory. For her story did not carry my (?) symbol, which would have allowed her answer back. At least about the undefined state of matter it was assumed to be. Before the Big Bang was spontaneous.

Not to follow the laxity of allowing errors create their own wake. Before contact, some small acceptances have to be laid down before the anti-matter and or fully charged matter of a God particle interacts.

All of which is held within the total hopes and expectation we alive today expect or wish for. When to realise it is us alive today who can secure a better meaning and understanding of what could be for our offspring, only to the good.

For when we reach "Natural Body Death from old age" and they later copy us. Much more enlightened, we can later exchange notes. For when those events for us all and for friends occur. We can be better made aware the progress our young have made over and above our efforts of now.

For one thing will be certain of what we give them in respect. In respect that our new standard of aiming to let them die of old age by not being in the situation we sometimes create. Like from war and religious murder.

Because we had suffered under human rights in the singular. But they by our good politics can now offer "The Rights of Humanity", to draw us all to the collective as the plural of one species. Then so on.

CHAPTER 18

The God Particle Theory

KNOWING FULL OF OUR EXPANDING universe, is not to be a constant. For the dilemma was reached about one hundred years ago. Leading to the setting of the Big Bang Theory. Hence a big bang, almost to be considered like an airburst explosion. With all the split components moving away from the core of the explosion and each other.

Then forever to be recorded so or assumed so to continue. Which might have been fine if my (?) God symbol was used as part of the primary description of events. So, we could fall back on something to support the originality of such an idea, even if to have been presented mathematically. When the Big Bang was put forward.

Even for things to have happened in that way, no consistency could ever be measured. For once the initial form of matter reacted in an instant, so too was the result in an instant.

Like if after the Big Bang occurred. Mathematics gave in one billionth of a second; the universe underwent its first phase. Which by description meant it was given to have form in the name of having separate units of space or room. For galaxy to form, but in separate motion.

As far as we can understand, each of the fantastic galaxy we see in the night sky are still moving away from each other in all directions. Which by now, if only one billionth of a second or 13.8 billion years later, we are told an enigma.

If an explosive force generated energy by following the standard of creating movement. Where the Big Bang occurred, especially after 13.8 billion years. Plus, to allow its remnants their right of movement of interaction and speed.

All galaxy formations should in effect be moving away from the point of their instigation.

They will in effect be deserting their point of creation.

But will still give the impression by stealth, they are moving away from each other. They must now be traveling at different speeds. Plus, to be creating a bigger and bigger void at where the air burst banged.

Which in all cases can be written up or already has been written up mathematically. Which might be made easier to follow, If God is not included in the equation by some senior scientists dead or alive. Which tells another story for all of us.

Now at last or at first, the bones of my "The God Particle Theory" can be aired. Which is no more than we already have. Except by my interpretation, I include God to be the factor in the only possible way, until a better Big Bang Theory comes along.

Befort the beginning there was a deep dark area of space/room what was and is. But nothing happened there, except in which was God. Discovered a mere four or five thousand years ago by the one species mankind.

Which meant God was recognised on our terms and by our understanding. Which was difficult, for God did not really know what he was to do at any time or at any juncture. Until his role was to be made clear to him as an act of liberation still unknown.

What might and then did occur a long time ago in the total silence, darkness and coldness of a void we can call space/room. Can be counted on the fingers of one finger.

Such an area from its own source was naturally set with a lattice field of the smallest pieces of matter, now known of by name only since 2012. Nothing else was there except God particles.

No comparison can ever be made between on the one hand a congealed form of all matter compressed to be no bigger than the size of a single garden pea. Even to be compressed to be as big as an orange.

Which when exposed was there to create the night sky as we actually see it. A tidy mass form of almost equidistant galaxy, starting nowhere and going nowhere, just there. Each seemingly allotted their own space/room to endlessly do the same thing. Until a better use is found for them.

Never to blame progress, but from 2012 we must seriously consider any new story that comes along. So why not start with mine. For in simple tones my tale has a better form of imagined structure than needs to be explained mathematically.

When I offered the terms boson with and or lattice field formation(s). The original plan was not mine alone but ours. For the suggestion led that God particles were almost set at random throughout an area of inactivity.

My part to enliven that plan comes from my own calculations. Not least in now realising we/I do not need an expertise in any branch of science to tell what I/we can see, even in the night sky.

Which is why I am not embarrassed to mention God in any context to release him from how we considered him in the past. Therefore, I can associate God and God particles to have an enlightened connection.

Like how I can visualise God to have set in simple plan and under simpler rules. What might lead to him finding interest in anything that might happen. Once he set all; the only single forms of matter, in the same diminutive size as each, a plan.

To be placed in lattice field form, spread equidistant apart in the same total room/space already there to accommodate anything that might yet occur. For in reflection, if that was done on my account alone. What else would be needed to occur before I might see what could happen.

Firstly, when to consider now, all matter already there was all matter. Be it lattice field spread or clumped together the size of a pea. It/they needed to be enacted, and bearing in mind, their situation of being in total dark, total silence, total cold and in total gravity, negative and positive. What next.

Which could only be to apply the lowest common denominator. All aspects of matter were given the independent act of motion at their own behest.

Which in target seemed to be the only thing God could do. If he wanted to see what and how the vastness of room/space already there could deliver to draw his interest. For in spreading motion to all forms of matter already there. The pending future was out of his hands.

Which could only mean, God set motion to wait and see what would or could occur without his input anymore or at any further time.

We, humanity, being the only other force in the entire universe to be able and congregate around what the future might bring. Have now failed God once more by trying to make the Big Bang Theory fit our plan for God's sake.

Alas the pea size of matter, could never work even mathematically. For on those terms there is no mathematical structure to accommodate one type of matter remaining in its place of origin. While others even of the same construct have moved or now live very far away from where they started from, just like the remaining elements of matter.

Whereas if all matter lattice field spread, interreacted under the one ability to move. Then on an untimed scale of movement. Which had to mean interaction, for in finding the God particle in 2012. It was rediscovered to be able and move 13.8 billion years ago.

Therefore my "The God Particle Theory" as an updated of the Big Bang Theory, which is now 'The Exploded Big Bang Theory' by me. Can no longer offer to be viable in scientific terms because it cannot be now supported mathematically.

Whereas again, if I use God to have set my, "The God Particle Theory". By the simple act of setting all God particles with motion on a wait and see basis. We now have a viable plan of how and why the universe in galactic form does what it does but never the why so far.

By not even beginning to understand, we by some form of our actions at various times along the past four or five thousand years. By or for no other reason than our personal habit.

Stimulated the object of our desires and hopes on our perception of God. Who by unrecorded return, did in ways, perform before some of us mostly in the singular. Which in turn lit two lights at the same time.

One for us, there is God, once for God. Who must now have found interest in a body or group that might yet fill the enormity of what "wait and see" would deliver. So, stands today.

When God particles were in the abundance of their form. Spread almost equidistant from each other in lattice field formation. In the cold darkness they naturally occupied; were given instructions of no kind except motion. What then along with the night sky of today.

Why God did bestow motion as the only act ever to be for the same and constant form of matter ever, God particles. Fits on several counts but with only one to count.

For if God knew of how time would be spent for the next 13 billion years. What could be the point of repetition, unless in Gods un-attending hands. In the short span of time, 800 million years long following the epic 13 billion. His interest was somehow raised yet his standing was not until now, then how.

CHAPTER 19

The Active God Particle Theory

MOTION AS A FORM OR shape or image in the style of movement needs a motive. Which cannot be self induced if it has no form. So, when God set all God particles with motion, it as an act was the first new event ever. But had to be carried, for the original and true standard of lattice field particles had no motion.

Therefore, even when wait and see was introduced as a back stop, to wait and see. If and when the lowest common denominator of God particles could not interact as they were. What could be applied in the same name of being indifferent so something could enter the wait and see range of waiting. By producing something else insofar as a single God particle dressed with motion moved. It might never have expended energy. For in dark space/room times ago; the positive particle in meeting with negative motion or in reverse, had but one name, matter or now God particles.

Unless the fact of motion as a result was pure energy or the reflection of energy, which is not to say it was or wasn't. Where we must draw a tangible line in the sand, is how is it easier to go back in time realistically. So, we do not have to close our eyes on what did or could happen at zero hour.

So, by offering my theory that God set God particles with motion stands on two counts. One, God is. Two, God does not know that yet.

So, in preparation to find out and in setting the theory of everything. The only way to begin is at the start under the only rules available.

Whereby God did not prompt any action whatsoever, for time was not an option or a range, but motion was and still is. Plus, irrespective of my mention to be positive or negative about the abundant God particles, now loaded with motion.

Needs no reply, for the time in mention is pre how the greatest of scientific minds came to the Big Bang Theory. Without being able to balance the books of scientific reality. Whereas you and I can. For we through me, have set a workable plan which needs no definable formula. For religion was not even around when God bestowed the full lattice field of God particles with motion.

Which in their own place, acted to react as they saw fit without plan or style to any imagined outcome. As nothing was measurable then ago, not even God. But his idea/plan was the only available set on a wait and see basis.

Whereby he could not be involved in anything. So, irrespective, when some or indeed all, which was not the case. God particles moved, most crossed lines to eventually crash and either combine or bounce off other God particles ongoing.

Then by eventually cross mixing as best they could; the combination of sole God particles together. Formed atom elements of different sorts and types without plan. But early doors such early formations continued to interact creating block formations.

Not as defined structures but confined by how far they could travel. Which when to count energy ratios if, limited most combinations of them, unless under exceptional circumstances. Which might have been of interest to God, except.

When after several billion years of types of interaction. God saw wonder in his own creation of doing nothing else but to give his lattice field of God particles the anti-gravitational act of motion.

Which by return and under a new clause, evolution. All such God particle formed the night sky as a rule. But still without form. By no example or from no lead, what God got back in dividend for his rather dull effort of letting things just happen because there was no other plan possible.

For God had no aim, for in being the singularity plus, he set time without knowing the why. Unless perhaps to see if matter from any size to begin with would or could return to him the factors of reason, cause, purpose. To enlightenment, then how so.

Which can start here and now if we set God the Active God Particle Theory, as best we can. At first in the name of humanity then further apart in the name of science. Which is not a conflict only a competition under the rules of vanity.

To balance correctly all to do is place our scientific rendition of the Big Bang Theory in one cup. Against my The God Particle Theory in the other cup, then set the fulcrum.

PART THREE

CHAPTER 20

Standing On The Shoulders Of God

T O BEGIN AGAIN AT THE start, we must recognise the main players as the cast. Set to win, but only by fair means, which are hard to follow, because in this plan there is only one player, humanity. But we are not alone.

What can be the explanation for the night sky, which is a magnificent display of time alone. Then in the same context why is the night sky drifting in aimless movement without any consequence. Which does not require a motive only reasoning.

Although the night sky could always have been a spontaneous experience, but for one thing. The ability of a small speck in the entire universe, to have built the universe. We of the one species humanity.

An inglorious species who while on the top of their game from about four or five thousand years ago. Went into slow decline, not for what we didn't know, but for what we thought we must have proof of to know.

Being an unqualified occurrence, measured only one way. Whereby we gave it to ourselves to understand the unimaginable size of space. Measured by its spread of galaxy. Plus, the unimaginable distance of space, which meant space could never be contested by comparison, only through gimmickry.

Yet we fell short in the clumsiest of ways when we came near the real reason of why the universe is so wonderful. Not least because at long last time produced the species humanity.

The key to open all doors of all knowledge. So, we can teach God how and what he must do to correct all our ills, even though not counted by God, only we in us.

For on all levels so far, God cannot hear 10.000 different religious pleas from the one species. Out of millions of other dead, extinct or still alive creature species who manage quite easily or did manage without God in any case.

So why should we be so important over or alongside those other creature species. Who by all accounts were far more likely to progress and change. Over how the chemical elements of galaxy changed ongoing.

Which is its own story of great consequence. For if other creature species, and they did change like us of humanity. But on their own lines, for all seemed to settle for pure and or natural instinct to be their line in the sand. They had reached their goal, humanity had not.

Whatever the reason in our case, it was blatant and unrefined, for we worked both ends against the middle. Although we are the unique species in all environments. Not least because we can and do use all of the continents as our one habitat.

We self engaged in forms of interaction which made us more unique. But by also following styles of natural instinct like other creature species. Plus, in being able and differentiate better than they.

Like in following the same restraints, we gained or created additional features to draw upon ourselves extra capabilities. In unique forms already documented not only here and now.

But from about in every book, written paper or study ever done. For when we come to realise, even without understanding. The sheer immensity of the universe by size, quantity and distance.

We revealed ourselves to be the only living source anywhere in the entire universe. Who were able and think above where our next meal was coming from. So now we had left pure instinct.

Not because we needed to, but because it happened. Which was and is pure progress. So, in line, when we did arrive at such a chance. We must take advantage of that case. By not squandering the opportunity of realising the why of anything or more so everything.

Which before anything else it is for us to set the ground rules, of all better future progress. Able to be obtained by any creature species for all creature species. Which is done when we now stand on the shoulders of God.

So, he too can show us our station, while following our directive to him of what to do next.

For when God did visit individuals or groups over the past four or five thousand years.

It was because after about 13.8 billion years of waiting. A new-ish insignificant little species, kind of said or alluded to things or ideas that caught God's interest. Over and above the backdrop of galaxy forming or uninteresting creature species having settled into the restraints of pure instinct.

By good return, at such times of Gods mild interest in us/humanity. God did nothing, for he knew not, except to now/then, instinctively know. If he did give it away, he was mildly interested in a personality. He would have wasted the event of what "wait and see" might yet deliver.

Thus, by maintaining the constant of no input, he kept the mystery of his own integrity.

Which covered all parts of the universe also.

When we came to the clear fresh idea of God. We were both aware and unaware at the same time of what that realisation meant until now. From my study, which is always our lead, whereby we can direct God to his podium, so he can give his first sermon by following our script.

On the premise that we, the species of humanity, have resolved to undo the random chaos within the universe. Set by us in the name of science in her own vanity.

By letting God introduce his own form of mathematics. Not to explain things, but to live and feel the downside, plus to experience the best end of complicated human emotions.

Set fair in representation of what drives us best. Even if to mingle in the paradox of "The Rights of Humanity"; and the expectation of "Natural Body Death from old age". Which when copied will allow God join us in form but under our direction to his taste.

CHAPTER 21

God Is, So Let Him Know

FROM ALL THE GREATEST EFFORTS of mankind. It was not until the first quarter of the 21st century we came of age. How relevant is that statement.

For in that timespan, we set the right parameters so we could begin at the bottom to see what would grow. Our first and only seed was the God particle, which is the collective of God particles always.

In quick succession we naturally nearly realised. God particles do not beget God particles. But in all cases, they needed the liquid of motion for the ability to move. Before we could fill the garden of room/space, already set aside for the wonder of combined growth.

Resulting in the night sky, in poor vision. A series of mainly white light dots above us. But when examined closely at a distance, the array is often so stunning to belie its reality, but why.

Although a wonderful feature in our discovery of why it is there and in parallel, why are we humanity, here also, eventually was given in reply. It is all at God's discretion.

Which is a fair observation, except where to set the demarcation line between God and us, but on who's terms but God's, set by us.

As it is more than plane there was other forces around before mankind got here about 3.000.000 years ago, more realistically in our present forms by development. From about 60.000 years ago. Then finally from about four or five thousand years ago.

Until about less than 10 years ago, when God found in us to be the time element to make a case for him. For until from ever then, God was in his "wait and see" mode.

Which ends now, but not between us as we live until we die a "Natural Body Death from old age". All can be told post then. From where begins God's own reality with the one and only species to realise. God is.

When to count 'in the beginning' dinosaur style, not a lot changed for God's interest to work. For if a galaxy existed for six or more billion years before it did something interesting. What would happen in 150 million years of different species of reptile coming and going in monotonous regularity lead to.

Above that story, what if a single species was to swim the seas of the earth. Reproducing in normality for the self-same 500 million years with nothing new to add. How interesting could that get.

What then when a squeaky newcomer species came along, a braggart group who supposed all they could see was for them. Even if to be tribal in their own eyes then ago, recently ago.

Groups to be so vain and brash to assume what they saw at any time was theirs in all cases. Yet were clever enough to think ex box. As I/we are here, what is our purpose and for who's end.

Groups smart enough, at least when thinking from the top down, they/we don't want this to end. But we do need those below us to maintain our status quo, but how to make ends meet to suit all.

Unless to be able and assure all of our tribe, group or clan from the bottom up. If they help us in life for the afterlife. We will raise their station in the afterlife with us, but to still serve us at our tribal God's behest.

Which did work as a deal. Until on the same lines, other groups paid a better dividend, which was channelled to be from their/our God to us especially. For what we had done pre afterlife to be rewarded post death on new terms.

All of which worked for thousands of years in this God fixation mindset. People carried the plan one way or another, until the picture was reformed. Fortunately, under the greatest of the same prevailing circumstances.

Which when we followed our God concept religions. We generationally honed them not only to suit ourselves in prevailing situations. Like how society was changing; and forcing some change by different criteria.

Often by show of hands generationally, perhaps because some religions were not performing well or overperforming. To already take away personal liberty or worse.

Maybe even because God gave no quarter to those of us who played his hand in our eyes of peace, generosity, love, benevolence along with other pious outpourings. We felt neglected, ignored and now abandoned. So now some felt we had nothing to give. So, God could keep to his corner and we ours.

If some of the above examples are sad even cruel. Remember God cannot lead to improve them. So never blame yourself, God cannot help to spite what you might hear. So never blame yourself.

At this juncture, God cannot even judge, so if you would need his help to judge you or your tormentors. Never blame yourself.

What we can all do best while we are alive in group generations. Is empower God in his own domain to heed us. For we wish no harm on others no matter how much they deserve. But we will tell God what to do unashamedly in our name. but now by his style and wisdom.

If and it has been broadly assumed, God is more at hand in the afterlife. Why query that option. Why not enhance it without bad consequences, for it agrees of our union with God.

On show, by at first indicating to God, we are the one species with the one expectation to die a "Natural Body Death from old age". Without having caused any unnecessary harm or hurt to any other human species member, whether they deserve it or not.

Which can only come when we adopt the off-centre maxim, God is. Always to be a connection with God but now on who's terms. Plus, to be fully aware the idea is to include our life experiences in terms of conduct. To be reviewed after our "NBDfoa" calls, by God alone, because God is.

By good fortune and bad planning, we have already usurped God. For in open debate, we set for God his homeland was heaven, sometimes called paradise. Then to make sure of no gate-crashing. We set he had another place of confinement.

Not as luxurious as heaven, in fact an inferno called hell, set on a fear factor rating. Which might have worked for the crime and punishment stakes, but never by God's hand under our rules.

So let it be said when we designate God, we also designate the nature and type of his address.

Which we can now post code as heaven 1 and heaven 2. Not to challenge, only aid.

Because of false associations which might have been made against God, by groups of people or individuals. Who might opt for the concept of hell. From where they can join forces that do not exist, to set opposition to God.

Which is too old a story for us to fool ourselves with again. By allowing those to be ungodly the option to remain so post life. Does not diminish the factors of post life judgement. Which by review will be a review by motive.

My stipulation in fact, asserts that when we die, we enter God's domain on his terms still under our direction. Which are to be open and honest. Not that we will now tell God how he must behave.

For when we enter there, God will now be aware and will have learnt to enjoy his great wait of time. For when he gave every single God particle that occupied the already room/space there the option of motion.

When using the motion aspect of their new construct, only if they used it anyway. In the beginning, God gave God particles motion on a wait and see basis.

Thirteen point eight billion years later, he was none the wiser to what might yet occur. Until the species humanity established a foothold in a tiny part of one galaxy the Milky Way.

So, bizarre they in we, named the total universe. Which did usurp God, for he did not know where to begin to make his own case, alone. But he did have several inbuilt assets we have yet to realise to him.

I had previously mentioned God did not have form or structure, which was true. Except he is all that is. How big can that get. But one of the last steps we must take before we release God to his proper task. Is to give him a proper shape and form, so he does not feel neglected.

But first again, we must check his personality for his sake. Bearing in mind God witnessed how the first two God particles then more interacted. After they had been set with motion.

Which almost answers the question God or science. For although science proved the existence of the smallest matter available. Enough so to give it a name or type to be in the boson field.

Then to endorse that image by suggestion in its their boson field form. The smallest of matter could be in a lattice configuration. When translated, means it was spread forth.

Being kind or like what God might have done in any case for a starting point at least. So, on that basis I will deliberately usurp science and all of her tentacle study fields.

By now saying honestly, science by coming to the same conclusions all religions already had come to. In respect that God had to start somewhere. Although the terminology of the God particle was a rational human choice. Even if at first entered by media sources.

Who by reference placed science to her proper position of only ever to be a servant of mankind following religions first and politics second. Destroying the myth, about a small trait of mankind in or about some of our scientific pronunciations. Which were sometimes entered to query problems we may have had about how we referenced God.

Science never had nor does she now have any authority to mention, even in passing about what God could do or not do. Nor to suggest if she could and God didn't, she was right. Unless her appeal was to the self possessed. Who in cases did not need a vibrant concept of God by religions to thwart their situation.

For in some cases, to be overtly wealthy, God was not needed to be used to suggest how personal wealth could be better used. Which will raise its own issue in later pages.

God is, and always is and is now going to find out for himself. Now that he has been endorsed by sciences God particle exposition.

Which is to be the beginning by explaining the end as it can only be done. Now that we have the full ingredients together to hand over to the master chef God.

Who when he dons his chef's hat and looks into the mirror. He will see 10.000 different religious faces. He will see black, brown, yellow and white faces, even in combination of the above mixed.

But much better he will see us all individually. Which is a true blessing to us all on his terms alone but still fed by us. For on that one to one basis he can record in likeness the single species humanity.

Alas he will also see face to face, mass murderers, torturers, abusers wanton killers. Despots of any political stamp. Who can order to kill in the name of Fatherland or Mother country.

So too will he see all the devout connected to all religions set in their own form. From wherein some might return a devout nod of their head in God's image to him. In recognition, they instructed one of their self same brethren. To kill for the very God, they now face up to.

So where might this occur on God's terms if to become a reality. Which is not such a problem as it might seem. When to consider it is we, all of us setting God his place from our plan. To be in heaven 1 and now heaven 2 also.

CHAPTER 22

Heaven 1 And Heaven 2

B Y THE STRANGEST OF COINCIDENCES all of humanity almost
drew the sane conclusions of God, starting about four or five
thousand years ago.

Naturally our species history can endorse the fact. But some of
us if tribally motivated, did have tribal fixations long before then.
Which were almost complete by acceptance for all the best reasons.

Why trouble God or better known then as the Great Spirit.
With details we will find out about in any case when we die. Our true
destiny of fate is at the behest of the Great Spirit.

Not a bad philosophy, perhaps, but the detail has not been
explained on Gods or the Great Spirit's behalf. Which is a detail, for in
our outlook regarding afterlife. We already accepted our Great Spirit
affects us and our enemies or other tribes, differently. Which worked
and still does unless the Great Spirit in God needs to know more.

To have previously stated, even if by hinting, God in all forms has
been with mankind for over sixty thousand years one way or another.
Allowing for our next big move, which is now, from four or five thousand years ago. When we gave God a face albeit tribally at first again.

Such a connection has another platform from which to radiate
from on tribal return basis. God was given to be tribal. Which laid
the foundation to think in terms of monotheism. When a one main
God society was dominant.

For our/their one God outnumbered all other God's of less importance for other tribes in our eyes only. So, if it can be said God was prominent to tribal issues. Plus, most tribes with one God philosophies, wanted God to close in on them. How to fit that idea, was borrowed from what we were given to expect in the afterlife owed to us all tribally.

Although naturally scaled from the top of any society down. An extra feature was added to our outcome when we died, even before the afterlife. For if we died in service to Flag or country. Our lot under due report from our superiors of rank. Would be decided when we reached the afterlife.

Which was a mixed up situation settled by a wonderful human ruse, of inventing the impossible to us, reason. So, in place of our ability to understand how so. We gave all matters of death to be in God's domain for judgement on our evidence.

Which could work, providing we supplied God with a name on two counts. One a place name where God could do his work. Two, in order for God to organise the mixture and style of those of us who were going to die in any case and what for. Our bodies lost to age or crime or war or cruelty. Could be settled and equalised represented by our soul one and all.

Who when we were to be made accountable for how we had lived. It would have to be in front of God in his heaven or paradise. Naturally a place where our lords and masters would also gain their merit.

But in order not to embarrass them or us, God could set the unsavoury of us, when they/we lived. To go to a different place of chastisement, so when we died, we then went to hell.

Plus, to be held in extension in our spirit or soul form, being a replicated image of who we were. But viable to God's desire one way or the other, but of our own consequence, while we were in our previous life form.

Heaven and Hell by idea are fair analysis of why and because when it come to that. Which is close to the best new options we can lead God to for his sake.

Having already established what we do not know but fits for when we die. Is not taken on lightly, for we ourselves are entering new ground, even for God. Which might be settled in this small way so we can feel better with our own opinion of ourselves, one and all.

Long out of God's control, we/humanity, constantly stir up events to shake the formal normality of the universe and all its goings on. Carried out regularly by most of us daily.

For we are all creators of pure thought. Yes thinking, no matter what about. We of humanity are the greatest force in the entire universe because we can and do think. That means all of us without limit. Although in some cases there are edges to the limit of the type of thinking some of us undertake. Overall, we are all supreme, because collectively our thought patterns are universe unique, which is our unique blessing of good harmony eventually.

To share with you/us, a top example of what the importance of our ability to think means. I set this tale without result or condemnation.

But if a senior religious person, a senior politician or a senior scientist, even a senior school or college lecturer or teacher. Set down or passed to us a test, trial, exam or quiz or idea.

All our answers would be judged by standards they work under. Nothing they passed on is original. In copycat style they simply turn the page for us. But worse expect us to follow their lead by their understanding.

Which could be bland, boring and irrelevant. Yet such people even if well intentioned, judge us on what they have passed on to us by their terms of reference. To the extent if we do not reach their standards or acceptances, we fail or worse, they do not see, they fail us.

More so because they do not read our standards and acceptances. Which can run on high ground or on the flat lands, but always in our talent, which is viable and real.

For we at our own desire can think in ranges beyond how we can be taught. Small time we can visualise, think, what an item of clothing might look like on us were we to wear it without trying it on first. Plus, big time we can think big about religion, politics, science and education on any lines we see fit to.

Providing we do not deliver thoughts about any of those subjects to cause harm or hurt to operators in those fields. By to guide them also, our, their ability to think in any range, makes we the species humanity unique in the universe, for we made it so.

A good place to rest our thinking laurels can be seen by how we have established a vast one code rule for everybody. Whereby we are now committed to set the standards in charter. We of humanity expect only "Natural Body Death from old age". Which is a thought process.

But in the meantime, we can decide mainly on our own account what we must do to get to old age without causing harm or hurt to self or others.

Which could be something to catch God's eye, although he can't do anything to help us now. For that would spoil the surprise when we meet with him at his gig.

Not to run before we can walk, but when we designate God's plan, with what we already tried and know. We will all be measured without exception, for the design of my plan is to set God in a place only he can manage when we arrive.

But before we can start at the beginning. I return to those of us young or old who often feel left out, overstepped or ignored. In line with our joined excellence, I set this poser.

If you/we sometimes feel a little down, just look at the palm of your hand. Slowly imagine a picture of the moon on your palm. Then with the earth then with the sun, now close your eyes. With that image in mind, you literally will have the best of our solar system in the palm of your hand alone. How good is that.

Which shows the pure magic of thought we human beings, who might not know our twelve times table. Can show to belong to the greatest order of species in the universe. Those to have discovered how and why. How cool is that.

We alone, you and I can form real and powerful thought lines on our own account. Without the need to be directed by politicians or teachers or clergy or scientists unless they free think like us.

But in fairness to all the above; and to show our level of understanding. By now knowing of our ability to visualise, meaning to think. We can join all forms of study only if we want to. Providing we make no claim to be superior as others might. For when we all now reach "Natural Body Death from old age". For God to be our host, we can set the stall.

We can all contribute to how God can react on his own account. Against all of us who gave him his new insights. By releasing to him a designed plan of conduct, based on our conduct while we lived.

Whereby all of us on equal ground when we die, can expect God to balance the events of our living. Which will have been made easier for God if we all made the effort to stay alive until "NBDfoa", even if it was hard for some of us because of dour circumstances. Who nearly fell under the pressure put on us by others often for their foul reasons. Because they did not like us or thought us different.

Which is not always to be a condemnation, for often our tormentors were troubled. Sometimes under circumstances as harsh as we were subject to. Alas sometimes because they were ugly of character.

So, when we charge God to his new duty for his sake, not to be overcome. Plus, in order to acquaint him to the evidence of the entire universe. Plus, to reassure him our set directive is to cast his duty in the proper context.

Comes from the simple fact that in all the time God particles were interacting in an assumed timespan of 13.8 billion years. Time only produced one valid species to be able and interpret God and his hopes. Before God reached the same now, conclusion. For he did not know what wait and see would or could deliver. But by finding interest in some of what had occurred, he began to realise wait and see would eventually deliver.

Even in or to the event the whole process of 'wait and see' was a subject and not a desire. For when the universe did start, God had no plan. Why, he was God, so may have waited 13.8 billion years over and over.

Which is of no scientific consequence, for she as a subject is not a desire. Only a tiny part of the drive in every single person alive today. With our ability to change any plan of time over any time period. For we found God in style but not class.

Which is why we now dare set God to task in heaven. When on our instructions but his style, he can set new standards. For in being God as God. We also released his real ability to express his scope. To be able and interpret every second of time past by any object, subject or person, but not in the future.

For that is the only format for God, which confirms the wait and see aspect of how we began, if to deliver any story.

In open reality God did not know how galaxy were going to perform even now. But he did know their makeup was entirely of God particles. He also knew new forms of God particle interaction, were added to the galactic mass in some places under different timeframes.

But in the next instant from about 800 million years ago, at least in our galaxy the Milky Way. A newer and changing form of God particle interaction took place. In the form of forming a new lifeform form of new matter. In the form names of flora, fauna and species.

But this time, of the new extra millions of nonchemical lifeforms, who used the natural attachment of evolution to extra account for the nature of some changes. Which were not of the old galaxy format, even though galaxy still followed their plan in any case seemingly.

Eventually, a single change, by following the same route all change uses. Introduced a new set of change rules from about four of five thousand years ago. Which although always a servant of the past. Became bold enough to set where the future could be now set in God's domain of heaven but with vital conditions.

To set the one standard for all people before we reach heaven. We must understand why we can call God or him, instead of it. How else might we address him, not as Mr Big Bang Theory or Mr motion setter. Nor Mr God Particle Theory, or Mr Wait and See.

Our reference unobtrusively draws God's image to be like us of humanity. Which is a better deal for God and us alike. For God is skin colour blind, nor does he need to keep slaves, nor to bully and torture or intimidate or put down or take advantage of. Nor does he desire or support murder for any reason of cause even if claimed in God's plan. Which is a fallacy.

On two small counts. One, God knows about every second and occurrence of the past 13.8 billion years. Which only can only be considered on one level, it was in the past. Two, God can now see he can be involved in the future only by what we of humanity have brought to him.

Which can begin in other rooms we have given name to, on our behalf a little bit. Then God's big time. Even though we set the plan, it will be in God's own haven of heaven one and heaven two. God can now join with our unique ability to think inside and outside of the box to teach us what we can further learn from our young when they join us post "NBDfoa".

CHAPTER 23

Hell, Heaven Two

D EAR GOD, THIS IS YOUR job, which has not changed until now. Though you found interest in some of us at various times along the progress of humanity. You must have mused at times at the way we mismatched our personalities.

There we were making it up as we went along age by age, generation by generation. Often inventing new God's on our behalf to suit our tribal personalities. Even to be more divided by some of our minor core beliefs about you.

But worse, divided about the nonsense of if skin colour or skin tones made a difference to our worth. But more in your eyes, which we still do not fully understand, but do on your say so.

For from various accounts through many of our religions. When you came in part sign to various individuals. Even if wrapped in their/our Great Spirit theory. Such impressions drawn, if not directly or on a face to face encounter.

We in part kept to our tribal identity about your visit. Which then ago was quite normal. Until it can be seen how some of us were scared by your appearances. Which in part indicated we were not collected as species; we were tribal if by skin tone alone or for other reasons.

Which was never a standard but a reaction, which often worsened as our human history shows.

From such bad and good experiences in the past about you and your effect on some of us. We put on our religious collars or hats to suit your message as we saw fit, using your direction or so some of us claimed.

Let's face it, what a disaster, in how from the same source of pious religious attitude, we humanity brutalised each other. Often on skin colour tones again. Then on the detail of how pious religious doctrine is interpreted, even of itself.

For your relief, I can withdraw any real blame owed to you. On the fair ground you by showing interest in some of us at various times throughout human history. Set you were interested in a new species. who made sounds of enquiry, never heard before anywhere in the universe.

You in facing us took to look like us automatically, which when found, meant you were dead pan. You never felt or realised we felt tribally independent from others.

You heard only species, not to need to know we had different ideas by diet, by habit by geography even by skin colour. For any extra verse in speaking to you or listening at such times was always of our tribal distinction. A matter we have yet to resolve. But now the end is in sight.

For now, we notice, we are in fact the same in the name species. When we release you to your chore of accepting at this stage of the universe. Expressed in part from a small section of it the Milky Way Galaxy.

Then a smaller section of that, our solar system, then a smaller section of that, our planet earth. Then a smaller section of that, our human rational to think ex box. We have a base.

You can only take delight, for with our story, we also pass to you the best of our human emotional range. Set in an array of bright lights that may cause you to be more interested in all of us than before.

Just before we do release you, I will point to the best of our conduct yea or nay style. Now arrived at by our good selves to be headed from all political, religious and scientific perspectives. For we will soon live in a new scientific range never contemplated.

By electing on our own account, both in all our religious and political ranges. Not to kill each other under those excuses. Because now "Natural Body Death from old age", is both of their objectives.

Additionally, by increasing our range to interact morally when setting the new standard of introducing "The Rights of Humanity", a plural concept, which reads unity. We can better identify our demons or bring them into focus, so we no longer fear them.

From the above, all can be achieved, at first with aid of our United Nations, to endorse my suggestions in the raw. Meaning how I meant them to be set. As cold fresh simple standards for us all to follow.

Which is wholly strengthened because I have not used any former political or religious standards or acceptances taken on side tribally. Nor do I condemn out of hand.

A point of serious reference when I give it for our U. N. to be able and set the core standard of any religion. To be sanctioned, endorsed and determined by the U. N. if they fail in aspect by killing in God's name or their supposed religious name.

Which if then any cross-sanction acts of religious killing under any name or for any religious reason take part. Such acts will come under the rigors of criminal law enforcement procedures.

Even when our U. N. correctly disenfranchises a former claimed religion, now not to be a religion for acts of murder, even killing in God's name. Such bodies or groups or companies cannot keep or reinstate their status under new headings. Like if now to call their former religion by a political name.

For in prior preparation our U. N. by already endorsing my religious and political maxim for all to expect to now meet "Natural Body Death from old age". Will have opened better doors than the ones she might have closed to murderers in God's name.

Of the thousand and one things yet to be done by us of the species humanity. Two of equal prominence need to be fresh aired. For both have carried taboo dust since we do not know when. Which means they have been in the corner to long.

So, in double consequence we must clarion both examples to destruction. For both are wrong, yet both right.

In fair play which will uncover other known anomalies. For when done all our dirty washing will be shown to spite the good, we have gained in this generation. Via those of us alive and sounding off to all our best advantage.

Number one concerns the tom foolery we show by how we try and alter things at the beginning under the wrong intelligence or intention. By grabbing the nettle without gloves on to declare the promotion of hate laws. A series of oafish political initiatives. Whereby an individual can be accused of hate in any context.

Hence hate laws, all to contemptuously say about them, is I hate, hate laws. Not for what they do or don't do. But because the idea has no structure. It can only run on misconception or at best to support the unworthy. With the correct presentation offered in self representation; the theory of hate would be neutralised.

Number two, almost on the same level as how hate laws were supposed to work, but under less supportable intention. When setting a barrier law to set the standards of being religiously tolerant.

For unknown reasons unless some extra historical significance had been given to any religion over others. Whereby to be Anti-Semitic is an affront in law. How can that work morally unless promoted by fools of conscience. Who think on one level only.

Which if on religious grounds only, can have upside down reaction. If and when the U. N. under new powers of direction, set it so that if any religion calls to kill in God's name, it then becomes a non religion.

How could this work if one group or several or none, only an individual. Gave out to be anti-Semitic in the sense of being a hate law issue. Could such a case be tested.

By reflection, if antisemitism was purely an example of a true formed anti religious attitude. Can it be against the law to hate a religion or religions. Or to hate the halo of a religion or religions.

Which becomes folded over when skin colour is brought into the equation of hate laws or anti religious laws or both. Which is then a travesty of pure moral justice. Because such rantings from the hate or anti brigade. Can become pure racist if any religion or political regime included all skin colours to their colours as a matter of fact.

Whereby if all religions mix and match, especially skin colours to produce forms of harmony. Yet draw opposition on geographical grounds. Which can be another form of hate or anti to be directed, if only against an idea over a reason.

Which is a scenario supplied mainly by the good offices of most political regimes. Aiming to satisfy the concepts of Fatherland or Mother Country, who by show often prioritise over racism or ethnicity.

In order for us to reset even reverse such trends. Although our U N has been directed to set new standards under our direction. She should better rationalise such cross wired ideas just mentioned.

Ethnicity including skin colour tones, which some people do and do not associate to be the same or of the same direction. Can be set in stone here and now again. We are species; humanity in you and me are the same among our obvious differences.

Which will be taken and given to God under that premiss. For in having set God's shape and style to be as he reflects in every single person he views. He will only remember the one species he was interested in. So let us feed that interest.

Religions will create their own consequences of anti-isms if any are shown to any religion. For all can be reclassified to be non religions. If they or any sect or separate group claiming association with a main core religion who sanction the murder of anybody in God's name, religiously.

Even if to propose they are clearing or cleansing the essential core of their own religion in God's name. For even without political mandate, we in the name of humanity are to deliver our plan to God personally in any case. But best through the good offices of our most abled control network.

Our religions still first and now our politics a closer second through the good offices of our United Nations departmentally.

Not to determine in finality on our hate law capability which is ill-used. For the reverse should be ably promoted from now. To offer its real and original intention as a proper force.

To bring into line those who miss the obvious of our true and real intentions to placate God for his sake and our purpose. For we are the first product of wait and see by any terms.

Therefore, to endorse our true integrity, we will show God how good it is to hate. But not skin colour or creed nor heart or honesty nor loyalty or love nor brotherhood or sincerity nor joy or happiness. Nor any great aspect of humanity, enough to bring a smile on God's reflection of his image in our face.

Hate must be carried to destroy the remnants of the users of bullies of overt bigots. Those who always see me before we, who always see the gain before the effort. Who close their eyes to the suffering of others always caused by others. Who look at the murder in war as a business opportunity.

But sometimes almost worse, they cannot comprehend on the obvious scale. Overt wealth as a sign is often a matter to stir hate over envy. Which in cause has led to some of our worst expressed standards in the name of humanity against humanity. For if want is stimulated by any means.

Any means might be used to redress what some could claim is unjust or unfair in representing the best ends of their/our rational and national political claims. Alas in to do so; the matter of divided wealth often only ends in producing a new and different wealth structure in the new society some of us strove to create in fair change for all.

Without change but in open reality. If and we have societies who carry overtly rich people among a God bound national climate of political settlement. Then perhaps from with change the only difference between then and now was on political lines. Who in cases might not need any God culture in their eyes. But still hold to some people in being overtly rich.

Without any consideration, when all societies through my "Natural Body Death from old age" standard arrives. Even to believe in God or not. But in case, God is to greet us as will be. All will be done in the time zone of heaven one and heaven two. Areas of time of new consequence. For there we might be tested one and all, what was your overt wealth for, for we have no need of it now. But tell me could it have been better used before.

Hate no, except when needed, anti-religion for no reason. For all will be left at God's feet when we meet in heaven one or heaven two. Which is where to find unused overt wealth.

God, if to be good mannered when we die and go to heaven in all cases. By then he will have the goods on all of us. Don't worry he is the master of discretion in all cases at reception and thereafter. Which amounts to a show of his true gratitude.

For even in knowing all things about then ago, he will be in eager anticipation of what our offspring; our next generation will bring to him also. They will have been primed by us who are to give the human species a new perspective by effect more than just image.

How we must value our self belief, will come from how we are prepared to not even settle our religious differences. But cement the concept of religion to be the laser beam to draw God's interest to us far more than we ever could before. For to set God in task is not to end all.

It is to set God a new role he will relish. For in waiting without knowing why, timeless. When we release him to heaven one, he will have a new beginning on real terms, for the first time in 13.8 billion years.

To think, a God particle configuration, humanity, set standards beyond the chemical reactions of other God particles so far. When they made galaxy, they also made us, humanity. Who also made God realise he had more to do than set God particles with motion.

From which in a timeline, a mere single generation later. Within a compressed living lifespan of around 80 odd years. A new matter form in the name humanity, let God realise his plan without information. But signposted, because he, God, set the first plan unknowingly.

So, we must set the route to finish it by who knows how. So why not now follow plan two with God leading without changing anything except to realise as motion in form was converted to the energy of pure new thought. Which was powerful enough to overreach all the assumed thoughtless efforts of formed galaxy.

Whereby when God particles continued in motion, irrespective of any idea of what to do or how. They on block, but in part. Reached a stage of interaction God was always there to accept.

But did not understand the why until the total effort and best effect of any God particle interaction resulted in producing the species humanity eventually, now arrived. Although entered before in theory, reality is a better story. Reality amounts to the one basic, time is not yet done.

For when thought patterns were able to be formed by us human beings only. In what range did they occur. Except on God's plane, which is why we can liberate God by any direction to realise his own task.

Again, without repetition. If and it is the real case, our unrecordable DNA substance of thought cannot be registered. Yet we conform in style to all other creature species who do have senses like us. But controlled within the bounds of pure natural instinct.

Then our range of the ability to think as we can and do, is unique in the universe. Afterall it is we who created the universe in all realities, which is a bottom liner.

Therefore, by instructing God to his task of setting order without destroying the aspect of how the universe is now. We by moving God to his choice of heaven to be his cloister is done so he can carry on with his new normal.

So, he does not interfere with what has been going on for the past 13.8 billion years. God did not know but had set all things positive on a wait and see basis. Which when found in cause by yours truly, the species humanity. God's wait and see really came into the picture, because in time we were the key to open the door to heaven one and heaven two.

For which credit due, credit given. So, in preparation we can expect God to set the best standards in heaven one and now heaven two. For his records and our sake.

By setting such criteria, we will have made the assurance our next generations can create the planet God would be proud to be responsible for. But still might be, for when he first gave all God particles random motion. He never could visualise what was to occur to draw his interest so vividly.

Yet to accept in true human humility style, he gained his new leads from the very same species who drew his interest a few short years ago when they/we were tribal only.

For which, not least because of our obvious collective attitude improvement, released to us all in the year 2012. By our endeavour, when we found we had a real beginning to now show God. We could set his role openly; we could almost feel his sweet human thoughts.

CHAPTER 24

Behind The Door

HAVING EMPOWERED GOD TO FORM his role and play his part. We must make slight adjustments to our wrong ideas about Heaven and Hell as we first read the story.

Having eventually, originally given to the idea God would reward us in heaven and punish us in hell. Depending how we had lived our lives earth style.

Always based on the assumption we were doing God's will in most cases. Also based on the wrong assumption God already knew everything about us in any case.

Which when giving that credit to God, we missed the point, that perhaps God gave us each a free will to make our own choices. But in any case, still knew all the answers of what we would do.

Although honest, the flaw of any like concept, was ruined in too many cases by too many religions. Some of whom on the lines of having a concord with God. Switched roles and did God's bidding according to their interpretation alone.

Even if to determine God would be pleased if they, some, took away his power base. Whereby they would kill on his behalf in place of God's judgement. For premature reward in heaven or paradise with God.

Leaving the open question of query. Does God know, did God know. Plus did God sanction any freewill base to decide for God and kill in his name. under a heading that was never introduced.

For God in all cases never knew what was continuously occurring over the previous four or five thousand years. When the one species of humanity accosted God over 10.000 different ways through forming religions. Some offering to kill in God's name and some not. Some offering to act for God some not.

All off key, for in line to assume God knew everything or everything was preordained or foretold. Meant we were never bestowed with freewill of any type or on any scale. How could we have been, if we thought to act for God, was our option. Which meant we could not act for ourselves.

Leaving the freewill concept askew. Because for 13 billion years, all galaxies had freewill, yet could do nothing to show the ability. Even when life species came along from about 800 million years ago. No freewill could be found.

Even when humanity came along in type and style from about 60.000 years ago. The cupboard was still bare on the lines to have been given free choice. Our gambit was to make sense of Gods full wait and see prospect.

Which has been led full on by our unique human ability to free think on our own account and associate our self made gift with the proper idea of God.

For God did not see any human form to be different from the shape or form of galaxy. Which almost proves my no freewill point.

God did not bestow the form or time range to how galaxy was made, why. God did not bestow how the smallest form of all matter, was able and regenerate and regenerate. Past the ability to create galaxy. To further regenerate and regenerate to create lifeforms.

For by regenerating to create 118 different proved of elements of matter, plus. It still had to be possible as it was. If when self regenerating in the vastness of room/space already there. Which in effect was a very large, Large Hadron Collider.

To the extent, in part the new existing 118 plus elements. Managed without any form of direction, to continue the feature of additional change from about 800 million years ago. Perhaps without further change until God's mentor came along four or five thousand years ago.

But who knew, God didn't, except in that same short time. God could pick and choose when he could be interested. With little evidence about other creature species shown as far as we can determine.

But in the lone case of humanity, signposted all over the world over the past 60.000 years. In strange cave paintings and rock paintings or writings. Enough to turn God's ear, to create an interest in himself.

What was the different God particle element to give me credit for something I never realised. What next, indeed what next, for when God had a peek at us along the way. He began to pick up some wrong signals from some of us. Like what was/is the wonder of God they, some keep alluding to.

Who is this guy who is going to sort out all their/our problems. Oops it's me, but I don't want to kill anybody or thing. So how can some seem to say I do and act accordingly on my behalf, how can that be.

For in class and type, although I may have given all God particles motion. If it was only on a wait and see basis, for space and room in the name time, I had plenty of.

Yet this one group, to have developed apart but in my name, have organised my wait to be a long wait. But now in such a way of interest I can move on. Plus, on their say so, I can now interact with them all by directing them in the future, post "Natural Body Death from old age". By their say so in my heaven one or now heaven two as well.

Which fits on all the lines I can now think on. Because their great ideas gave me cause and reason for myself. Creating a far better concept of when I now watch what the galaxy will do. Even if to produce better mentors for me than now. I can set where this can be done by their suggestion but now on my terms.

But knowing it is alright to start with the plan they left me as my own. For in the new realisation of heaven in reward, or better by my own term in recognition, I can meet head to head all I bring there in heaven one.

Plus, so far, I will follow the suggestion of there being heaven two. Where reward will be harder to find. For there I will use, human, my information species standards. To make those I call, realise why they are there. Which will be factual in both cases.

For in both instances now. Having heard the resolve of the only action species in the entire universe to give me an identity. I will use my office, having already taken on the reflective spiritual physical form of every single post life remnant human species member. To set them all in their new place. Set by their own conduct before any spirit form or soul form, was allowed form, only under my direction.

Because with the scales to have fallen from my eyes, I can now run with the first ideas created four or five thousand years ago. But to alter nothing, because when the tribal species humanity, then/ when ago, organised my role. Even if at first only committed to tribal circumstances. They even did not have to unlock it.

My realisations were there in part automatically, I am God. I set the universe in motion from its lowest ebb. Where else to start if not at the beginning with the lowest common denominator. The smallest of all matter, God particles latticed throughout the room/ space to hold them.

With nothing to do or nothing in want, until I gave each God particle the option of motion. A small activity discovered/realised, to do, by one of my favourite species, humanity. Who in the timespan year of 2012 opened new doors.

Who also pre 2012 had already given the universe a time ratio rational. Which is another good reason why I will spend some of my own time with them in my heaven one and heaven two. Where we can better acquaint with each other, this time on my terms but led by your ideas.

In part I rest this book in our idea of God's hands. Beginning when we all reach "Natural Body Death from old age" on a wait and see basin.

AFTERWORD 1

THIS AFTERWORD IS AN UNFINISHABLE effort on one main count. For in essence, I will again be speaking for you vis-à-vis. To become a familiar experience carried out on the same grounds as before.

I ask for a greater effort from us all. My theory of heaven one and heaven two is a serious result clause. Owed to when and how God can set the real beginning of our future.

Therefore, by future guessing, my aim is to set the best standards we can achieve pre death.

So, God might accept us in term post death, but on his terms still directed by us.

Which must remain our ultimate goal, because reality started when we were alive four or five thousand years ago. When we released God to begin and understand himself.

Plus, from then ago we set the rules and standards of the universe in God's name; and by the timespan we made for us all. Which although only 80 odd years long. Begins when those meagre years are spent by all on four levels.

Level one, operates on a purely human species level, which is a direct follow up of now. Whereby nothing is to change except to realise things will and can only improve in ways not yet realised.

Based on how we can all understand our efforts can work now that we have "Stood on the shoulders of God". Whereby we have gained the resolve to force change by setting "The Rights of Humanity" to be one of our new cornerstones of reliance.

Plus, on the rebound religiously and politically. To now impose our born expectation of reaching "Natural Body Death from old age". Set by the one species humanity, for God's own sake. On the acceptance, God, who must have set a plan of time to deliver to him answers for what he did not know, from a wait and see perspective.

Which duly arrived a long time after God might have let time begin when he mused to give God particles, the building bricks of all types of matter, motion. But still did not know why or what for until about four or five thousand years ago.

Level two, might yet be a far better realisation for God before us. For I have set it to refer to be or occur in heaven one.

Which before anything else, is a self explanation of how and why we of humanity. Can or could or did connect with God before he connected with us.

For on his terms, in all the time that was used up before we interrupted him four or five thousand years ago. With the start of our idea of religion or God in religions. He had no hand in anything over the previous 13.8 billion years.

On those lines we must reacquaint him to his proper role in heaven one. For we found it long before God. What we did not know was how to operate it except on human terms, which could be biased.

For our general thinking was based on the main principle, things would be more or less the same in heaven as they were on earth. Except they will go on longer and be somewhat better than what occurred on earth while we were all alive.

Which alas was fed from points of view held by the higher or leading class of each society. Who saw heaven to be a place of their reward, whereby on merit they would be able and enjoy their personal treasures and trinkets. Amassed while alive and living in their particular timeslot.

Hence many examples of ritual burials throughout the world both in history and time, generally set to leaders in society. Often with the addition, some leaders, would still be served by their minions as before. Which was considered to be their reward in the afterlife also.

Unfortunately creating too many falsehoods, which although always under review even today. To create the proper structure and style of how some societies behaved. Most old plans and planning, although by offering to their God their idea of God's desire. All missed the obvious of what mortal death really brought.

Not least because we continued to connect the experience with our ancestors and their hopes and desires. It was only when we now realise, we were God's answer to wait and see. On the grounds we took only 80 odd years ongoing, to set God in plan to spite all setbacks. Which can now be realised in heaven one under God's new lead supplied by us.

Level three, in being heaven two is a story that needs telling, which might be the last. For now, we might see how God operates on his own account.

Although we, humanity, fixated, even if in God's name, to the plan of heaven and hell to be post human life stopovers. Whereby heaven was for the good souls and hell was for the bad souls and sinners. Which is almost too tidy to work, unless we could better differentiate.

Done on human terms only, which was another of our big mistakes, on the lines we again usurped God. We could only imagine by human standards, which failed more in hell than heaven.

For we did not know what we gave God to contend with. In heaven one to look easy was hard. For if it was to represent the good of conduct only, how could that be reconciled. When we in that class had to change direction without really understanding the why.

Of course, conduct is the first sign of being good, being the base form guide we were laying down for God to decide upon. Which should have been a sign of how we all lived and the way of. But just for self.

Unfortunately, the mess we left God with for placement in heaven one, might make strange bedfellows. Bearing in mind the open standard we have set God to decide upon.

Good yes, how, who knows, except now God, for he is to be the only power who walked every mile with each person as we lived, that was always God's real job.

Good yes, how, God knows, even from us. For our first real modern declaration is not to kill each other. By adopting my "Natural Body Death from old age" maxim. Owned fully by all religions who now fit our U N's directive to determine the most basic religious concept. Of not to kill others, otherwise a religion in doing so may not now be a religion.

Not to confuse God again, but to allow some small laxity in our "NBDfoa" prospect on the religious side. It must be given by us under the most extreme cases politically, which means politically only.

Even if a religion had been downgraded to have no religious status. They in their redesignated form cannot claim to be a new political force for other ends. Their only application before the U. N. to regain their religious status. Even if to rename parts of their religion, is of never to kill human beings by any means.

We accept no subterfuge whereby ex religions can claim political form, in order to be able to kill at political discretion levels. Which we must cede to be on political grounds only.

Alas, but to conserve human integrity, all political systems in that class only, can by personal desire use the ultimate failing of mankind to kill others. Even if for unimportant reasons now but were important at the time.

Which is not a plea to God or religions, nor to be an apology for past deeds. My limit is to show how unsophisticated we remain when left to our own devises. Which as a line in the sand we have often tried to stabilise. That needs a new final consideration.

Unfortunately, when to kill each other under any reason, we sometimes mix and match our emotions too often in the wrong context. Which must be set now to hold their own ground with our line in the sand to be drawn.

Never to now kill religiously is our best standard. To kill politically if desired will lose its potency in the near future. When the reasons to kill will be exposed as wrong through our realisation. We all can only now expect to live in the same 80 plus year life span range.

Dangerously and seriously, emotional killing which is prone to cross barriers. By style and reason for some of us, can induce us to want to kill by return. Even if murder is done politically, it can draw emotional responses.

But when done on a personal level, like if to a family member, like if to a child in a family. What then in response if from the heart of the family. Who now may not consider reason only cause. And in fair consequence, look not to God for judgement. But the realities of life, living, even death, to settle matters.

To maintain the advent of reality, such dreadful situations have at times been reviewed under political review through the auspiciousness of applying standards of criminal law or justice by another name to settle highly charged emotional situations. Which should have no barriers at this stage of human development.

All we can do if to try and maintain our "The Rights of Humanity", plus preserve our greatest achievement yet when unilaterally offering the image of all to expect "Natural Body Death from old age".

With those there, installed, how to settle the control of our emotions if stirred by murder of kith and kin. Which has been a reality for far too many people not over the ages but in contact with their version of living within an 80 plus year lifespan at different age intervals.

Never to down grade high emotions, but in fair balance and in deference to victims' family and friends. All our first concerns must be directed to their corner without judging them.

For perpetrators, all our standards must be the same, but under control. Whereby no pressure is ever to be put on the family or friends of victims. Who too often are ignored with regard to the emotional turmoil they have been put through.

It is worthy to remember, like it or not God has the goods on all of us in any range of conduct good or bad. So, in reference, not to please God, but let him know, our emotions sometimes carry us. As if claimed by some perpetrators of random murder, who may expect to suicide bomb their way into God's favour emotionally.

Without regard not to those they murder, but the parents, relatives, friends and others who also suffer at the murder of kith and kin and friend. Which also is a now God free situation, for religions in God no longer kill in God's name. So, to kill in the name of your/my religion is only a criminal act for different judgement.

How then under judgement could we seriously set perpetrators of cruel murder to be set anywhere but heaven two. Unless to compare extreme motives even if unseen or unconsidered. Like what really is the value of extreme wealth.

Like if a person of the best of character who lives in the world of extreme wealth. Which is a credit situation on all levels not least for the individual concerned. For in most cases of incredible wealth, they are what they are.

A situation of funds being available to people, who on good terms worked hard and hard.

To develop their talent or expertise or energy or skill, which eventually drew their reward.

Which always stands on the firm ground of quicksand. Because while growing in size and depth. Such great fortunes made are also losing ground. Not for what they are doing but for what they don't do.

Although most if not all very wealthy people often donate vast amounts of money to charity, which is a good tax break option and perfectly moral, even honest. Which is not the main point, especially when to understand, their option of life and living. Is also generally encased in the 80 year lifetime bracket.

Never to be a threat, except to realise sooner or later, we no longer bury or inter people with symbols of their wealth. Which was to depict their standing in the communities they once lived in or are now going to in reflection.

Which could affect some of our very wealthy by how they lived before, when now in heaven. For here like all of us they stand before God. He who knows how every second of their time and for what and who over the past 13.8 billion years.

God the only being now, who can operate in the one moment of time in two vectors. One relative to those of us alive and living today and now on a 80 plus year lifespan. Then to be still attached to all the previous events ever to have occurred before we of the species humanity. Set God in answer to his own plan of wait and see.

Which puts him in vector two at the same time and in parallel time. Which when translated means at this moment he is in heaven one also.

Having already being in operation there since our year mark of 2012, when we found his God particle(s) had been set with motion a lot earlier than then. So much so that we activated God to follow the trail of what "wait and see" left, until we showed God how to read his own plan.

Which when by gratitude shown. God has always been on our case from at least the past four or five thousand years. With more to follow, but now in hard tack style.

Even generated by us, not least because although most of us thought we were doing well by being good, as who knows how.

We mixed trends, measured on the same levels of how we acted or reacted or behaved. Not now religiously or politically, but to be rich or poor by range. Now setting a dilemma for God only in heaven one.

Bearing in mind God must work things out on his own scale born of our plan. But must be able and show some of us the error of our ways if we make any. But only morally, on the terms of our self made morality codes. Which generally and still works for most of us who were and are just also rans.

We of the silent majority who had to put up with things as they flowed. Many of us individual yours truly, to nervous or scared or awkward or ignorant. To at first realise anything we did or said had no impact or could have no input except to continually save the world over and over again.

It is we the underlings, who always sought change, who best tried for change, who always hoped for change. By doing nothing more than following the broken trail all the harbingers of greed left behind or in their wake. Even if not to know they were betraying themselves.

Not that success can be a failsafe, but what it can do. Is place people of the same metal as you and me, to be of less consequence in Gods eyes if by misrepresentation; and their/our own eyes also. By relaying a sense of failure to us, in respect we were not able or good enough to do as we/they did.

Never to compare the opportunity success generated on its own behalf or sometimes supported by people of the same arrangement or class. Plus, by association often on political levels. Whereby better aid and assistance was provided by people of the same political party arrangement or class, also.

What we should have already relayed to God, which we did on bloc but out of sync. Was as the one species humanity, all might be delivered to us of our worth in God's heaven and hell.

Wrongly assumed by us, for we took to decide for God. Whereby the best of us would Go to heaven for reward. With the not so good sent to hell for God's punishment often on our terms so we thought.

Nice and tidy, but in the just in time network of trying to solve problems. We then, now gave God a better form of our understanding to now work with. For in his hands, we thought he could better cope.

Whereby if we suggested to abolish hell but not all its worst connotations. God could then place us all in heaven, but now heaven one as before. With hell to have been changed to heaven two, to still hold the usual suspects, self-scared with their previous conduct pre "NBDfoa". Now God could serve moral and honest justice for all under the one roof.

Before that door is opened, although never entitled to, we must give God our genuine assurance. We will not query or question how he intends to examine how wealth was used to generate any event pre "NBDfoa". For only God can recall in accuracy what did happen at such times.

We can still ask in hope for God to reflect on his decision about the relationship between the overtly rich and desperately poor while we all lived. Which in heaven one is not an issue. When both factions can take pleasure in God's company and each other for if there were issues even imagined between them while we all lived. There are none now.

But as a pointer when God reviews the aspect of extreme wealth, more so on personal levels, owed to when holders lived.

Criteria of use or non-use must follow certain roles. Like were parts of personal or corporate wealth used to fund war or terror activities. Were parts used in squander, bordering in the opulence of waste.

For all wealth in general was assisted by the toil of others. Who often gave the welfare of time to accommodate often very worthy styles of generating national and personal wealth, it is just to what degree we balance the scale.

In the positive side of being negative, was wealth gained at the expense of neglect through the channels of providing a dividend over care. Plus, on the same negative theme. Though some people on personal levels donate hundreds of millions of monies to good causes.

Is that enough done to counterbalance the fact that the remaining funds in the billions of money. Still procure interest through investment from the unnatural scale, money begot money.

While far too many people in the range of billions of our fellow species humanity. Languish in hunger, while we watch the planted seeds of investment grow their own dividend.

Which is hard to swallow when it delivers no nourishment to keep some of us going. Meaning in stark reality some of us might die in the infancy of thought. Unable to make a sound for God to become interested in.

While the sound of gold jingles in some pockets even if many, who may have tried to help. But didn't know how to, except to replant their excess of money in the name of corporate returns.

From which we can satisfy ourselves, God by our direction, even in his domain of heaven one, can rest us all in conscience by what he knows. For at any and from all times he can then move on to what we once thought to be hell but is now heaven two.

Level four. Now to be the real heaven two, has but one standard use. But on the same terms as all post life devised can expect, even if unknowing. Where we can check on how God has followed our timed suggestions. Which gives credit to the whole 13.8 billion years the universe has so far lasted for.

To remind ourselves for now, we have God on our side. But we must remember without embarrassment. From a real and solid base line of living for only 80 plus years. We stirred God into action.

Almost leading him to endorse the full aspect of maintaining the only way he could enjoy our company, set by the best of us. Which means the best of any species ever to have lived, who had the same chances to enlighten God as he needed to be.

So, he could at last if first see the best results of what "wait and see" delivered. Which was set and maintained by our human rational. Which has not been fooled by a definite product of ours, our sciences.

Which in self denial set their standards in error beyond the limits of her/their mentor, mathematics. Which can be let lie when we experiment, why there is to be an additional place. For God to evaluate, every single person who has lived and died on this earth in any case and in any timeframe.

Which can be shelved without harm or hurt at God's pleasure. So, God might then recover the thinking, attitude and efforts of how we all contributed to God's self discovery in new ways over the past four or five thousand years.

Though led by us again, things only became clearer when to realise, four of five thousand years of humanity can be realistically compressed to be 80 plus years long as we now live. But we dared set God to be as our ancestors thought four or five thousand years ago.

Our best efforts from the times of now to make good any errors made by our ancestors. Can in a trice be made clear and right when we abandon old habits of accepting hell to be part of the plan we made for God.

Which is done when we in God's name, turn hell or the old style punishment block. To be now Heaven two. Giving God full charge of all the reaches of humanity who by their own terms of engagement. Set a chore for God and God alone to deliver by account our worth post human death from any era.

My reasoning for the above stems thus, I reclassify hell to be heaven two. But wholly on human terms so God cannot be compromised further. By the already number of people, who do not believe in the concept of God.

Therefore, if by mixed or tortured emotions, some, to display their disgust in God. Fall to be anti God and ally themselves, to a form that is given not to be of God, in hell.

A place of mis design by us humans, who in the spirit of setting God his role, forgot God will always be in his own command. To deal with us when we die naturally from old age, never to have realised only now.

Once God is to do our bidding and settle on us each the measure of our reward if deserved. He must balance the books for his sake, on one count only. Which is to set all the suffering we accumulated over the centuries of living with God, even before the past four or five thousand years.

For in suffering as so many did at the hands of misquoted religious doctrine, misdirected political objectives or drives. Even by misdirecting national standards if to promote murder and war unabated. We all still bear the burden of cost owed to God's judgement on his lines, which is irrecoverable for God's sake.

Needing to be tidied up especially now to enforce God's role and keep him interested in the only species to draw his interest so far.

I have hinted in many instances; God will know in any case. Which is factual reasoning, balanced by how God believes even if tied to a religion or not.

To make God aware we know of him in two guises. One as God our judge. Who in gratitude for being enlivened by another form of God particle reclamation. Eventually producing our species humanity; the only ever to give God a task, being a factual standard set only from the perspective of being able to heed God's plan set by us.

Even though, some of this, our great species, who by already following all leads to behave as we do, they do. In being human, except some, in the most complicated of ways. Use their very great intellect sometimes to deny God in all forms.

Which of course is part of "The Rights of Humanity" to do so, but only in our new plural haze. Like not to believe in God, has to be fairly justified collectively. While at the same time running to believe or not to believe are concurrent without opposition.

In other words, God is. Which becomes a true focal point for us alive today. For to be alive in these very times, means we are entering the best phase timeslot. So, our young and next generations can improve on the immensity of understanding we have already brought to ourselves first, then God.

So, in consequence we must set the future for the benefit of all next generations. It is not enough to pat them on the back and let them carry on in our blindness.

In order to enliven them all, even with force, connivance or deceit. When we offer them our God concept rational, it must stand on solid ground. By no more than insisting their input is vital and valuable.

By effectively showing them, they are part of the whole as each and every one of us are. Therefore, our aim, their aim is to congeal, but on the grounds their input will be counted on how they improve on our failed efforts so far.

We have to tell the best they cannot opt out of our/their plan in the same way others might wish to. Like the bully and bombastic. People who ply their trade or standards, and in consequence by having heard about the threat of God in heaven one and now heaven two instead of hell.

Would suppose to opt out of this God thing we species wide are involved in, when nobody can. Especially if to avoid the image of God's judgement. Without blemish, all we must convey to our young is they are involved.

I personally set no standards for God, but we can, which covers all ground. Which is why we need the input of all our young to contribute to God's need. Of wanting to put things right that were wrong on two counts.

One, we didn't know, two, we didn't know how to know. For almost before we could read and write, which is not a requisite. Providing we can listen in kind to the good reason of reasonability, which brings us all together better.

I send no threat to our young, some of whom in you and me are well spirited in the value of being naturally good. But often see the other side of the coin. Where bad gets the dividend and worse does better.

Which is why I can now say under the most natural of situations, you/me have not been ignored, even if at times it seems so. But much better we are not alone. Especially now you and me. Yes you, even if you feel intimidated of bullied or trapped in a corner.

You can help me pull the rug from under those who do intimidate and bully. Not even to know and understand why they do what they do. But God does; the God you and me released, when we took it on to realise, there is better to follow in cause.

Which is not us making excuses, but us all, me and you included. Who took it on the chin to spite what we came up against. To give others like us the chance to grow and mature even if to carry bad experiences with us.

So that when the time comes, we will be listened to. Because we put more in than we took out over any given timescale even if as short as 80 plus years.

Never to forget only when we all go by way of, "Natural Body Death from old age". We give God the option of where he would set us all from his honesty in heaven one or heaven two.

Plus, he already knows of every second of each of our lives as we now live or once lived. But will be pleased enough to follow our guidelines of who how and why individuals are to be put in heaven one and heaven two.

But never on our terms, which might help some of us. Who can only see to brutally destroy those who brutally affected our lives. If to have murdered any of our kith or kin for their own cruel reasons. Even if some vile murderers were to claim God's hand was involved by instructing them to kill.

Before I continue with this Afterword rendition. I set this reflection, which might deliver the key to the future unchanged but now changeable.

My work has been set in heart honesty to picture the universe as it should be seen but not through our eyes yet.

In the highest name of mathematical science of politics of religion of humanity for their/our cause in the name God. I state categorically, God is, which although a flat one liner is huge in perception.

For he is the only medium whereby we can imagine the immensity of space in terms of content and distance which is time. Yet we/humanity are so small in station and by time. How then can we relate to God.

By two associations, which almost began in the year 2012, when we found the God particle. Which by now I have made that an old story in part. Proved by how God has listened to us in our species guise over these past four or five thousand years. To learn by acceptance in the one way only to suit all future projections.

So, if we gave God the option of heaven to be there for continual reviewal. He accepted in good grace and by return so he could relate to the proper standards. So even he could evaluate what his "wait and see" produced in the positive.

Which was a charged multi piece of combined God particles matter, now formed in the species name of humanity. Now at last settled on the only two levels we can understand, one is in our domain of now and one is in God's domain of heaven one and heaven two.

To be set as a record office and a pay station. The former almost like a handwritten case note file, whereby now that we are in heaven one. Through our own thought pattern in our soul like form, sponsored by God in gratitude.

We can self appraise; and he can value each of our contributions from any time in history while we were alive and trying to progress our species humanity, however we could.

Therefore, heaven one worked on a reward basis, perhaps. Meaning each person was there because in God's eyes alone, we were worth it, but set by our standard. Which may automatically hold in equal sincerity people from throughout the ages, who might have had to denounce God for reasons we will/won't find out about from God. Who does not sit in judgement, leastwise by our old standards.

Heaven two might pose big problems for some of us, if ever we thought of it to be hell. We erred on two counts, one, it was a place of damnation under domination by God's cur as told.

Two, it was a place of deep punishment, where our human form abusers and users and murderers and despots. Would get their just deserts. For by realisation, we set such criteria as a means to an end.

But under the very real criteria, if God was to punish miscreants, yet heaven was our place of reward. Then God in his wisdom by our say so, was not responsible for bad deeds. They were set by the matter of what we at first thought hell should be like, even four or five thousand years ago.

Which in name was a place not of God, but God's enemies in our eyes. But like all positives even in the negative. We gave that hell had its own judiciary, which was not God, only God's cur.

Hence as a place of real damnation, when in error we gave hell to be what we made it. A gathering place for those out of favour with God or in context to be in direct opposition with God. We even usurped our own intentions of why and how we discovered God in the first place then in any case.

If in good grace when God placed a soul in heaven one, it might have automatically soothed the hurt if done to us individually or collectively while we lived. To give us respite, not to use our anger or fear as weapons of retribution. Which runs well for us and God.

Almost on the same lines, heaven two, now instead of hell. Which hinted that some of our worst examples of humanity, might try and make an alliance with the cur of hell. Against their conduct yet to be reconciled by God. Which might never have been an option in any case.

To always be sure God never had a hand, idea or inkling in what bad people planned to do. It will be best to be able and assume heaven two was a place not of reconciliation or torture nor chastisement. It was God's place of reference, but a little more in terms of how and why, set for us humans alone.

Which should make the picture, all that God could ever do was generalise the best end of our human emotional scale already done in heaven one by us there. The small fry who never gave up. Who never doubted the mystical idea of there being God, the instigator of the wonderful night sky.

Then who only after about four or five thousand years, drew God from his lost cause in waiting, to "wait and see" what might yet occur. As the almost end product of how time was used since God gave the lattice field of God particles, motion.

Heaven two is only populated by the same people we always are in the premier species humanity. Alas no matter what the reasons or circumstances to be there, is only for God's reasoning to attend to.

Even if to include the worst mass murderers by genocide or ethnic cleansing or through or from religious reasons of discontent or spite. There they stand.

Even if in brethren they stand beside historical and modern day rich people. Who may have tried to but did not do enough by way of reducing their excessive wealth. Which blatantly and vividly allowed others die of starvation. In places on this earth, when their excessive money could grow in interest when crops could not.

For there was not enough investment to turn the plough while the bombs of war did their bit of paying dividends.

Heaven two is still a good old fashioned holy place. Only now her attendees will have a long time of reflection to see if they could have done better. Which might yet be filled with light coming from over the horizon.

Blazed across all the reaches of the two heavens, set by not those there, but us at the living end of humanity, we, still alive plus those yet to be born.

For in their name, and already on their file before some are old enough to know. They will be able and start out in the positive now knowing their ideas are set to be collective. Under their double endorsed following "The Rights of Humanity".

Plus, in panoramic form, many will be born into the real situation whereby none will ever need to fear any religion. For none now will offer murder as a fast track to God. All have taken on my maxim to live to obtain "Natural Body Death from old age", without having to have suffered the indignity others have. Even in our parents, grandparents or ancestors.

Also on the same lines, our new young will be less encumbered politically. For in her/the youth of politics she/they also want to connect to the same ideal. All their adherents if of any skin colour, trait or trend or religion. Can bow to "Natural Body Death from old age". Not having suffered slavery, abuse, torment or other draining experiences while we live.

A better and harder deal for our young to tackle, for they will eventually bring more to heaven one than heaven two. After setting their own young, onward and upwards. To better tasks than those of us alive today, passed on to them.

Which can only make God smile more, for in point. When they send less and less to heaven two, those there will by then or now. Have begun to realise, somehow, they messed up. Which will always only remain a matter between God and them, unless.

Heaven one could be a place of calm and restful harmony, where loneliness is only at the desire of the individual. Casting a form of pleasure over them, for nobody is alone sitting at the right hand of God.

When half suggesting in half representation, heaven two might hold the worst example of humanity. Cruel people along with the odd person who might have at some time carried ill used excessive wealth. No comparison can be made between either party because God's reasoning is applied in his own style.

My inference, which I leave for God wholly. Was to imply that excessive wealth tending, can be wasteful and hurtful and dangerous in some instances. Plus, it does not represent the true character of all the people in that class.

I judged, which is never to suppose I judge as God might. On the lines if money begot money, where to stop. For if a person needs sufficient funds to survive in forms of comfort until they die from old age naturally. Then to be penniless in heaven one, but ever having a better time than before, is all answers.

Why need to bring excessive wealth to the brink of death. Not to know if heaven one or heaven two really is. Then if heaven two was laid before me on God's say so, why. For in both heavens I would be broke, is that not enough.

Never to test God, but realise this, we/humanity have made sure of one fact, God is certainly going to be fair in assessing our conduct, because we are fair.

Which then might leave the case if a vainly rich person was to find themselves in heaven two. It must be for something done pre death, pre the magical concept of to expect to die only in old age by natural body death having never to have abused.

Which could read was wealth gained from the blood and sweat of others. Who at the expense of rich negligence suffered badly, perhaps not as badly as for the want of a slice of bread. Not paid for out of the interest accumulated in the dividend range of servicing money.

What we might hope for, not in danger, is for our young and new generations to keep asking one question all over the place all the time. To whom it concerns, "what do you need so much money for". Then in jest adding, "you can't take it with you".

Excessive wealth can be a disease of sorts, only those in that class are mindful not to pass the disease on. Which for them is a pity and many a tragedy.

No claim can be made against those in the good fortune of reasonable wealth even excessive wealth. My theory of if God put some for being rich, in heaven two. Is not to be set against those who did gain their wealth by all the best means allowed.

It is more likely to be set against those who work in the darker fields of crime to reap their harvest of excessive wealth. Who could have worked the fields of intimidation even murder for their monetary gains.

But even if not, God will only set heaven one and heaven two on a reflective time basis. Heaven one, if under our terms to be mainly for the good of heart. Means just that, for it is there the whole of human history in the positive can mix, how good can that get.

For in mind's eye, although only a thought, it is now there in heaven, just as real as when the first two God particles with motion interacted. God can tell his own story. Then again and again, for have you seen the night sky, wonderful.

If heaven two is negative or anti positive, it also shows the night sky. But is it seen there or are all there locked into counting head by head all they murdered, even by neglect. Whereas the vast majority now in heaven one. Who by good choice do not need to be concerned in fear about those in heaven two now.

They are in God's care under God's own defined ruling without any guide unless by style.

They are in Heaven two because God said so.

What is there to fear from the ranting of a normal man, who happened to murder and steal in the name of self or for Fatherland or Mother country. Over we, brother, sister or friend, who just kept on trying.

For with such people if in heaven two, although they can still look over their own shoulders. You/we as they, will not need to fear revenge sprung from your/our victims. For most in the same company you/we are in, share the same God our keeper.

While there is every chance the dread in heaven two over and over. Is to look into the mirror of time while ranting as could and did occur. But now nobody hears or salutes an empty future of repetition and repetition, of not to be heard or seen except by reflection.

Unless God might ask some of those in heaven one to suggest, until then. Heaven one can enjoy watching their next generation play better moves to the future than we ever could. Which will round all the squares for God's sake first and ours second.

For God now knows why he set "wait and see" when he gave God particles motion.

AFTERWORD 2 (A)

I, LIKE MANY WRITERS, HAVE told this my story from my own perspective heavily weighted emotionally. Which is how I think, how I care, but with a little more. For when I think by my own style. I tend to force feed others with my thoughts.

Often taken to be arrogant, pointed unbalanced, unless you, my/our dear species read between the lines. Not to plus or minus me, though feel free to. Your task is to cement all my stated ideas into policy. On the three main topics I have written about, with the fourth being the best.

For the fourth is you and I of the only species in the entire universe. Who have exercised our self-made ability to think, not only outside the box, but it is we who made the box. So, in no false modesty, under the only example to apply.

When we, if through me, attempt to set a rule a code a standard even big time, all will be done with hand on heart and God in mind. Which is the only understanding we need to carry if we are to build a future based on human conduct and how. But we can still leave some of what might follow in mystery.

So, to make no bones about my style of writing, which now has to be shifted into legislation over fancy. In good deference to where I was born. Dublin city in the Republic of Ireland and in the year of 1945.

I can code all of my little extra ideas to be set as Dublin City Accords, D C A's. With the additional bracketed code of (P) for a political accord, (R) for a religious accord.

By previously stating I considered our religions to be the prime mover. Of how and why humanity advanced in such spectacular style over any other creature species, stands. But now on the proper lines, if any religion leans to any expectation of God in any way whatsoever. Then God must be given his status as he would be God.

Which is a boundless statement but needs final research here and now. So, the concept of God does not become stale or can be manipulated. To have levels of concern more to any group, nee religion. Who claims an affinity with God, too often on their terms first.

Therefore, henceforth under our international endorsement, we can introduce one of our new main. Dublin City Accord statements vis a vis.

Dublin City Accord (R) (P), to represent God in form accepts in all priorities, God is. Though pointed, the remark has no sharp edges. Whereby for others who do not understand my intention and the concept of why we need D C A's about religion. Is so people cannot now say God is mine or ours. Therefore, we heed God in our own way to murder and kill in his name for us and he.

Which by reverse code, plus, when I added the bracketed (P) to that accord. Means there is also a political ruling to follow, to be treated here and now. The political version of my Dublin City Accord (P), relating to God is. Is there to hold that statement open as God is, to be a final remark about God. For who knows about God's desire, wants or knowledge in any case.

Except that God figures big time in all human considerations always. Therefore, God cannot be allied to any particular human group who consider themselves to be God worthy alone. Which might imperil the factor of all religions if misused.

Another, perhaps the most stringent of Dublin City Accords, is better first aligned to any and all religions on the one theme. Cleverly shown to have been devised by mankind. In order to clear God's own ability, to later decide on individual human conduct. Like when to reward such/any people or person for their deeds while alive.

Therefore, in all cases allied to the religious concept of an afterlife at Gods discretion.

Another Dublin City Accord stands to read thus.

Dublin City Accord (R) States categorically, all religions or beliefs with a God ratio. State as a directive, all adherents, followers and believers are to be assured "Natural Body Death from old age", guaranteed from and by our religious creed or tenet by any style.

Which at best supports the concept God is. without setting God is, any human thought or modes of conduct contrary to offering "NBDfoa" for all.

Although all religions are simply defined, we must draw on the better side of our political reasoning to enhance that supposition. I make the above assumption on behalf of all religions and all political systems so far used.

Simply defined, religions are not to play on their complexities. But if as they all rely on or ply to an afterlife scenario, then that must be designed based on the good of the human character. For if and when the afterlife becomes relative to humanity.

There has to be a standard enough so for us to have attracted God is, to us when we die, as how we see it. Which might show up better when we almost duplicate a Dublin City Accord politically, hence.

Dublin City Accord (P) (A) also states all political systems plans or drives are to get all party members, adherents or constituents to "Natural Body Death from old age". With the addition on the same subject theme.

Our Dublin City Accord (P) (B) addition on the same subject of old age. But now not having suffered the indignity of slavery, torture, intimidation, bullying or worse even murder. Section (B) is not to be a crossover, but as a political direction, we can with great effort obtain such goals.

Whereas if some religions opt for self debasement as a form of penance to be in their format. It is unworthy for us to set our assumed political objective, to override some religious practices. Providing they do not infringe on other people in the singular or otherwise to their group detriment.

Without danger, because I have laid a clear path to how we must reach to improve both religiously and politically. Although I personally will always maintain we owe more to our religious causes than other lines of enquiry. International politics must now stand full square for all our sakes.

Essentially, I cite our United Nations to fill the role of vital and pointed change under the heading of species unity.

With no bones showing, her main Dublin City Accord follows as thus, headed thus with due reference to the United Nations.

Dublin City Accord (UN) (P) (1) clause. Is set in stone; the collective realisation by updating the dated human rights accord, circa 1919. Into "The Rights of Humanity" standard. Readily accepting the plural concept of applying the same standard singly. But in consideration to apply internationally to all under the one banner.

Without considering the mundane of our skin colour differences, our ethnicity expressed one way or the other. But in line to that concept. We can at first add clause (2) to the original (1) already offered.

Whereby our Dublin City Accord (UN) (P) (2) clause, is to accept we are one species, hence, "The Rights of Humanity". But only with our, to be declared, national or regional traits to have been entered nation by nation. As standards exclusive to that or those societies naturally.

But in form to show our developed moral and cultural standing if at inauguration of our United Nations in 1945.

Which is to become the stalwart of all future considerations on all national levels applied internationally by our U. N. to encompass "The Rights of Humanity" in its proper order.

Our U. N. under the Dublin City Accord (UN) (P) (B) directive, will now have to form its own shape far better than ever before. For when to adopt my/our realisation to enter "The Rights of Humanity", at best means to include the plural of people over the singular of distraction.

Thence the singular of me, should now mean we, as we can now think in the plural. Which is always to be a debatable rational. Unless me, proposes to enter my singular of the right to pursue my own religion as I see fit.

Which can be more than a double negative. For if a person of any religious claim, sets they can kill or murder either themselves or others by suicide bombing in the name of martyrdom to gain God's favour.

Which then cannot be answered politically, for if they die in their acts of murder. They cannot answer if asked. "Why do you think that it is all right to kill in God's name".

Which effectively means one of two main things. Someone else will speak for them to sanctify God, their religion and best of all God's impatience. Plus, to indicate suicide murderers are so important. God cannot wait to have a cosey little chat with those involved, even after 800 million years of waiting in all cases.

Which is an open affront to any religion ever. A total affront to God always. What type of God would wish to witness day in and day out the broken and smashed bodies of men women and children. So, he could settle in comfort the murderers and or their spokespeople who set the task of murder in God's good name.

Knowing full well God is higher than that; and in keeping with the international standard our U. N. can now impose by consent. I give a new and true Dublin City accord, to its our U. N's metal.

To be read in draft at first of a misdirected type. Because of God's infinite power base if to be God. Plus, if it has been our un-set task to find God. He must be attributed with certain characteristics. Primarily with one we can understand because we are open.

The inference is of patience, which can only refer to God over any other imaginings. Not least because of all the timeframes involved. Spread as I had directed before, whereby many religions are thousands of years old, yet we individually on species terms are much older.

Yet again have our meagre 80 plus years to come to God or not, but always. Eighty plus which must include the plural of we over the singular of me.

For which if we murder in the singular as a person, even though our victims are in the plural. Now our U. N. must step in to balance the books to both suit God and the plural of humanity.

By following the written trend expressed now by another Dublin City Accord. My/our reading is thus. Dublin City Accord (UN) (P) (R) (1), as a primary political directive, it follows, God, a defined concept, who in the assumed profile of being involved with countless religions plus. Under the ability to post life perform on behalf of all religious adherents.

Is to remain a genuine post life fixation to meet all the requirements of said religions, therefore and thus, this said Dublin City Accord relates to God in that context religiously. Plus, to preserve all religious integration.

We the U N fed in projection by the Dublin City Accord (UN) (P) (R) (1), set it that if any group uses God's reasoning to kill or murder in God's unnamed name. Such perpetrators of said acts. Are not acting for God. Therefore, in context to be religious. They are not acting for their religion.

Which now in name becomes a non religion. Therefore, to claim murder in God's name or cause. Automatically denies the idea the religion involved in any way shape or form, is/was a religion.

Therefore, to kill on such terms, apart to decry your/their/my religion, is not a religious act. Now then becomes a criminal act only, which can then be judged on United Nations terms politically. But to encompass all separate national states, who murder or kill other than when necessary.

Which is to protect "Natural Body Death from old age" encompassed by "The Rights of Humanity", being forms of our creation in God's name. So, he can judge us by what we next deliver.

Our next Dublin City Accord (UN) (P)(R)(2) in parallel with clause (1) of the above. Makes all aware of death in its only natural way from now on, is naturally from old age. Which is done on positive, negative lines religiously first, not politically.

Not to speak for God as the U. N. cannot. But to have continually avoided in reference God and religion. So far done by allowing our former human rights permit, set all religious rites under religious tolerance.

Our U. N. reneged in duty, which can only be repaired by usurping God. But now backed up by adopting in first choice our new "The Rights of Humanity". Which points to the obvious, whereby if religious status is to be classified under the relief of not to kill in God's name.

Then section (2) is the part of the Dublin City Accord (UN)(P) (R)(2) to help clarify our intent. Which attached to serious historical misinterpretations needs direct action. Although given and designed as a gap filler if to cover anomalies pre death on any scale.

Even if now a negative, but to have died in the name of clan, group or tribe. By protecting and serving self and others. When to carry out normal aspects of interaction. Like through the hunt or to defend tribe or clan. Always had to have its own relevance, when the new concept of religious countenance came along any time over the past four or five thousand years. New tactics were called for on no uncertain terms. Like if a religious group was to have been unceremoniously persecuted.

Often from internal sources, perhaps over policy or definition. But almost from when religions started four or five thousand years ago. Even when following such habits, a general theme began to form. Whereby all in compliance with their/our religion would be eventually subject to God's ruling in any case.

Being a fail-safe to cover any errors made when we all were in lifestyle contact. Endorsed by the unique religious acceptance, we the collective of any religious society. Post social life, would meet with our God, imminent.

Who would then set us in heaven or hell depending on our conduct while we lived. But for good measure, by a mixture of ideas suited to the time of history we lived in. We gave God options based on our imminent meeting with him.

Often set up by our religious clergy, if we were to be subjected to die by the hand or reasoning or perhaps our enemies. Then our imminent union would have been brought about by our martyrdom. Which in kind hand was to read we died for our faith.

Though a very workable assumption from when. The idea of being a martyr to one's faith. Lost its sincerity when martyrdom was and is claimed other than from religions also, but from when.

Although a true religious connotation historically, now that we have set our U. N. to manage both religious and political aspects of how we can now expect to die from old age only.

Without blemish we have set the aspect of to be a martyr, a needles exercise. Not as a requirement, but as we all can expect to live and be of influence if we want in our 80 plus year lifespan. Our union with God is imminent in all cases when we reach "NBDfoa".

Never to be any sort of chastisement laid against old habits of some religions. For when we introduce my/our Dublin City Accords either in direct form or to be D. C. A. (UN) by title. They all best work through our religious considerations first.

Which is not to interfere with the idea of God. Except to enhance God as God, which should be the case.

If what our Dublin City Accords offer for the first time ever. Is that humanity have made God universal. We have taken the mundane of being self cantered tribally or ethnically or of different skin colours. Even of different nationalities to be of little consequence to God.

Now with God in our team, we have a great way to promote human unity by destroying any slight clauses that promote our differences. When done religiously, we open all doors to God in all cases perhaps, except politically.

Which will become another great armband we can all wear. But might need more and better attention than we have just given our religions.

AFTERWORD 2 (B)

As a post 1945 realisation on my own account. I can suggest about my Dublin City Accord (UN) offerings. It might not be needed to add more to those just laid out. For, they all are but one. Running to be the outfall of "Natural Body Death from old age".

With or through politics, we may not get to add any D C A's, for in type they could be too petty to work with, until. That will be until we post haste alter to remove our mixed up cause of holding to a dead and flat maxim as human rights.

An old theory introduced circa 1919 to give a mixed bag of nationals and people in general the same opportunity. In holding that the term human rights, met that requirement, we missed the beat on several levels.

When the original purveyor of such an idea, the League of Nations, first introduced that plan it half ticked one of the right boxes. Alas when the League failed, there was no way or plan to reschedule its ideas.

So, when a new body the United Nations came along after the world's most bloody war ended in 1945. We unfortunately used two of the leagues' hotspots and reapplied the human rights mandate along with endorsing the concept of religious tolerance.

Having run with them since then we can only count our mistakes, for both have run to apply to the ideas of the individual. As my human rights, as my religious choices.

Seventy six years later might not be the best time to complain. Except it might have taken that long for any of us to try and realise we did not get it right politically then ago or since.

So, in style when our UN pulls the pin, perhaps dressed in DCA livery, to update the version of human rights into "The Rights of Humanity". By reconnecting to the plural of community, we/they will at last first, helped ourselves in ways we always intended to.

Another first, by introducing my/our plural concept, we will keep in check the ability of the/a plural committee deciding for the whole. As may have been done in the past when forming to control Fatherland or Mother country.

Plus, in order so a plural committee on religious lines cannot option to set God's own plan on their lines if to kill in God's name. By relying on the same standard of religious tolerance as part of their/our human right.

My, our, "Natural Body Death from old age" maxim, already set, covers every aspect of our timely death. Therefore, no plural committee can decide otherwise. But many will try on political grounds only.

Being a weakness most of us carry, not least because if religions have failed us so for, then not to be of that class. Many of us rely only on what politics delivers, even if to war. Yet often from that very haze, we have no idea as to why.

Proved far too often in the past, when in fact war was done without objective. For if countries were to fight for any reason whatsoever. As soon as the last combatants in the name survivor died. The effect of war had no connection anywhere, which on political lines is uncountable. For if nation states are un-religious by choice. There are no boundaries in which to bury their dead in all cases. Plus, in all cases there is no reason to war or to kill for there are no objectives, unless only on political grounds.

What we, humanity have been slow to realise even with our UN updates, more needed. Stem from the small fact we only really live in a single lifespan range until better comes along.

AFTERWORD 2 (C)

I F WE HAVE NOW MADE a composite plan joining all the best elements of most true religions with the theory of most political ideologies work. Because we have dared combine most human affairs under direction of our United Nations. Then we must guard that progress by including all aspects of our concern, so we do not overplay our hand.

For me to speak or more openly write of science and her dual subjects. Should best be almost considered in the abstract, for that is her mantra.

If to start on level ground, we should accept science is not a subject she is a topic. Its personality is to deliver known facts as they become known. So ends the long story of science which must now be reconciled.

Science in her true name to be a data provider should have only one standard. To provide data as understanding becomes known or is exposed.

In simple terms, at any level of human understanding will be seen the horizon worked by human ingenuity to have limits. Effectively science and any person involved in the study of any of her tentacles, branches.

Stretching from simple chemistry to areas like physics, nuclear fusion or cosmology or bits and bobs of other interested parties. Which in all cases amount to one completed experiment.

Whereby in all realities, science as a subject is a given number of elements, objects or items.

Reacting together to produce a given number of results. Which has always been her limit.

So now begins science in her proper place. Historically, science in any of her guises has always been a bit of a celebrity on human terms. For she began to explain some of the mysteries of life.

Who many of us had already accepted what we did not understand in form or by event, was in our religions then to God's safe hands. Which still works even after 2012 when we got the green light.

Alas over the last 150 years at least, with science doing more for our welfare and in a sense our religions and God was given to do less. Human vanity seemed to take control of events, which was better done through the double vanity of politics joining hands with the celebrity of science.

Making new alliances which were nearly settled in the magic of the year 2012 once more. But were again stalled because with politics divorcing from the soul of our best religious countenance. To take in hand the blindness of science which was bland.

Because the only voice of science ever, was political. For she is not her own entity, she cannot support herself in any way. For she is only a topic of human interest mostly leading the ignorance of politics by the nose.

All to always remember about science, is she is a series of events already there, already laying around. When a spokesperson in her name delivers a data realisation even in formula. All she has done is assemble the jigsaw. If she then gives the result of her efforts into the hands of a political recipient. That is her metal.

What she must learn not to do is confuse our religious views in association with God, with how some of us only take a political stand. For in that combination, she will be of less value to the greater cause of humanity over her own vanity.

So not to dismiss her out of hand because of her newfound celebrity status. I set this factual plan as a scientific clause. But first I set to chastise her for other small matters. She can no longer pretend to study in the future without to consider the concept of God.

Which I presented a case for when I indicated to counter the anomalies of how mathematics is run beyond its own understanding. When I set it so all formula past, present and from now on. Must carry my God representation symbol of open bracket, question mark, close bracket, (?), in their written form.

Be it there, then if and any theory comes to offer a plan about the future that cannot be met but might be viable. Scientific vanity will be spared, for no voice can utter "I told you so".

In one small swoop I can now show how good science can be but does not yet know it. For when in 2012 via the Large Hadron Collider under CERN sponsorship. We splattered matter to produce an image of what we called the smallest of matter possible; the expected boson or popular God particle, we were there. At the beginning of time.

Which was not the religiously or mathematically appointed Big Bang Theory of how time began, even scientifically.

What was met in the LHC in 2012 was a photographed piece of matter in movement, apparently. Although nominally expected when visualised to be already there in lattice field form.

Science under her own banner has so far been slow to marry that occurrence to be of any relevance to future thinking about God and what for or why. Perhaps because politically, she cannot think above feeding her, their ego. Be it celebrity led or self-acclaimed.

Where science seems to go cold about the image of a God particle in photographic form seeming to leave an energy trail. As an item. Is that so far there is no way whatsoever to further that experience to its obvious next phase, that is experimentally. Therefore, science must now fall on her sword.

For even to extend the range and scope of the LHC it can never prove the other part of the God particle theory. Whereby the items were lattice field spread.

Which I can now relate to be a fact. For in my mind's eye, I have added my God symbol (?), beside the proof photograph of the single God particle. Which shows the full lattice field form of their final distribution.

My experiment already done has no scientific or political connotation. It is raw science in the lateral field of reality. For even though

I cannot mark my experiment in formula. My terms of reference in all cases explain how we can see the night sky.

But much more with that as a reality, ex of to extrapolate back in time. I can set our beginning ex of mathematical formula to have been set without purpose. For that was the only way God could operate before he let the night sky grow and we showed him what for.

Science modern verse keeps telling us our galaxy the milky way is big, big, big, but in class is only one of millions of galaxies in this vast universe of ours. Which creates this scientific anomaly, about the room/space available to accommodate them all, then how.

Alas to muddy scientific waters we now have a situation whereby it is considered the million even billions of galaxies involved, are moving away from each other now. Which in seeming indicates they are expanding but into where? To be a matter under review.

Fortunately, since 2012 we can consider, as God particles were lattice field formed; and to be the smallest of matter. Which could claim the title to be number one in size. Then what allowed them to form on mass so they could be split later.

Without the luxury to experiment, plus to accept their lattice field form, without assumption we can imagine they already occupied all the space/room they would ever need. But as known dark space was cold room was static space. Was capable of change but how and why.

We know the how but then the why or is it we know why but how. So, if we had all matter compressed the size of a pea, to then create the night sky. There is no how, even if why is involved.

For the Big Bang Theory cannot now work mathematically if the universe is what it is today. Which is not a condemnation of thought in any sense. Merely a recognition that the size of the universe in time cannot be accounted for mathematically. If one form of matter in the same coat remains at source. While the same form of matter grows at the extremity of the room/space to contain it.

Whereas if we begin to accept as we must, God particles are, were a form. Then all to do is motivate them. Which could only be done under one set of circumstances mathematically.

They all had to acquire motivation, which was never a human term of reference. Their stimulus was nothing more than to be set with random motion. So, if nothing else, the entire lattice field spread of God particles. Already occupying the room/space for them to interact in, could now interact.

However we would wish to title such an incident of God particles getting the aspect of random motion. We cannot alter the fact such forces who can contain the whole universe let alone our own milky way galaxy. Must come from a place beyond our reasoning, like God for instance.

Which in turn or by return would need to be defined in any case. But again, in subtle recline, for God would like to be told by any form to be able and communicate so. Of what follows now.

AFTERWORD 3

T O REST SCIENCE ON HER laurels, we must give her fair judgement, but in harsh reality. For she very nearly threw mankind off track. When we realised it was for us in our species form to enliven God. Who in effect is the master of science, but through mankind only.

All we must do to bring science on side, is to be aware of our own failings, which can also run in the field of vanity born of feared ignorance. For from her splendour, if like me we take to challenge her we can sometimes seem to fear her in the form of envy, which although taken to be personal if by others. We need people like me to bring the best out of our next generations. Although we can mix and match in the same lifespan range of living together in the same 80 plus year time band.

More often than not, we cloud their merging opinions by our very conduct of now. In display by how we manage our religions our politics our wealth our sciences and then God. What real lead do we give to our younger generations?

Which by a strange coincidence, we can enliven our young of now, in the same way I can now rest science in comfort for what she has done for us so far. Providing all associated with every branch of science so far entered into, are God aware.

Which is not just to apply my God involvement symbol (?) to every old or new formula. But consider in real reality. The formula of what why might be. Formed from the following setting I now give in the name of humanity. Which although direct can be and will be simply explained at the only times it can be.

Post "Natural Body death from old age", being a marker for all the species genre humanity. So, we can hear God's answer about what drew his interest in us over the past four or five thousand years particularly or from earlier times.

Dear science, take my ignorance in hand and know this. I can only admire you except in your arrogance. I am in awe of so many individuals, especially from the past, I am not against modernists as such.

But the old school had nothing to work from. As well as to make the implements of what to experiment with or in. They had no prior references except those they made themselves or borrowed from each other in name to try, try and try again. Wonderful stories.

Of course, modern scientists are far better schooled, some with broad shoulders able to be stood on by some of us wishing to see further. But not if they break their bond in the quest for knowledge by falling to theorise about aspects of the universe we will never come across.

Especially if to deny the concept of God, which in concept at one time went hand in hand with science. Perhaps until the celebrity of science played her cards at solitaire.

Science as of now has no mysteries but does have grey areas. For if some scientists, more from the past than of now followed God in concept and religion. Their standards had to be of a higher rating than perhaps some of our modern class scientists.

Who when in full study are only counting data, personified when an experiment passes or fails, which still delivers data. Even though we can now reasonably study in the theoretical fields of science. Instead of closing channels as some do.

In abandon, we can open all channels to include all possibilities based on an incredible series of events even unset experiments. Whereby any number of peoples individually or more, have had unexplainable memories of events in the full range of what science sometimes gives us.

Although counted, such events seem to lack only one thing, a formula ratio. A code to set parameters every aspect needs to have. Except perhaps God, that is God of now circa 2020, even though we only found God in 2012 by the best effort of science ever.

In fair praise to science as a body, knowing she is in effect a willing part of the human psyche set by us. The best service we can deliver her is to set her to understand her own needs in good form.

So, she does not turn tail to us in order to self promote, by reminding her she is not in competition with any of our religions or even God. She can then begin and help us prove of God in form but never why.

That is our job started in 2012 by science, then to be set better by our following generations to their young in the same arrangement.

Although this my plan has been tried before as many as 10.000 different times over the past four or five thousand years and longer. Our focus must be maintained for us to assess the total importance of our multi-generational lifespan in the 80 plus years we have.

We must never become part of any organisation in name to be of a religion, of any political persuasion of any scientific connection. Who would conspire or just do, anything to shorten that span of time I have indicated we all deserve.

With that supposition already covered in prospect to become active if by Our Dublin City Accord (UN) (R)(P), with additions. Then we can move on, which is now but by another name.

EPILOGUE

I N THE BEGINNING WAS A vast area of space/room populated by matter, which is substance, which is almost everything. So, we in our present frame can visualise the scene, we can rely on the good offices of science. Who by the simple means of experiment in the year of 2012 showed a state of matter in its most diminutive form.

Which we had already pre-named to be the God particle if findable, which of course it was. Of no small consequence the image we received of such an item was almost like the tentacle of a sea creature. With one limb to carry the famed particle of matter befitting to its name.

All to do since is fit that image to its own historical setting, whereby up to its/their discovery. They in proving they were recoverable, as per the experiment. Gave sign they were a flexible part of the whole.

Whereby if they were recoverable, they then had form prior to such findings. Which can be taken first hand they always were, and now, always will be.

So, in the beginning was a vast area of space/room populated with God particles. Doing nothing, for they were not motivated. Although a very valid statement, our first and best attempt to address such a scenario as short in time as less than 10 years ago. Gave us a start point.

When the theory of mathematics led us to believe in fact all matter had been compressed to be the size of a pea, then to be in a fixed point of where. Plus, to have dated that configuration from our human year count to be set in time 13.8 billion years ago.

All needed was to name such a singularity, which was so as the singularity. All then, was to get it in time from then to now. Abely done when it was considered the universe of now started to form from the interaction of when the pea sizes lump of all matter exploded to shatter and form the night sky of today.

Of course, around one hundred years ago when God was still considered big time. All to do for the best of reasons was to appoint God to have set the pea of matter in motion by inducing an explosion so some thought.

In scale, because the universe was considered to be vast, even big. A ready idea of to set the start of time by an incident. Was to name it as The Big Bang Theory, set like an explosion.

Although loose fitting the name and idea stuck with the obvious acclaim given to God to have started the whole shebang for his ends, but what ends.

Alas in modern time and now big time, many have fallen away from the idea of God's involvement in anything. Almost exclusively highlighted recently by some very senior scientists who for whatever reasons.

Gave out, the Big Bang in previous form. Was not set off or instigated by the fair hand of God, it just occurred, it was in fact a spontaneous occurrence. An idea which seems to be growing by those in the celebrity of science who work in the theory of physics but cannot now see the reality of God.

With no need to dismantle the Big Bang theory as we should, as science should if it was then spontaneous. For if the Big Bang did occur it would have to have God's input. For there is no scientific way some of the events that did occur under the big bang. Could have occurred without the input of God's desire over scientific design.

Which moves me on to 2012 and the results of the LHC experiments of finding all God Particles. For that was her result. To find one as she showed us was to find the route to all.

Hence all the room/space already there was populated in equal division by God particles. Visual perceptions can follow. But in line now they were inactive, perhaps for all time even 100 billion years or more.

Until spontaneity kicked in, but why 13.8 billion years ago instead. Unless it was God who kicked in 13.8 billion years ago as the lowest common denominator. Whereby instead of adding or giving or bestowing motivation to each and every God particle. He simply gave them all the fuel of motion.

Which had no definable reason unless to ply God with answers he did not wish to know until they were offered to his interest in what God particles, could or would or might deliver. From the sole events of their interaction.

If the above offers how and why some senior scientists are entitled to denounce God by indifference because of how science works. That might pass until I read my story.

Like all I cannot start; in the beginning, for we all started in the middle muddle. Not really, but close. So, in consequence, in order to create common ground or at least to make a case for God to maintain our human integrity.

I set this my Big Bang Theory plan by exploding that myth. To set my alternative "The God Particle Theory". Which has substance because so far it will give cosmologists a better view to be able and understand the universe as it is now from when.

In the best tradition of revealing secrets and telling stories, my exposition will display a time mark anomaly. Whereby my theory was realised about one hundred years ago. By a giant in the field of science.

Who would have reached the same conclusions I now draw. Had science through any means possible been able and reveal the God particle in his day then ago, as we did in 2012.

I take nothing from great men of science like Albert Einstein, who's talent is unmeasurable on two counts. One, his scientific thinking range was beyond the norm of its day. Two, he had an unerring belief in God on two counts.

One, he followed his faith in form to be one of our 10.000 world religions. Two, although very emotive. By story we are led to believe in his later life under care because of his physical frailty. He continually looked for the image of God in reality.

Which leans in one direction only at such times. Bearing in mind he died in 1955 at the age of 76 years by all intent under the conditions of "Natural Body Death from old age". My adage to indicate his hearty mindset.

If I set my "The God Particle Theory" from the reasoning of a 2012 scientific occurrence. I make no connection with what Einstein might have thought pre 1955. Except he was not armed with the scientific events to have occurred since then.

Therefore, without any attempt to include me with him on any level, except we are of the same wonderful species humanity. What I see post the discovery of the God particle which is only a 10 year old revelation.

Is they in the plural, were evenly spaced as per lattice field fed in the room/space already there to accommodate them. Except my reasoning as per, has to accept they were not as then motivated, why?

Unless we dare bring God into our mathematical equation, to set why on course. By ceding if God particles were there, now proved in 2012 and in the night sky. How did they get there, which is not of my concern except for you.

No, they were not always there, they were only to be the beginning as the lowest common denominator. But they did nothing. But they had no motivation. For which if to continue our story. I now break the seal, which once and for all, alters the delusion we as species were a product of spontaneity.

We are a product of evolution which is time. We are a product of time which is reason. We discovered the concept of God which is cause. Which Albert Einstein knew, which is discovery.

Not to overplay my own hand. But for me to say now, God set God particles with motion, is a scientific and mathematical fact. Which destroys without harm or hurt any proposal of not to believe in God from any time ever.

In any case I move my "God Particle Theory" forward on no principles except fact. For when in 2012 we found the smallest of all matter by size. We went nowhere except to realise we had a beginning.

Our next plan to set the universe as it is now, becomes easier even mathematically. For now, we do not have to create reasons for what we do not understand like we gained from the defunct Big Bang Theory.

It failed on the small principles of time and distance. And there is no subterfuge like pretending time started all on its own, hop skippity jump. Whereby galaxy formed under different timescales producing the same results except they didn't.

Alas. without dissection, but as said. Even if it can be tested, the one supposed piece of all matter, said mathematically to be the size of a pea in first form. Was to spontaneously expand to form the night sky eventually. Where is the formula for the impossible.

Measured from the construct of the pea lump of matter. Like were all the hard bits at the centre of the pea, with fluffy bits as its mantle or crust. Then what was their speed ratio. For some bits would be still wandering about near where the singularity was. While other bits would presumably be at the limit of universal expansion.

Not that we need to split hairs about such matters unless they force some of us to draw the wrong conclusions about God if that is a point of reference. But not to include God at this stage of my guessing. Is a collective failing, when to consider as stated by myself, we owe virtually all to our religious countenance as our drive to seek God.

Gained in various forms over the past four or five thousand years without prompt. For it is us in our species form who are of interest to God providing we maintain our best equilibrium.

Therefore, and thus, when God gave all God particles motion for no reason, not even his own. Because of their actual distribution in lattice formation. When they eventually interacted, they set the one trend in seeming. To form the galactic mass shown in the night sky.

So, under the wing of good mathematical formula is, but in my case, there is no need too.

Set a ratio of how and why there are too many examples of galaxy just like each other.

From which without examination they could not have formed from any combination of events supplied by the Big Bang Theory, distances considered.

Which leaves it for God or humanity to give us better answers, so if we can suppose God might renege for now or he would show his hand to soon. All to do is invent our own story which does not need to be explained mathematically, morally or socially. For it might be.

My God Particle Theory almost stands on one principle only but set in timescales of different duration. Because there were limits into how and why the motivation of motion was haphazardly used.

If we, you and I dare visualise the state of the universe now and count back in time of how. Do we come to a singularity of empty space/room already there or nothing, except just waiting to expand. But in that nothingness is all matter combined, the size of a pea. Perhaps ready for a Big Bang to motivate action of some sort.

Perhaps as I assert, the space/room already there was fully populated with God particles equidistance apart. In type, three dimensionally spread, meaning their distribution formed a vast sphere or cube shaped area to accommodate all there then ago.

Not by count but if we can notice the night sky presents us with a number of galaxies in their own area of space/room already there. Then is it not real to consider as they are, they could or might only have had the one prompt which was motion but contained.

Not by any limit at instigation but in what happened when God particle per God particle interacted. Which created their own result of now developing their own galaxy area in the previous vast area of space/room which in effect turned to be the Universe. Which in turn is a lattice field of Galaxi.

Where when once God particles changed when they combined through interacting under their right of inconsequential motion. To form other configurations of matter, uncontrollable except by limit.

Such forces under unique circumstances, when to further combine and interact through the medium of movement. In further combining to create boson, quarks, nuclei, protons electrons and others to then become atoms. A fixed form of matter, although different in class to each other.

Such atoms also ever active, self combined to create the separate class of elements we can sometimes count accurately today. But were still able to mix, combine to further create the essence of further development which is mankind. But first we must rewind a bit.

If only to remind ourselves, when such forces of God particle interaction grew, all aspects were new, even to God. For he had tied his own hands until something happened along the way to draw his interest.

In the meantime, by time, several fixtures were on the way. For without explanation by time or consent the further God particle matter in the name elements interacted. What was the spoil of past events and in what order. Which might be mathematically found if the right criteria are set first.

But first what must be seen is not necessarily the obvious, for it had been hidden a long time. So, without setting formula plus without using my open bracket, question mark, close bracket symbol (?) to represent God.

But if we grasp the following without trepidation, we can only score big points. For more than in the obvious. We have identified in type all galaxy seem to be in spiral or in vortex assembly.

Which must indicate even early doors, when interaction first began to take hold. Motion or the expenditure of energy was at cost. Whereby if in the extreme of cold of darkness even soft gravity.

Movement set its own charge. Whereby if, and this is not a constant. But if energy is expended in no class but to self. Where does the residue go or fall. Which must be reasoned in most cases, it arcs when set in a three dimensional frame. Which could be the proof of weak gravity.

There again if such dead matter has a no formula form, for in total darkness and cold no tales are told. So, if dark or spent matter energy, congeals in the arc, then if a spiral is formed as per the appearance of most galaxy we can see in the night sky. Shown to us by the medium of light.

When in rewind mode we are in the dark again, then we can assume, though in early spiral. The core of such a form in root form has no movement, which is the start of where black holes are made. Which is where heavy gravity lays.

By no more than playful annoyance have we/I solved any clues about God. For even if God did not set the Universe to be a lattice field of galaxy. That's what we have got. With another big question mark being formed about the more recent discovery of more and more black holes.

With the possible trend forming, whereby there is more and more evidence to indicate they are all in the spiral centre of galaxy as they are discovered. Still carrying the mystery trait whereby now if residual light comes under their influence. It will be trapped in the certainty of heavy gravity. Which by all accounts seems to be substance without form.

Although I suppose, although science supposes under her own rules of provable data or formula mathematically appointed. She will have to appoint her own mediator to contend with the reality of how her rules of engagement must be changed without alteration.

For in present mode, she is close to pressing our self-destruct button often aided by sources she ably supports operating in our political fields.

Which is part of my reasoning of including mention of one of the world's greatest scientists Albert Einstein, who will not cover sciences blushes.

To indicate me and he agree is an awful excuse for someone like me to use in any context to try and improve my standing. But to have known he was deservedly awarded a Nobel prize for his insights. Even though he was off key by assuming in shape the universe was essentially set in its present form from who knows when.

His understanding in part was galaxy were galaxy and always were since time. Which in at such times was a general view until a better idea in proof came along. Which it did headed by another Nobel prize winner.

A scientist in religion, Georges Lemaitre, who was to become a priest. Who set in motion the current standing of accepting the Big Bang Theory as a first point of reference to the present state of the universe, but in reference to its situation pre any recognisable form.

I set no comparison between such well known scientific personalities except they were contemporise. Georges Lemaitre died in 1966, they had met each other and were obviously familiar with the state of science. But as essential laymen, they would have crossed notes in cordial discourse.

Although great in stature scientifically and personally religiously sound to the extent they both followed the concept of God. By scale, they may have differed continually but without malice, for they in common were men of inquiry and study.

Again, I do not compare with either and or others who study in any field of science. My points are to be set before them specifically for their own good. For when alive, how did they think of God, which I am not even going to ask.

Except to offer my own plan now, about my "God Particle Theory". Which comprises. One, the room/space to accommodate the lattice field configuration of God Particles, was at any point of time already there. How long, is out of our range to contemplate.

Two, God at the time, beyond any consideration. Set each of the same form of diminutive matter with the flued of motion, ex of further instruction.

Three, such forms of matter there were, took in motion, undirected, to move. Which in turn led to contact between the same elementary sources. Which through the simple acts of physical contact or scientific interaction. Then formed their own ability to reform and reform, taking a long time to build its/their style of presentation.

Four, eventually, they through motion, brought the night sky into form and the species humanity to enjoy it. Who in we, began to work the wonder of it all out or more precisely, for?

I set no mathematical clause to belong to my "God Particle Theory". For all the whole thing means is time began and humanity discovered that fact. I personally do not set to be disruptive but stand on the firm ground of faith.

Faith in humanity, faith in you me and we, all of us. Especially our young generations now and yet to be born. For we need them all, so when they join us after their "Natural Body Death from old age", occurring post their 80 plus life year range. We can all remember how the shining star of humanity attended to our needs better than ever could have been done under the worse circumstances some of us left them in.

In good style when our young begin to grasp my understanding of my Presentation of" The God Particle Theory". They can relax themselves by not having to consider its relevance today.

Because although from now it will always be there, it can remain in shadow, when to consider God will always find more interest in us if we show him how to behave by example. Which was always his aim or was it.

Although I had entered Albert Einstein who in good faith was Jewish, along with Georges Lemaitre, who in good faith was Catholic. I make no claim on any religious basis as to who or what. But I stand for all religions or at least most of our worlds 10.000, providing they hold to a God is, reality theme.

So, without any religious connotation, when I mentioned in brief, Albert Einstein at the time of his Nobel award. Held to accept the universe in form was as it had always been, with a bounty of galaxy filling the night sky. Naturally God's work.

It is honest to assume on his behalf there was no reason or cause or style for him to think any different. Except perhaps now on one level only which he may already know and us not.

For if he accepted God's message religiously yet could produce scientific formula ratios to astound at any level. Why would he need to think or train his mind elsewhere. Which although to cut my theory of now out. What can I, we imagine would have been his thoughts if my story was laid before him about my God particle scenario. Which open God's wounds.

Because of defined time year age differences between Albert Einstein and Georges Lemaitre, although they met. Nothing can ever be made of their separate religious beliefs to be detrimental.

Even when Georges Lemaitre got his Nobel prize for illuminating the Big Bang Theory mathematically. Which still holds good Ground today as a backdrop to ongoing studies. No serious firefight broke out in scientific fields about who or what.

Which can cloud issues. For if hot is cold or black is white, we should be able and describe the method or style of such observations, so they do not cause conflict. Especially between the supporters of parties, while their principles never would dispute even though. As well as holding different views they held different religions supporting the same God.

With their regard to me, it is obviously non-existent. Unless they now are beginning to understand the whole thing was and will only ever work. But never definitively, because the beginning might only start after the end.

To associate myself with such great men of science and God was done big style in the name of us, humanity. Better defined as the species humanity. Better defined as those of us alive and living now.

Whose main task is to cure the past of her ills as they fester unabated, not for their worth, but for how we feed our own ideals. Because we far too often overstate our worth above the value of community. By excessively supporting the me aspect over the we aspect of conduct.

Unfortunately, drip fed by our own hand of misguidedly applying the negative of liberal autocracy as our medicine. Being a curious political addition, having crept into our rational of expecting to have to do the right things, if set by the right class of people first.

Who once having set standards, allow knowledge or understanding run amok, but in what they perceive to be the style of being liberal? Which at first gathered the belief to be a political standard whereby in theory. All men were created equal, but not politically.

To be liberal as a political medium from about 200 years ago and counting. Was at first set to be a style of political management. Whereby considerations were given to most religious concepts of all men being equal in God's eyes even if he wasn't looking.

A kind of gentle ruse without malice, almost as if an unseen set human idea only, was to include all peoples politically under the one set of rules. Following the theme I say, you do, for we are all equal. But me, I mean one of us must lead. So, in consequence, when I direct to our equality it is done according to the standard of our worth.

Which was never a standard only a result. Unfortunately, almost, under most liberal proposals, religiously or politically led. In order to keep up momentum, such systems took their lead from anywhere offering.

So, if science was to propose, in all sense's equations were all equal. How could religion tied to God or politics tied to leadership. Offer any objections to what science offered under liberal study, producing liberal results.

Which when viewed through rose tinted glasses gave off the image, science ruled. She did not vi with God, why, God could not offer proof in her class. But she did take to politics in an aid per aid manor, of helping each other out. On the scale of one paying for research and the other producing her own results. Which works if one turns a blind eye and hears no evil and the other sets her own standards of producing liberal results experimentally.

Whereby if results are equal, they are liberal until posted, they then become autocratic. For a result is a result positive or negative. So, when science speaks for herself, she represents us all politically.

Meaning, under such unwritten codes of conduct. Because science operates in the dark area of our common ignorance. She in time when passing the baton to her main supporter, politics. Sets her rules to be constant in the laws of physics.

Resulting in strange readymade acceptances at most on the political calendar. Whereby if standards are set, even theoretically. They then become the norm, but piece meal. Which when to be liberal as if through our best political standard to be, when needed improvement is added.

Our United Nations, which only holds political charter, except when to direct religious fortitude in the near future. Is given her proper colours, to carry my "the Rights of Humanity". Being a direct replacement for our dated acceptance of human rights and religious tolerance.

Protected in full by my fixation for all to expect, "Natural Body Death from old age". Being an obvious reference to all who will achieve that end post our term of natural living. Which is a real human objective set by us of the one species humanity.

But allowing for us to at first realise our big mistakes so far, like introducing and following the unworkable of following Liberal Autocracy. Which always fails because it does not see or cannot follow that if we all are to reach "NBDfoa".

Each move we make has to be self originating, or at best to be done in accordance with all to be equal in death as we were not in life. For in death from old age, we will be able and carry our thoughts which can receive the full energy of God. Moreso God can still receive our full energy.

Which will be hard to deliver if purveyors of liberal autocracy try to stifle God in his, now our domain also, heaven one or heaven two.

For which we can set this poser on political levels only. I have been reluctant to name individual historical scientists. Who will always remain the backbone of humanity and our involvement with God. No praise is good enough for so many giant shoulders to be stood on.

By mentioning Georges Lemaitre and Albert Einstein and the range of their great works in part. But in an odd way, whereby Albert set a cornerstone formula ratio, then Georges set an almost opposite standard. Yet both were awarded in equal proportion. And why not. Except were they in real agreement or did they both apply liberal autocracy by unseen standards. Then what if they had known to add my (?) for God symbol, which could only open doors.

What now, where now. For if we were led to believe there was/ is a progressive future for all of humanity. Because we did not follow the best symbols of science in E=MC2 from Einstein or the "Big Bang Theory" from Lemaitre but cut new ground for God's sake let alone ours.

By turning our task to reach God the only way imaginable, post life. By setting our star to shine post life. We have already produced the biggest formula in the history of time. Therefore, even without consequence what I next write as a synopsis. Is not only to enhance my thinking, which like all should always be mobile.

For to be static is not only negative, it is to follow the cause of all other creature species tied only to instinct proper. Which although to display a form of motion through learning. Pure instinct as its own source, for those in it, means they are spent.

We of humanity are not. Therefore, when I utter new ground, it must be worked on by the same people in you and me. But from now on, on our terms. Which can only include the concept of God. No not only to follow the concept of God as a box ticker.

My theory of God is our theory of God. Not least because in my pure ignorance, when I stood on God's shoulders. I was amidst a host of great scientists, politicians, religious leaders, a few obesely rich people, plus many, many of my contemporise.

Who all looked forward in good faith. But alas some of us, perhaps in being fearful of what the future might bring. Were prepared to leave too many doors ajar, just in case. Which was in part safe ground, but not sure ground.

Although we can at leisure find the right door to all proofs and realities by the simplest of acts. Which in God's name and for our sake, I had evened when I set "NBDfoa" our standard.

I cannot claim any measure of gain over any other person, for I hold no memory of any individual conduct, owed to any individual while we lived, I am entitled to judge on. My memories are personal and almost irrelevant. Except without merit, I know of God religiously, politically and scientifically.

I know of humanity historically to the best of my ability to try and understand. Where I can differ. Is in some way beyond my own ability to really comprehend. I have been able to rationalise even God's purpose. Which at my level is reasonable if to consider one small fact only.

Why, of our 10.000 world religions, most formed over the past four or five thousand years.

Most leading God by their rules on his terms. Then Eurika, I've got it.

That's it, it is or has nothing to do with us one way or the other. When God set all God particles with motion, he then left the room. He never once in over 13.8 billion years looked over his shoulder.

Until a single species form, humanity, drew his interest, from which, why and because he grew into what he is by what we are. The only lifeform ever to look God in the eye and say thank you.

For until we met God's only desire, he had no form, motive, inclination of how time could meet its own obligation of presenting him with a viable reason of why he gave God particles motion. But then ago, when ago, for what motion might produce to suit God's unknown intentions.

In simple arithmetic, not mathematics, God was asking of himself what am I. even when knowing full well he was the already master of the room/space already there, already populated with God particles. So why look for more, except to look into the mirror, a what?

We can never know, but I/we can lead God as we, to be able and at last settle for what we offer at least this time around. Until a better plan comes along but delivered by who.

If to be brash and assume all God needed was direction, then we are nearly there. After all we tried over 10.000 different ways to lead. Never to realise originally, 10.000 cannot be divided into one and produce whole numbers.

So, if as I suggest we are the one species, our 10.000 world religions leaning to a God concept. Can now become a one species God concept. Which when to assemble a line through the middle on our terms and with God's needs in mind.

By no more than the process of physical, but to God's scale of introducing a standard of reflection. When God looks into the mirror of species. In our case the black, brown, white, yellow or any face he sees, is his. Which now begins to aid God as much as we, for if he did not have a plan before he set God particles with motion, he still hasn't, but at least now we have cleared God of his first need, for an identity. Post such a realisation on both counts, we each must now set God his ideals. Which follow almost the same lines but from different angles.

If God can identify with us and we he, we must both realise the same result needed from different angles. But under different restraints. For God that is harder than for us.

By good terms, we of the species humanity, in general do understand that for God to realise his own standards, but under the restraint of who or what he is dealing with. A place of connection between we and he is needed.

Hence our offering of heaven one and heaven two, which will help hide God's blushes on the terms. For if he was to suggest a plan, although in his range which is everywhere and of all time. He might have forgot it is for us to reassure him rather than the reverse,

His real job at this time is to listen to us first to see our plan, then any other plan offered. Providing it follows on similar lines to ours. Which will become his and our master plan until other times, perhaps only owed to the single species humanity.

Although I have dared speak for humanity. My credentials are these. I do not kill people; I advocate no human should ever. Religiously, I believe in the unity of humanity on species terms primarily. I believe in the concept of God alone and through thousands of religions but under the God is ruling.

I set heaven to be of its own consequence in our names, I have set heaven two instead of the excuse hell, to be also in God's command but under guidance from us when needed.

I Believe in order to separate the fact of species to be apart from the reality of God. Must be worked out on a one-to-one basis, but with scope.

In the range to realise. If God is God, it is for us to make his case on the same basis he is not sure of yet. For if he already knew all we say he does, his game as said before is already over and not very interesting.

Whereas if we are the first to realise God is. Then we can suppose, God's first intention, although involved. When he set God particles with motion, was to set the true wait and see collective of to wait and see what picture could be painted in the future for the future.

Without compromising God first and God second. Which can stand because when God was first in setting motion. He was also second because he already can now recall all our deeds while we live and lived over any timescale. But only after we the species humanity gave him directions.

In the only way this feat could have been worked out by any species, who themselves created their own relevance. At first to group, then to the individual in group as group species. But under the real clever bit.

Whereby we were able and realise for the first time historically and ever. It is we alive and living today who are the only group in the entire universe. Who can set God to his desired involvement with time on any level. Who can still make it interesting for God.

Because even when in heaven one we are irrepressible. Because even for those in heaven two. Those of us in one, might still take it on to direct God to his conduct regarding some of those in heaven two.

Filling all God could ever hope for when he gave God particles motion without motive, for wait and see was the only standard of time, long, long ago. That is until a product of God particle interactive connection and reconnection.

Eventually produced a collective of lifeform forms of matter even if to be modelled by new forces like evolution. Which did not necessarily follow the pattern of always adding new bits made from God particle interaction.

But overlapped some of the same pieces with the magic of allowing some form emotions which by sign had no form. Because amongst the same species of humanity, we unbeknown, can range the intensity of personal emotions from zero to 100%. Yet cannot define their intensity.

Which in part means as they are of our response they were not supplied by evolution. Which if they were they could be scaled by DNA profiling. But bigger and better, not due to, but with evolution no longer pulling our strings and DNA an open book. We do not have to make sense of our personal thoughts, but God might.

With little more to achieve except on all our behaves, if we try to concentrate on the importance of living our lives from within our 80 plus year lifespan of now. We might learn the future will prove a lot longer than tomorrow.

Plus, on the same scale, when we get it right and set our young to set their/our stall better than we so far have managed. With their role to be vastly enhanced, for they will start owing nothing to the past. Except the taste of how we failed them, but now without shame or fear or embarrassment. For at long last we value them for who they are, our best future lead.

SYNOPSIS

I RUN MY HAND OVER THESE pages not for the last time but to remind myself, although of little consequence, my input may be of no relevance to anybody but God. So have I written this for myself or for us humanity. I do not know, but I must care.

For when the dust settles, no matter who set the tempest. We will all be accountable for what we have done or been involved in while we live; and in the case of our forebearers while they lived also. which already broadens our scope.

Which might seem cumbersome, except to remember the real reality, we can all remember yesterday almost minuet by minuet. Then history as it was supposed to have affected us all, but often by our plan only having left its own wake to be realised.

In many cases being a good backdrop if we can balance it with what tomorrow brings in any way shape or form. But under intention, which is a driven form of force beyond normal human understanding.

But is a good indicator of our uniqueness in comparison with all other lifeforms in their creature species groups. From whom I was able and draw a straight line through our differences apparently. My assertion being they could not or did not, but we did religiously aspire, which when levelled meant we sought God.

Meaning by result we sought a route, a meaning, even a cause to our existence. Not to cover why we were here, but what for; by bringing God into the picture.

Although a sorry story to follow by the nature of our blundering over the past 60.000 years of our real existence. Whereby era by era all we seemed to do was to improve on how we could kill each other. Not perhaps a solid foundation on which to build a culture philosophy on.

But in having no instruction book to follow we at least survived, so much so from about four or five thousand years ago. We cut the shackles of pure instinct owed to all other creature species, we drew our own line in the sand reading Gods and religion or religions and God.

Although classic realisations, it needs these last few pages set in my order of chaos, to bring some form of unity to this wonderful species we are. Proved always by how when we get knocked down; the best of us in us all. Dust down and carry on until we get knocked down again. But always to get up.

From which in this brief, I will set our counterbalance point to start from the year 1945. My birth year, plus the end year of our planets most dreadful World War. But in better hope, the year our United Nations was inaugurated.

Though a defined time slot, not everything fits which is important to realise. For in making end statements, it is well to be reassured their reference is to an ideal rather than a calendar setting.

At the same time and in the same mix, my references previously stated when given now, are always delivered on the pretext. We do want to improve under the same heading of being the only species form to have come to the idea of God independently but together.

Which will set the start point of this synopsis summery. To come from me alone but collectively. Because all I have to say is the result of thought collectively, by a single style owed only to humanity.

My thoughts are ours whether you/we like it or not. Therefore, by reflection only on my terms, which are ours. I set in numerical form the whys and wherefores of how to set any and all political constitutions.

From what I now write, it can be corrected or updated from what you have just read. In the first instant my "The God Particle Theory" is a factor delivered by our human studies of self. It is therefore a foundation stone of all human thought lines to be. But is not needed by my style of delivery to make a difference.

For my track and style is to count on each and every person's lifetime, if to run to be 80 plus years long normally. Expecting to only die a "Natural Body Death from old age", no strings attached.

Except those conditions are to be enhanced by all not to have suffered slavery, intimidation, bullying, torture, murder or worse like being ignored or forgotten by being left with a low profile.

My obvious aim as it should be seen. Is there to bring us all together, even to notice some of us have different desires and wishes; and may not wish to follow such a code.

Which is fine by me, but as I am presenting my thoughts and ideas, my auto set is to include us all together. Recognising we are different in many ways by self-choice, plus than by natural circumstances. Induced by climate, geography, diet, habitat and other reasons perhaps like culture. Often supplied by the above.

Highlighted at their zenith by how we carry over 10.000 world religions, age ranged over the past four or five thousand years. But most in line beholding to our imagination of God's desire. Which draws me to start my count of correction by entering the term God, to be my list number one.

ONE Coming to the idea of God was a very sophisticated way of trying to account for the fact of today. Which when looked at closely was a unique trait of us humans alone. Even though when we first came to the idea, we did so almost under the same circumstances. But tied to our tribal preferences, which is a comforting thought. For it signs we are not really that different.

Fast forward to circa 2020/1. We find ourselves in the best position ever, because our God complex is answered in proof almost daily, by the insincerity of our own making. Our scientific fields of study.

Who beyond reflection make up silly stories about the structure of science and her ability to determine great stories about the universe. Mixing dark matter or the lack of, with weak gravity or uncountable speed and time ratios. Backed up by the miscreant of her mentor mathematics without including God.

Then without a by your leave, offering the almost silly remark that time is/was spontaneous. No push or shove was needed or used to get things going. But for parts of science to still stick with the; there is was a formula ratio pattern to how science should be presented. But not to include the human concept of God.

Which is the core of my, it being number ONE. For when to think of the future even towards our death, come what may. The concept of God must prevail, especially now modern verse. Which is translated by me on our terms thus.

Somewhere along the timeline of humanity of no more than 60.000 years realistically. Held against all other creature species of a timeline running from 800 million years ago. We in being the only ever true species to be able and rationalise, even beyond our ability to understand.

Came to the matters of cause, reason even why, which automatically calls to the how of now. By every fixation when we drew a line under the concept God. Meaning God is. We unbeknown gave God his first identity which stands. Because nothing has happened to change matters.

From which when to accept the concept of God as I do. I do not need to answer doubters or pig-headedness that may be laid against me or others who accept the concept God is. So, if in place we, people like me, hold to the theory of God in concept that's it.

When we speak for God, it is in and on terms. We are not apologising for those who do not follow our God ideals or even religion. When to realise we are essentially directing God, then the shadow of doubt might gain light.

But in any case, it is never our need to gain your support, even if you in us were to use the excuse most religions are unclear about God. Therefore, God is, or God isn't, as a line of approach. We in me even through me, do not have to count your opinion nor do we have to consider in the negative ever.

Especially when we run with the passage of time on our side compressed into our/your lifespan of now. Which is a game changer, because by now we have more realisations before us about the surety of God than we ever had.

Allowing people like me make up our minds. But to give you the liberty of your choice which can be now ignored. Under the scientific evidence something happened beyond the reaches of science a long time ago.

Without malice for those who do believe in God, we are working "The Rights of Humanity" as they are meant to be run. Therefore, when we believe, we do not have to justify that cause even to God. Certainly not to unbelievers in God.

Becoming a matter to be cleared while we all wear our religious coats. For when a religion says yes, it says God. So, in consequence because of our worlds 10.000 religions. We are all covered one way or the other religiously. Thus, allowing me now enter my next heading two, as a near final remark.

TWO   It is a fact to consider. most religions over the past four or five thousand years had a fixation to an afterlife situation. Generally, one of reward, whereby adherents or followers on reaching death by how so ever, would receive God's own reward. But if life conduct was an issue, damnation might be their/our lot.

Unfortunately, we worked such plans in the wrong context. Whereby when bad people were to be dealt with. We gave it that God did not deal with them, instead God's fallen angel was to punish those called too or left at his door.

A wholly human fixation, for to even consider there was opposition to God in such a way. Allowed for those of us in turmoil make an ally of what essentially was God's enemy in the cur of hell.

Unfortunately to become a pliable way to almost rationalise bad deeds, for here on offer was a place of refuge for people who set to be bad. Under their own rules, which carried the bonus. If they made a pact with the cur of this bad doer's place hell.

Then in death they would reach a designed degree of comfort in a place of what should have dealt misery to sinners and not saints.

Although this fixation almost stands verbatim today. Which is almost a charter to keep to any religion and be bad or of just be bad and do not believe in God but the cur of hell instead. For if the cur separated himself from God. Where stands for the theory of God in the first place, then in any case.

When to run with theorising about heaven or hell and of who's entitlement to either or what for or why. We leave the field open in the wrong context even if thought to be right when following the shadow of wrong choices.

Therefore, without choosing, even choice. We must come up with better plans to fill God's cup. So, his results in judgement tell of our ability to lead him to more of his desire than we led him too before. Mainly because of our self-doubt, worked more by nonbelievers.

My/our offering of heaven one and heaven two instead of heaven and hell as places of confinement, work better. Because it releases God to follow our future leads and ideas.

Led now by one of our/my plans to show God how we can think 21st century. Whereby we, humanity, have set in religious fixation the best plan ever. Whereby we of our God belief religions and others. Resolve never to kill other human beings. Enhanced by our religious acceptance. We of all religions hereby expect only to die "Natural Body Death from old age".

That is almost as far as we need go religiously to indicate to God our good intentions are there to set immovable standards. By the same token, not to be religious holds the same outcome. For by intention the object of the exercise is to show God we understand the concept of the future for our young and yet to be born.

Has an overlap context whereby each generation improves to the scale of setting God's always wanted standards, at least to be explained. All we/I am doing now is to show God how we might yet learn not to kill each other religiously at first.

By having been now set again, we do not need to worry about the aspect of killing even if by those not to call religion in their name. For to kill beyond any religious cause, has its own level of control cast from the same understanding of us maintaining our 80 plus year lifespan as a figurehead.

At least now our first line of defence to wanton murder. Has been created by the simple idea of counting on heaven one and heaven two to be places of sufferance at Gods total discretion.

Which for now allows me to close the issue of my second reviewal about our religious identities and move on to point three.

THREE Politics is a far simpler realisation than our religions. But is often harder to control or rationalise. Which will be now shown in example when I lay in honesty the same standard just refreshed in item two.

I set the standard to be expected on all political systems just laid down on all religions, but with her own reservations. Whereby under the same heading, all political systems are to also protect all adherents, followers, constituents and others.

To the extent they, each person can expect to die a "Natural Body Death from old age", which is nice until to consider the complexity of politics over religion. Complexity in style but not by intensity.

Simply because we have given politics to punch over her own weight by misinterpretation alone. We have let some political systems assume they are a better source of providing solace to their member states than religion actually is.

Which I now make clear in this short passage, by laying down the factual rules of concern we must all heed. Certainly, from now on which has always been the elephant in the room. For politics has no legs without the support of religions through God.

When split thus, we can all see my meaning and more so my intentions. By setting all political systems to now also adopt our religious ruling of setting all people to expect to die from old age also. with the same good limitations of not to have been abused in getting there.

We will have set a Planet Earth universal standard. Whereby we of humanity have set a path worthy of God's thinking in the first place, while waiting. To hear and hope his product of time produced a capable compatriot. Able and give him his first leads of what to do next.

Not for God's sake but ours, when I set our religions and political ideals with the one and same standard of expecting "NBDfoa". My clause in one part was open ended, strangely to cover the weaker of those itemised achievements of ours.

Politics alas does not carry the integrity most of our religions do, but can improve. If only to try and fulfil my/our directive of not to kill other human beings. Which must be delicately set so she does not bury her head further in the sand.

Shown by how in far too many cases, some very prominent nation states do not follow a God is, theory or maxim. Going for nonaligned religious statehood, then even further to carry that cross not to believe in God or the concept of God as a defined political standard.

Which is both a human right and complies with my offered to be introduced the update. Fixating to "The Rights of Humanity". A plural connotation to confine the overlord element of applying Liberal Autocracy. Dictatorial autocracy. Regal autocracy. Even Religious Autocracy.

All elements, although fully entwined as the one, offer the explanation that such deeds of whatever to follow. Have been sanctioned in accordance with the core conduct of the beholder.

Therefore, they stand, which is fine when I offered in coded law, all religions in God harmony set it for all to die under "Natural Body Death from old age", an end one liner. For by reflection that option states, in the meantime no one is to kill anyone else for any reason, religiously.

Which of course works very well in all religious zones by today's standards. Which again will be settled better by another political wing of ours, our United Nations inaugurated in 1945. For under political rulings she will be able and determine the sanctity of religious conduct stated.

But before then and including how our U N will be able and determine religious status only by example and decree. I will set my ideas of why and how politics may have to kill humans under any say so at least for now. Which is not to be a true example of how our new adaptation of "The Rights of Humanity" are to work.

Unfortunately, if a Nation state calls not to be religious and follow their concept of political harmony. They have every right to express their will and protect their standards. Providing they in general consider others as themselves. But only in reference to all the people involved in their/our nationhood.

My point of national reference being, as I am, you/we are our nation. Therefore, if a nation is to be a nation, it must at least count all heads within its boundaries to be nationals at least of their flag.

Which has no issues religiously because God is not involved, which creates our political problems. For with no God in view there can be no national future in view. For all political decisions are to or through the head of ungodly states, exercising their personal views.

Which at best might be set for the good of the very land their flag covers, but not necessarily the people there also. Which by default allows others, even with religious backgrounds, offer to help and defend those who might only be under political abuse.

For with no future projections available for those locked into non-God belief philosophies, where is there to turn if murder is to befall you/me at political discretion. Where or when will our political leaders tell us of how worthy we are for killing those we were ordered to kill for a flag that has no future.

Then for those we killed in the name of politics, at least when we die, even at the hand of politics, we also will be the same nothing as before. As perhaps our country is now. For it like us has no future if it cannot associate with us through our young who are our future. But only when they too realise, they in we must now include a God theory to our future wellbeing.

Not in placation of others already there, but when to realise at very simple levels. Other creature species intently set their plan by running all to continue at least in style as before. Which is its own idea allowing that under the premise things might change in time or in the future, we are ready or are we ready.

Being a progressive fortitude on two fronts, one we are still going, two we are in the game of change at least evolutionary even though we do not know that, but we might have an idea.

Although a strange cross mix, my other creature species references are entered to cross balance how, where why they are hanging on. Yet some of us in the human species range are already giving up, at least politically. For we are being tied to dated political concepts of counting the dead before we think of the living.

Fortunately, within my 'three', this third political thinking box. I can mention our United Nations and its full new role of to protect our "Rights of Humanity". Especially because of our/its new appointed attitude to all religions. Whereby without personal comment she is to set a fixed pattern to always include all religions from now on.

Done by remembering one of our first U N tasks after setting "The Rights of Humanity" is to endorse the overall concept that no human being can kill another human being for any reason.

Which is brought into full control religiously first. Whereby no person of any religion can call to kill other humans in God's name. If so, then our U N can declassify any group religious name to be a non-religious group.

For to believe in God in any way shape or form is to show God we are prepared to set a plan for him so he will be able and consider the worth of every single person by conduct while they/ we lived. Which is a self acknowledgement, we value the best product of times development under any rules, being fully ours in any case.

For we are the only species who have taken a 13.8-billion-year story; and turned it into a 800 million year classic. To compress and condense it to be an 80 plus year epic, beginning over the last 150 years realistically.

Then since 1945, then since 2012 when science produced her first results with a brilliant exposition of connecting our 80 plus year lifespan of now to have started 13.8 billion years ago.

All of which is sure to be packaged in the right order by our U N when she realises. It is far better to listen to her creators in us/humanity rather than to rely on what she thought was her mentor in politics.

Which if aided by science as both parties seem to pretend suits them. It now becomes vital for us to put science in a nice place of contemplation. So that when she gets the urge to dismiss in contempt some of the ideals most of us hold religiously or of God.

We can elevate science to have her own box ticking area under my title heading number four, which in a way is a promotion for her. Because in giving her title it allows her to assume she has her own voice, whereas she speaks only in shadow.

For her words can come from the lips of genius, as in many cases over the centuries, or from fools. Not for their foolishness, but more so for not counting on the logic of reality. But in deference to science, I can summarise her in my slot number four.

FOUR Science in being relentless is barely a figment of our imagination. For she has no aesthetic soul. She cannot self-impose, she cannot self-determine, nor can she self-react. For all of her tasks are already pre-ordained without being pre-set.

For when her only name was to be a God particle, 13.8 billion years later that is all she still is. Except now to be several different combinations of multi-God particle configurations, but not in creature species form.

Because those/our configurations are, were later adaptations if through processes of evolving, which is not the same as the scientific act of evolution. Assuming evolution began at the instant of time when any two or more God particles interacted to produce change.

Evolving, though to include the almost same process of changing, loses its similarity with evolution if they cannot be mixed and matched. By the same process of joining with different combinations of God particle, although not the norm, is a marker.

If evolving means change and it does. Then if science is a counter of change, she must be able and always run formula in all cases over all timescales. If not, science is not, which is not my full statement yet.

But when to realise we of humanity evolved as we did. Who counts if in comparison of how all other creature species evolved. We could draw on imagination, which in obvious seeming, has no God particle credentials.

Knowing full well evolution is still a practical proposition. show on several different levels across the whole band of creature species including humanity. Is a rational acceptance, but if we borrow my mention of the word imagination and turn it into the reality of thought.

What or where is the crossover combination of God particle interaction with an idea of thought which could form the full story of all God particle interaction so far without ever having to consider motive.

Which becomes a very unsophisticated way of saying science is limited, our species humanity is not. Not least because we can think in the irrational, the unprovable, the unobtainable even to set standards by any mention.

Whereas science is tied to formula, which must have a theorised rational, sometimes proved by experimentation. But now exposed in the crudest of ways of how science fails herself first, then us. But led by us or at least some of us who operate in the name of science before humanity.

Not to lay a heavy hand on science, but now in my class 'four' for personal reviewal, she or her best representatives in some of our senior scientists. Have no power of attorney to dictate in political style. Whether God exists or not, for she is not a product of evolving or evolution.

She is a tough old leather faced comrade of ours, able to be used at our discretion only by whomsoever. But in hand with all of us, for her only product in delivery is data. She cannot manipulate her deliverers to enter their story over her own, which is always to tell us our own story without invention.

Invention comes from within our own collective ability to think even bigger than the size of the universe. Which if ever was in God's domain only, is nearly ours now of which we will find out more in heaven one or heaven two.

Not now to be formal when to discuss God in any context, but we must also give science and her expositions credit for what they were, more than what they are. For in are, all they seem to do is associate with the arm of politics as her ally. Who in context offer her science to be more aware and progressive than the main religious concept of how we think about God.

Which almost turns the last page of this open account of how we should gather to the concept of God. Over other distractions like politics and how we view science in her capital form to have always been thought as one of our foundation stones. Under the terms and ability to supply us with answers we always hoped to find but were always just out of reach.

Because of our own doubt, whereby it seemed easier to give in rather than to stand up and be counted. Being a positive over a negative, which draws me to my item 'five', cast in the negative, but seen to be a positive.

FIVE What if we/me/you or I do not believe in God, politics or science. Where then is our voice, which can only be an echo. For to stand for nothing is to say nothing, how could it be aught else.

I make no specific claim against any person who in conscience follow their own trend, even if in set counterbalance against other claims. My points to be made are there for choice and not argument.

But confrontation cannot be shunned if the parameters of any square are born circular.

My best contribution to limit discourse and keep opposites in balance. Come from the general theory of my relativity. Whereby we each in the fields of humanity, be we religious, Godly, political, agnostic, atheist or lost to the autocracy of other ideals.

We will all from now, be it from 1945 or a little sooner. Be it from 2012 when to me we discovered self. When following to find proof of the God particle phenomenon. Even if not to count for some. That crucial scientific moment was a feature nobody can deny, unless to deny self. From which although a small tragedy can be cured post haste.

Never to deny any person their choice even if deemed wrong. Their personal value is still counted one to one by my own realisations so far recorded. Which are framed and presented in the simplest of ways.

By claiming for all people to expect only "Natural Body Death from old age" religiously then politically. Naturally included all people of all persuasions or none. But my real plan was set in the same mention to be fulfilled in our 80 plus year life span range first.

An unerring period of time, just about long enough to be able to accommodate our individual attempts to rationalise the whole event of time we have so far studied. But not to the advantage of science, a wonderous attachment for our amusement only.

For although we need science and all her attachments within our 80 plus year lifespan time range to aid and assist our comforts if we can afford them. We do not need her to compare with our personal flair of how we discovered the true mystery of God. If over the past four or five thousand years or earlier.

For in that small last sentence, we show first class our species superiority over other creature species. Plus, why and how we far outshine science in any of her guises. For in name to have considered God in context four or five thousand years ago or before.

Then to be fully able and discuss God in family and friend familiarity while in our 80 plus years of actual living now. Even if to deny God. We transcend all levels and styles of control we self-applied over those past histories.

For when to look into the mirror of life's reflection. All we can see is yesterday and nothing of tomorrow. Which though very viable, is not what we should count, because in doing so we most failed, not least because we began to take direction from the past and what it did to us rather than of what the future will bring when we download the app.

To be put into the hands of our young which means we will almost have to renew everything. But now at last under their guidance. For when our 80 plus years is done. They automatically take over under their own wing.

Carrying new refreshed ideas of where to start. But now at the real beginning. For they move with the best story ever of how, but not why God gave all God particles motion without pretence.

Irrespective of that clause, they also move in an atmosphere of never having to consider killing others of our human species for any religious reason. Strangely endorsed by our U. N. A refined political institution which although representing all political persuasions.

Might, under the most extreme of circumstances. Almost have to allow some member states to do just that. If they feel they must maintain their political state integrity from within their own standard base of morality historically applied.

But fortunately, now, post 2012, we can if through our U. N. set time limits on individual national caveats. Set before our year of knowledge date time mark of 2012. If they were to call even while to join the U. N., they could continue to act in part to maintain their best national interests. Whereby some felt it necessary to kill enemies of the state as they see it so far.

Which is never a test for our young, especially when to consider at this present year time mark of 2021/2. Throughout the world today in every flag bearing nation, are young people who could hope for nothing more than to reach "Natural Body Death from old age", in expectation.

Therefore, without charge, we can and should endorse that trend and fateful expectation to rest easy on the minds of our young. By backing up my offering in this abstract tale about the surety of

God. Offered now in brief as my last settlement so far but to be section Six of this epitaph.

SIX To be a short reprieve. For now, when I write, against me it is for you to support murder as our primary degradation. Along with to support slavery, torture, brutality, intimidation, bullying, causing emotional stress, even wanton neglect and all other negative attitudes to each other.

Often set up on the grounds of ethnicity, by tribe or clan or skin colour shades. Simply to set a defined picture representation of why we can treat people different if we feign nationality as our right.

For even if we assume to operate within the U. N. but outside her standards as we propose to set them. We will eventually come to a crucial point of impasse. Offering no apparent point of acceptance which can now only pivot on the one axis.

Which is to be the concept of God 10.000 different ways, but now only offered in the form God is. Which is not a religious call but a call to religions. For they will become our best barrier to put up against wanton human murder in any name, even martyrdom or suicide in any cause.

Even without any sight of God so far, humanity in the species form us, have always just managed to keep going. Which allows us the privilege to ask any questions we like about who why or what. Although always done with relish especially over these past 150 years, we were never in a position to begin and really answer until the year of our God particle discovery.

Which led people like me to be able and see through the mist of where the future was hiding. So, at last again, a picture could be offered to explain how the future could continue while accounting for the reason of the past.

Being a giant undertaking on as many levels we must look into, so when we eventually gather in heaven after "NBDfoa". All discussions about what we did not do, will be there for God to decide upon. But never by our judgement individually.

For at that juncture, God who has taken note of every action of every second of time we individually have used pre "NBDfoa". Will council us one to one on where we think we should be put, even temporarily, to languish in either heaven.

A delicious inescapable place of settlement for all of us who ever lived in the name of species, of humanity. Of tribe of clan of ethnicity of skin colour, but who were free thinkers all the time. Because in our species form, we formed over 10.000 different versions of the one God. We were capable to lead, so he could follow his own results.

Although I deliver this next passage under its own heading to be order of delivery number 'seven', hinted to be of benefit to the whole species of humanity. I insist in the singular, even without authority. For that is where God works from.

When to remember each and every single person who can be called in the name species, is as species is, like God is. For in the time-span of wait and see. God's own game plan can be delivered by the one species so far to have named the universe. Hence number 'seven'.

SEVEN   Seven is me and you meaning us. Which when read means each and every single person ever to have lived and those yet to be born. With the real addition those yet to arrive in our group will already have benefited because the three or so generations working together in our 80 plus year time bracket.

Who have by now already decided to adopt "The Rights of Humanity". Plus, under all religious and political plans run with setting all adherents and followers to expect "Natural Body Death from old age" without having suffered the many indignities some of us normally expect. Because of our deemed worth if set by the judgement of our peers is all we got used to.

For some of them at least who at such times thought we, their servants and slaves, were in fact God appointed to serve them both in their name and his. So that such appointees could then better serve God in return or self-serve in duty. Blameful or blameless, God in heaven will decide.

Remembering it will be by God's judgement on our lines when we all reach heaven. That we will receive Gods best attention, we lead him in not only for what we did. But more so for what we didn't do. But always under mitigation expressed morally.

Which becomes a reflective condemnation on the several worst levels humanity works on. One, it was not my fault, two nobody told me, three, they, he, said. Four, I was only following orders.

Alas often endorsed by the positive signs, five, it was my choice, it was my effort. Although rounded. Such arguments and discussions when setting a case in the singular. Sometimes disguise the fact although we are the first species, the only to have named the universe.

We cannot appoint ourselves to be over important enough to determine we created the universe or deny that fact. Which means but one thing and little else. We are our own agents to come together with God finally. Not necessarily to suit our ends,

For when I say we created the universe, it only implies we recognised it in time reference to be a sequence of events that can now be traced. But in style to have had or to have evolved to be able and recognise its intention which is God bound in all respects. But only set by any creature species who could offer such a plan.

Although no single person can set God's plan on their own account. Which reflects what our 10.000 world religions have been trying to do. We must balance that full anomaly by using the same individual group who sometimes opt not to believe in God.

Which is only a poise taken from the fact all religious perspectives when first created, carried their own support and supporters. To automatically create a negative situation form, from the unreliability of dressing God in 10.000 different coats. But worse, in making God see only one, over 10.000 different reasons.

Which then burst its banks of restraint, perhaps more so since 1945 when our readoption of human rights and religious tolerance. Instead of setting standards, destroyed them.

On the simple premise our United Nations was now to work for the plural of community and not the singular. So, by adopting old singular concepts with hidden support. Like offering the maintenance of religious tolerance in the singular.

When allowing that choice, we also allowed the personal choice of not to be religious by choice. Which of course is a general standard and must be maintained, but now under the right intention.

Whereby not to believe in God gives no leeway to act or react for or against God. We/I will gain no special leave not to believe in God. We gain no, nor never have had the ability to act as if we were God. Even when to imagine we were following God's orders.

For when we flip the coin the other head will not tell us what we want to hear. Which might relate to our/the other imagination with regard to the cur of hell. Who has no part in setting our personal standards.

Unless we make it our own condition to deny God through supporting hell, which is a good sign we do not believe in God. But then where is personal choice. For if to follow God's cur is our means to deny God we then believe in God. Which is part of following "The Rights of Humanity".

Not to believe in God is so negative, it implies we, whomsoever, on reaching that verdict. Join hand in hand to all other creature species who also only use pure instinct to account for the passage of time, futureless.

It relates you, us to such species who by time have lasted generationally for over five hundred million years. Yet still do not know about tomorrow let alone yesterday.

Whereas without distinction, we of humanity in using the good offices of our short term generational ancestors. Almost know every second of God's interest in us shown and given over the past four or five thousand years.

But much better, we can turn their past into the relevance of our 80 plus year lifespan. Which has been the only time needed to bring us to the true concept of God in God is. Always to be a positive. For we can never disprove God until we at first accept full proof.

Not on God's terms, for when he set God particles with motion, he only hoped to find himself. Even under the non-activated plan of wait and see. Which was fully active for 13.8 billion years so far and became a reality in 2012. When the single species of humanity popped the cork.

Which will set the beginning to be what it will become when all of us in the name humanity. Come to realise, yes, we did get it right when we named the universe to uncover God wrapped in his full splendour. Yes, it is only we of humanity who have empowered God in the only two ways possible.

One, for us, who let God now know we know of him and why. Two, for God, who by return can now use his heaven one and heaven two with us in mind. After all it is we, who showed God the door. Though left ajar, it will still be from us through our young and their young to take it off its hinges.

Because by all futures, our young and we can move hand in hand with the rest of our ancestry into a new era of time. Which might yet be the next development of how God particle interaction is set to work.

For in taking 13.8 billion years to produce the species humanity, an offshoot of the genre creature species. But who in seeming advanced from that cradle, to be the only species so far to imagine by the processes of thought and thinking alone? We are not alone.

Who by our own standard need to reconcile any thought of idea about the why and how of our environment, which is the entirety of the universe? Which is the night sky. Which shows change and the prospect of further change.

Therefore, without blemish, we can extrapolate from what we already know to have happened, into what might yet occur. Even if to alter the parameters. Whereby old style the past is/was not always what we remember. But in reflection with the future yet to be determined within new parameters.

We can now rely on the fact, with our young involved, plus in that we at last have refined our previous 10.000 opinions of God to lead us into the future one way only. But never in expectation. Even though we have made it easier by setting God to use heaven one and two positively. When we round all the corners, we will realise it is us of humanity alone who are the only so far to set the standard. God is.

SECTION TWO

MY CONCLUSIONS

DEAR READER ALTHOUGH YOU HAVE been treated to an insight of your own conscience and consciousness by my delivery so far. This next passage presented in the singular by yours truly again. Is an attestation, whereby what is now said, is a distillation of my previous utterings.

But held now to be the best of what humanity has so far delivered for your enlightenment. Now at last backed up by the reality of human vulnerability. Covered by how in general we all try to improve certain aspects of life. Some of us are not sure of the reason as to why but know it must be done.

Alas often leading for the same people in the individual, to follow false trails often laid down for them by others who may not have got it quite right just yet. But who for various reasons carry on sometimes in the belief of, what they suggest or allude to, is right?

If not for themselves, then from their own good heart, but sold on the idea they also serve. Therefore, their involvement sometimes in being selfless, can lead to confusion when their suggestions are overplayed by the people they suggest for.

Which can be stabilised here and now but not by me only. Which becomes a negative positive, for I am the only person to add to my own script. Under the reality check, so far, even unseen, I dare write in the singular for our human species to take heed of collectively.

I must follow my own trend, therefore when I now start at the beginning, I start in the beginning, which always was number one, which is always God.

But from now on we do not have to attempt and equate the phenomena. Except to realise that if proof was ever needed about the surety of God, it is now at hand. Therefore, in title number one this time. I will set my last theory about God. I speak for nought but the species humanity.

ONE God is, being a reality. But not of mixed consequence, for in that reality to work or to be viable. In any context, we, but in this case me, are entitled to represent the total of our single species past and present. For no other reason than I do.

Being of no value except my story is the only one offered start to finish. Whereby I have set the full plan of God's desire to fill his own offering of what "wait and see" delivers. Done now to accommodate and account for the wishes of each one of our worlds 10.000 plus religions.

Which were more responsible historically than any other medium, to have advanced, even separated us from other classified creature species. For in or through all religions, we carried pictures of what the future might be for or bring.

Tying at first all religious concepts with aspects of God. But unbeknown, at such times mainly ranged from about four or five thousand years ago until today. We did not grasp to make things work all round, religion and God are inseparable. No matter what the call, except, providing all religions gather to accept the one reality.

When they utter their own verse, no matter how or why. Each religion from whenever, is, are, were fully beholding to the same God. Plus, that one and same God, was in full need to be shown by any living form. If at first developed from about 800 million years ago, what his role was to be. Which becomes the following.

On how all future religious thinking must be now based upon, recently proved by historical representations. Of how when we did come to God, we never at the first time or since realised. God had no motive, even though he set the standard for time to begin. Whenever but not why ever.

For to realise God is, is to realise all existence in life forms, is simply a matter of time in running, but under the good control of a medium almost as mysterious as God. The factor of evolution and evolving. Or by any other name.

But fist again, my, this title ONE, has been set for us to understand, even if we don't. Our invention of God was to discover God in reality. Which will be shown in better proof when I go over in less detail than before, the influences our religions our politics and our sciences has so far had upon us.

But in better settlement, I will give my account of why I set evolution to have been a process of real value of our wellbeing. Not least because it was never a figment of any imagination. It was a process of change without alteration.

Set on its own wrong path when we assumed it had a cause other than to follow God's "Wait and see plan". Even undirected, which it never was, but it was there to be found. To be at least a peg we could hang our thoughts on.

I have to accept the theme of evolution sets two main channels. One counted in my rendition about God and associated religions because of its mystery. Carried in this block analysis already given the subtitle ONE. With the other interpretation dealt with later, but of the same significance.

Talk will later follow about the scientific discovery in fact of the God particle. But in my range of discussion now about God and religions. Without sanction, although I join the concepts, their union is tenuis. Which will be better shown when I code religions on their own behalf.

So, in the meantime, when to mention God, even as God is. My statement follows God as a source, beyond being a force. Is the entity of time itself, which over the past 13.8 billion years has become my acceptance. God in his own sense is and was the creator of all movement in the entire universe.

But because of the enormity of that consequence, it will be for us of humanity, to relay that message to God. So, he might begin to understand his unthought of reasons for setting all God particles with motion which was never a religious concept.

But before we move on to my number "two" listed reasoning about reality. If I now set what may have been the first other process of movement, evolution, now in this God range of my reconstruction.

I must set in stone for future debate wrangles. To offer opposition to the concept of God, at least about my 21st century rendition of the fact of God. To be a non-God concept or to hold a non-belief in God or simply not to believe in the concept of God. Carries no representative opinion worthy of use against any person or group, who follow at best to accept the concept of there being God as per the creator if.

In modern verse, that simply means by my terms alone, unless added to, but only on the same basis I offer my opinion.

All to remember in any way shape or form. Is we already accept we do not understand everything that goes on in galaxy let alone the full universe? So how can we opine not to believe God or the concept of God when we have the heavens to behold.

Which must draw from me at least a measure of scornful disapproval. Whereby in voice without condemnation, I have to lean in full measure, for those who do not believe in the concept of God per se. They have no human right to expect that opinion to be listened to let alone be given any credence.

For in essence, they will have turned their back on the reality of humanity as a feature, to have become the only species in 800 million years to have discovered reason and cause. Through their/my understanding of where God fits in.

To declare not to believe in the concept of God never was a human right. Which will soon be repaired when we adopt my new maxim "The Right of Humanity". But in between, until we reach there again. For me to down grade anybody not to express their own opinion is done in good faith.

For in my direct statement about how I believe in the concept of God. I am not saying I am right, and others are wrong. My issue is to stop people from forsaking their own future which will be. But not at my hands nor their own.

Their future will be set from the real complexities of what happened yesterday if set by our ancestors and forebearers. For when and before we were born or planned or happened. All they ever had as the future was us. Which is a great imagination.

Therefore, without command, when I say if not to believe in the concept of God lets us all down. That stands on the not so sure ground we/me/I were not the future. Set by our forebearers to finish their plans from where we could meet with them in the not-so-distant future to at best enjoy our mixed company. Or at worst be set to pay perhaps in kind for the not so good conduct we may have used before we met the proper future head on.

Although whatever we believe about God, one thing we must take on is the positivity of the product. For which under different terms we might have science to thank indirectly. But until then I will close my number ONE rendition about the certainty of God. With my half-educated guess about the other magic evolution supplied to our conditions of existence.

When taken honestly, all I might suggest about evolution as an act, object or subject, is it is involved from the very start of time. By being involved in the matter of change, induced or otherwise. Which might bring it to higher regard than before when it was misread and mismatched.

If evolution means change, when the first two of any number of God particles interacted, evolution in one form or another was involved. But where is her magic against God's.

Bearing in mind, we have to consider realistically, evolution as an act, object or subject. Continued in the one form of change in each forming galaxy as far as we can reasonably realise for 13 billion years.

By taking the same mix of interacting, and interacting combined God particle clusters to change their form to be among 118 different elements to have formed the billions upon billions of different star form galaxy.

All telling the same story of evolving change to create the same matter of events billions upon billions of different times, yet in the same universe or the one universe which of course is God's universe. Or at least that is what I tell God.

Although God had the same ally of evolution side by side for 13 billion years. He never knew of the why. How could he, what form of so far chemical interaction or reaction could voice to God anything other than to react or interact.

It would seem evolution was getting a little boring on its own account, but at least she stuck to her guns. Until a powder flash occurred from about 800 million years ago. Whereby the chemical end of the normal 118 plus of now known elements changed slightly, in or on at least one small part of at least one galaxy, the Milky Way.

Although still technically chemical in form, when newer forms of matter configurations began to appear in lifeform forms. In seeming, following their own trends of reproducing to be now un-chemical at source. For these new products were now self-inclined to self-habitat to meet group specific needs if before desires.

Without real change but in style, evolution from about 800 million years ago twined to serve the old style galaxy system of mixing and matching. Plus, to also serve this different newer style of lifeform configurations.

Which seemed to have eventually developed a post evolutionary stanza. Whereby different now lifeforms of evolved elements. In part found themselves to be independent of how evolution used to work.

Here and now from about 800 million years ago. Creature species formed to their own needs as if that was their new impetus. But from now almost 800 million years ago, evolutionary change formed a new pattern. Whereby change was not always the result, but ideas might be.

Without any ratio or pattern emerging of notable concern in that whole time, except the two forms of evolution ran side by side and still do. One managing chemical evolution, with the other giving ground to social evolution.

Whereby the products of, in giving of a different aurora than ever before. seemed to have reached beyond the best of what evolution could offer. By out evolving evolution in being able and associate in better style over these past four or five thousand years the concept of God.

By using new tools not supplied by evolution or God particle interaction. But just good old fashioned usage of how we had developed our new talents and attachments. Without any reference to evolution or even God. For now, we had the idea of thought, which almost self- manifest on its own account. For there is no chemical name for it even to have been set by God.

Without claim almost effort, we of humanity, in theory almost self-created under the very eyes of God. Which meant in theory we were around at the supposed start of time some 13,8 billion years ago. How else would we know about the situation then ago if we weren't there? Which is not a real question.

For in this exercise number ONE, my intention has been to show our relationship with God on his surmountable terms. Which is a must not for us but God, for in waiting for 13,8 billion years to hear a voice again. We cannot risk the story told by those who do not believe in the concept of God genuinely.

Therefore, before I move on to my next station TWO, which in a sense refers to religions separately for one element only. I set this standard to be a positive for God even though we of humanity have to set God his own tasks and methodology to solve our problems.

We can now lead God to create his own acceptances about how we, but in the singular of me or I socially. Who must take a stand on what can from now only be Gods desired terms so far. Even when supplied by evolution, which we know to be almost as old as God in all cases.

How, can be maintained when to consider the true aspects of change offered at least over the past 800 million years. Resulted in one, owed to factual evolution. Whereby change in culmination was to offer an end pattern of conduct for all creature species.

Who essentially were to satisfy themselves with the end product of continuance by way of procreating in all cases? Yet were still able to follow evolution as it happened in all cases. Except in the one and only case of how humanity in we, that means all of us whether we believe in God or not.

Threw a spanner into the whole setup, by how we showed we could still operate on normal species terms evolutionary. Even though we out evolved the system when we activated our, the unread ability to think beyond imagination.

Which was and is a standard evolution cannot match, for her limits even so far on God's terms, can do no more than revolve around what our 118 known of chemical elements have already delivered.

Although she still effects change, she is not in the same class as of how humanity in we, are still able and attract God's interest even if we do not yet believe in the real concept of God. Which when we look into the future past of our religious countenance, all might be able to feel we are standing on the same firm ground our religions were thought to have prepared for us.

At least from about four or five thousand years ago first. Until they were misled modern verse by the same people in we, who over-played our religious hands. Because some of us thought our religions were historical. When in fact they are of today only.

Shown first hand when we realise our religions have no histor-ical religious resonance. They are utterly connected to those of us alive and living today. Those actively using our lifespan of 80 plus years to still influence God. This time with the full generational sup-port of our young, who in tandem with us. Will be able and comfort God; we will try harder.

TWO   Religions in form owe us much more than we owe them. But what I suggest they set to our plan, will repay us in dividend.

Not least because they by effect and effort were and are more responsible to stimulate God better than before. But now 21st cen-tury style. Which in a sense can be mounted when we set the one standard for all religions for all time while we live.

Therefore, irrespective of their, our understanding of how we relate to God through religion. When we set this my overall plan on firm religious terms. At a glance we will have turned 10.000 different religions, who in essence follow the same God. Into 10.000 religions with the same outlook and almost expectation.

For when my plan is introduced, it transcends what we made to be different historically, into a viable realisation we can all move for-ward at our own pace. Which as ever from now means from within our 80 plus year lifespan. We really are the one species who found God for his sake.

Therefore, to set that realisation and by return. My maxim at first on religious lines stands thus. Religions on bloc are to set the expectation for all followers of any class or style. To at first expect, religiously set. When they, we die, it will follow the style of "Natural Body Death from old age" only.

Plus, in good measure, and still on religious terms. To add the moral standards, no person of any religion should have suffered the indignity of to have been a slave, of being tortured of being intimidated or bullied or downtrodden. Even ignored even to have been murdered.

All of course are reasons designed to placate God over how any unclear purely religious understanding of what religions are for, when they are not only our link with God. But are God's way whereby he can link with us.

By such a token, I have just stated, no religion 21st century style. Can now promote for any of their adherents, followers or believers to kill any other human being. Which means of the species humanity, for any reason. Not even in God's name.

Have I just spoken for God, no. Have I spoken against our religious administrators, no. What I have done, is set our plan of God into operation. Whereby if asked, God can answer fully," yes, do not kill religiously".

For to do so is to tarnish the only way we can come together, which is post life. But now under my terms described by you or whomsoever in the collective class of humanity. The only species who can rationalise thought beyond what evolution could deliver in 800 million years or trying to.

But best of all to realise that when I set God particles with motion. Their return was to produce a means to answer my own questions of why or what for, if only to give me substance I deserve. Then the event that realised that cause will still be able and help me enjoy what I allowed happen, even when unsure.

With no strings attached, it is, was, and might yet be our religions which were, are the force we need in hand, to be able and follow the trail we have blazed for God to follow. Providing we give them credit for their projection into the future. Beyond how we can rationally think or thought.

Not to be heavy handed, but when we now think religion and God, we must theme such thoughts to read, God then religion.

For although in a sense they gave us the concept of God, we over decorated that clause by applying a coat of many colours, which by result gave us 10.000 different options of God. Being well and good, all to do now is make that story fit.

Which becomes much easier when to realise if we keep in plan the individuality of a single person with the individuality of God. All to do is associate that image in terms to suit our thinking species.

Which can only ever be met if we are all given the same time chance as each other. Which when translated properly means nothing can change if we die prematurely. Therefore, to fixate as I have, we are all owed "Natural Body Death from old age", will stand us all in good stead.

Never to be a barrier even for some of us who might find it hard to grasp what I write or allude to. But in good heart fear not yourself. For in you/us to die of old age naturally, allows our union with God work. No matter what we did while alive.

Providing we did not kill anybody, providing we did not knowingly subject any of our peers to slavery or abuse or torture or intimidation. Nor to have knowingly bullied, coerced even to have ignored by uncaring indifference.

Bearing in mind, some who do, may have started their journey under such circumstances for them to be untrustworthy of their peers. Which is not an excuse or reason, but once cut, the scar left can be a sad reminder of what was not deserved.

Which is never to be an easy fix situation, unless when to realise we in species are a true wonder. Providing we keep in touch with the reality of now. A timeframe means whereby we can all quote current events only to have a bearing on our understanding of what the future is for.

Though not to dismiss or forget the past pre our own experiences. What we must take on board in review, is to consider the effect of the past on people such as we, who never really experienced some of it. But when others, our contemporise who feel they may have scores to settle. Then we must intervene even for reasons we might not fully understand.

Which in or from our new religious awareness, allows us to forebear with each other before we condemn. For by accepting all religions through our belief in the concept of God. Can now accept

God's proposed future role for time to continue in any case. Afterall who can deny our existence of from about 800 million years ago when creature species came into being.

Who can deny one of that class of God particle interaction, were ripe enough to form a ready- made picture of what time past was for by setting a plan of what the future would bring? But on who's terms and why. Which fell to be produced by our 10.000 world religions but now to only one workable plan.

One which must include God, but now on his terms which have to be made fit. Which they were in the wonder of error. When we of humanity in broken glass style assembled the picture of how God could be involved with the only species ever to have given God a purpose for himself. Which might be open to improvement under different circumstances if offered.

But in the meantime, it will be up to the likes of me and you to make good sense of what we in humanity have been doing for the past four or five thousand years. Which was to set God with a viable plan and style of how he can continue to learn from us for him.

Which when seen what our religious mould has produced. We can relax and take on board the measure of the plan we have already offered to God. Which can only run by imagination, which is a bit like free thinking. But only on human terms if tinged with religious expectations.

Never to downgrade good intentions, which is doubt. Why we must promote the concept of all religions in the God is theory of under-standing. Will self-manifest when to realise, they are the only offering whereby we can free think almost about anything, but mainly God.

To explore that medium in its own field, it is easy to notice our religions are the only way whereby we can come to the idea of God's supremacy. This time on our account only, for through religion is the best way to promote raw thought.

Which as we know by style is an unbreakable fixation of per-haps why and how humanity is unique in the universe, as far as we can assume. Because we now know the order of the universe even in chaos, is a permanent feature.

Expressed scientifically by the fact that all God particle interac-tion so far. Has produced in general, only about 118 atom structured elements of their own style. But can never tell how or why in a later time setting, a new form of elementary mixing emerged.

Perhaps to have started about three million years ago when by line of decent, even if evolution was involved. Humanity arose, to be the only force in the entire universe who could name the universe.

Through how we, if through our invention of our religions, were, are now able to think them all to the wonder of God. Which by effect is starting at the beginning, for if there is or was never God in place to have set God particles with motion.

Science and politics could never have been produced to offer doubt to their own existence. Which is why my beginning of not much longer than 80 odd years of living, plus all of us in that range of living in any case. Had to have historically set the plan of how any-thing could work. Which ongoing, we called them all our religions.

Although I had indicated often, we sort of came to the/a Great Spirit supposition about God at least 60.000 years ago. Which still runs in some places today and cannot be judged badly.

For in that run of time, we better refined the core of that con-cept to be now God. A more defined character. From which and in union with the idea of the Great spirit, whose task was to take care of us in the afterlife. We simply promoted he and God to have greater influence than we ever could have, unless set through God, our later single definition.

Without further examination except what this is. If we were roused enough over the past 60.000 or the past four or five thousand years in parallel. To come to the idea of God and his aftercare for us in all counts, then we must say it is/was our religions to be the source of our main motivation.

So now there is no reason to argue the odds of what they might say or come up with. Even when in mild reality it is almost now our politics is to have taken over socially. Sometimes on the grounds of her association with her nemesis science. Not to worry, they will have their say as my later listings of three and four later.

So, to finish on my numbered two listing, religions. I will set their themes to rest. When to consider the enormity of how, if

60.000 years ago. We began to give thought of how the Great spirit was going to care for us afterlife.

Then as little as four or five thousand years ago, on the same theme, we refined that ideal to the new final consideration, but in God's name. If he was to attend to us in afterlife. It must be to judge us in standard for our conduct while we lived.

Never to be a rule, but only another human thought idea. For if now to be in God's company post life to claim our reward for time well spent. That must be it. Unless how would God treat the less worthy of us. From which we through our thought patterns sorted that problem out for God.

If we were or could be bad, so too could God's kith and kin associates be. Therefore, on his own account, but by our reasoning. He must have cast his former spiritual associates to be the masters of their own fate, but not in our/God's place of refuge we called heaven or paradise.

When almost at the same time, we realised reward came with retribution. Then that could not occur in heaven together. So in good style, we for God built for him the darkness of damnation deserved for those who we thought were not up to God's good standards.

They by their efforts alone, but often on our say so on God's behalf would suffer in Hell. A place of damnation. Strangely out of God's hands of control or so we were happy to leave it so.

That is perhaps until about in this modern era circa 2012, something of a true scientific nature occurred. Whereby we, yours truly of humanity, found it necessary to round all corners about religion and God. For what we were running with did not compliment the best scientific efforts of 2012, whereby the God particle was first recorded.

So, in order to maintain the integrity of what that revelation meant. We needed to take a short review, but in a style we cannot answer. For when we thought heaven and hell, we were blind to the immensity of God.

How could God only do half his job by only attending to the supposed good of humanity when we lived and are now in God's domain of heaven. Then to leave people we, we considered to be bad in God's name for others to chastise.

If heaven and hell have been of God's concern since God knows when, set by us. Then let us reinstate God better to his own understanding, so that when he reconnects with us, no blushes will be the order of concern for either party.

Which is why when I concluded religiously. Heaven and hell are not the issue, but heaven one and heaven two are. Because at a stroke we have restored God to the only place he can be religiously. To be able and set all our, any creature species efforts at total attempted understanding in their/our order of significance.

Almost off cuff, we have re-empowered God religiously, even for those who do not believe in the concept. For in a trice over these past ten years since 2012, we have changed the habit of disagreeing with or denouncing what could not be put in our hand for individual inspection.

By the simple expression of thinking of God in name, we of humanity almost now rule the universe. Shown in simple style by this skit. If any creature species dies, the best they might have done while alive, is to have propagated, so their line instinctively continues, that's their lot.

We on a different plain have made it so that when we die naturally from old age. We still have a role to fill. Shown by how we have religious connections beyond the powers of pure instinct.

Such power being expressed generationally by how we of the same stamp can generationally relate to each other at first religiously. Which means through God, then by experience, which means life and living. Although at a pinch we sometimes get it wrong, we now know we are right.

For when the time comes to set the clock, we now understand the only relevance to God in all time is of our conduct while alive. Which has always been the only means whereby we can relay to God his most important religious role of to determine by our set rules of our standing when we die and now go to heaven one or heaven two only.

Which is only carried religiously, because religions are unselfish in concept. For their first name has always been service. Although we got a few things wrong in or through some supposed called or claimed religious outlooks. Our main religious themes have been generally good.

But in order to prove that case, from now on when we go to God it must be on his terms set by us. Which is a lot simpler than when announced. For to set our terms first, is to show God what he has been looking for in 13.8 billion years of waiting.

Before we reach that pinnacle, we must associate God to our conduct, so when the time comes, he will be able and set our plan as he should, if he was deciding on his own. Let's face it, God must be done with waiting, at least at this stage, because we have most of the answers.

Therefore, in kind return, we can move to the penultimate stage of God's understanding so far. Which has to be aligned to what is on offer, which only comes from humanity. Even if we do not agree, like not to believe in the concept of God.

For which the danger is, we, that is all who do believe in God if through religion or otherwise. Raise Gods awareness, he will have to include all of humanity whether we like it or not in his reckoning. Which is a product of us who do believe in God for all lifeform sakes, not least because from where we all came from, whether we liked it or not.

Religions without real consideration, offer the concept, God as our discoverer, appointed us to follow his rules. Which are what, except to be set by us. For if God was involved in any other way about how we thought. He would be doing our thinking for us. Is he?

Which as we all know is not a reality check viability, that scenario leaves things in God's hands only. Which again is unprovable because we of humanity are here. Creating the picture there are other reasons or motives to accommodate God. Which by now are nearly lost in time unless we of humanity take charge.

Done when we share God in heaven one and now heaven two, also to follow our unique lead. Whereby God is to follow our ideas because of the unsighted confusion laid down by the millions of other creature species. Who are not yet ripe to offer their plan. But alas worse, they now never will be if my diagnosis is near right.

When I grouped them all to follow the prospect of procreation only as their core incentive. I was not being dismissive, all I set to do was to declassify them in comparative human terms so far. Which is a story to be better told of by God.

Afterall when he found interest in us of humanity on merit. He had at least 800 million years before our appearance to be interested in other creature species if they made sounds to draw his interest. Plus he had the previous 13 billion years with the forming of galaxy to contend with.

Which again was slow but ran on the self-same similar lines, galaxy per galaxy. Only changed on mass but to be the same as far as we can understand. When further God particle interaction increased their background ratio, when new elements were formed from one to the one hundred and eighteen, we know of. Which turned out to be a predictable forecast.

Though I have almost directed galaxy were of little interest to God by how I present my case. Then the newer configuration of other creature species did not ring any bells. My plan is not to dismiss such enterprise. If to consider my real theme is to promote God.

Then by giving them an angle on equal terms with the species humanity. My real aim is to enlighten God, of his intention, which must have been near to at first be recognised. Then to have his role defined.

Was he to be like all galaxy by character? Was he to tie himself in self-interest to only procreate? Perhaps if he was and is, he was waiting to be shown which route to follow and why.

In steps the unity of humanity, who by trial and error religiously, have at last compressed the meaning and aims of 10.000 different world religions into one. Which now carries the name species.

Although God will have the final say, it must follow under our direction. Which can now only occur in heaven one or heaven two. Because when God particles interacted to produce 118 recognised full atom elements. God's scope was always there in parallel, but he did not operate that clause as far as we can assume.

Which allows my, his plan of wait and see, was set pre time, to cover the full extent of time. If just to see what happened in the meantime. Which resulted in religion. The only means to be able and mix with God in any form, but not by any means.

Which is perhaps why our religions above all else have been the course we can take to liberate God on his terms anew. Because their combined guesswork of coming to the idea of a post life situation with God hit the mark.

We now know not all angles were right angles. But we were left with enough to be able and clear the air about what might happen when we would have reached death by any means.

By using the good offices of how to understand God will help us in other fields of study about personal query. Which does not have to be complicated. For it will never be necessary for us individually to know all the answers. We are not on test; we are not to be examined. Which does not mean we can hide in a corner and still share all the goodies when handed out.

My only implication is that it is not for any of us who may not know the answers. To be used or exploited by some who think they do know all the answers. Which revisits some of the unsure ground we once walked upon.

I can now offer my version of why most of our religions are worth their salt. Although repetitive, most came to understand the lifespan of the individual was not long enough by span to hold God's interest.

Therefore, by return, many in normal recline, for they had God on their side. Simply did the sums, God could still be involved with us when we were to die howsoever. Then even better, he could set us in quarters for how we behaved while we lived.

Alas our version of accommodation, ran to be we would have been assigned to heaven with God or hell with God's cur. Not to have realised then ago and after. To be with God in death, meant we were all with God only. For there is only one God to contend with, but no cur.

So, with that piece of magic to consider, plus because our single lifespan of eighty or so years is all we may have in comparison with other creature species. Plus, in our species generational form, which is different to all other creature species also.

God would have to concede, because of the way we humanity intermixed generationally in the thought field stakes, unlike all other creature species. On our say so, he will have to create the position of how and where we can re-interact to suit his needs to keep learning from us before he takes the time to be our professor of thought.

This time not led by us, for time enough will have then passed so we can justify to God why our religions are so very important. Not least because they were our motivation for the likes of us not to abandon the concept of God. So, we could journey back 800 million years to catch evolution at her least influence and remain there.

Which for, me or us might be now, for if we do not believe in God. All that we can do is hide under our pillow. For we have just proved religiously, God believes in us.

Plus, by non-demand, we have come to realise through religions first. We have been able to formulate a formal way of how we should interact so human progress is assured. Which will leave it for our young in our next generations. To carry us to better and better ways of community between us, the species humanity and God.

But just a little before that happens, we now have to move on to my number three heading which will be like pulling teeth, for number three bleeds politics.

THREE   Politics is another name for hit and hope, for she has little direction and fewer morals. Her call seems too always be me over the ideal of we. If we are to continue and enhance any ideas, we may hold about the real future of humanity in any state.

We will have to better realise, in order to direct proper change, our rules of engagement will have to show their foundations. Which at long last have now been set religiously first, which must run in parallel with my political presentation.

Whereby all political systems in duplicate, must now introduce, almost under the same terms. My suggestion already offered religiously. Whereby all political parties, systems or styles. For the benefit of all adherents, followers, believers or activists. Also set to deliver for all, the same fixture regarding the subject of death.

It now becomes a political declaration; all connections can expect "Natural Body Death from old age ". To be the new exclusive of how we each can expect death without other influences being involved.

Although linked with my religious clause, this political rendition does not necessarily follow the exact same case note. Because political systems do not have to follow any God clause we expect from religious connections.

But just in case, if as stated one side is not to kill religiously. Then the other in politics should not kill morally. Which is a bigger picture if to consider the true responsibilities political direction holds for her adherents. But as a must, so not to alienate the general thrust of politics, which is to serve.

By me suggesting politics should deliver the same expectation we can expect religiously which is linked to God. My thrust of political mediation, when read to be of major concern only to those alive and living today until "Natural Body Death from old age". Endorses the integrity of how politics should work.

For when we set my plan politically. What we are saying by suggestion, is if we cannot sort our problems out in an 80 plus year cycle of time. We have no hope ever of solving it, them, by falsely removing, often the means of improvement in our living, political enterprise. Who have nothing more to do than improve the lot of all subjects until natural body death calls.

One offhand but highly positive way we can use politics to lay her own foundations is through our United Nations. Already suggested, but when we set her to determine the limits or basic standard of all religions.

Whereby if any claim to kill in God's name, under soul searching by our UN, they can declassify any claimed religion who use such tactics. To be a different non-religious force.

To help set and guide such standards, we can remind ourselves. It will have been our United Nations under political direction only, who would already have established our new "The Rights of Humanity" maxim in direct replacement of how human rights is misused.

Being my reminder, we are to consider mankind in the plural over the dated concept of applying human rights in the singular. Which means we must also take care in the same way with how we view and operate religious tolerance to suit ourselves, also in the singular. Almost shown 10.000 different ways.

Politics will still have much to do but must learn to mind her P's and Q's. For as a source on her own account, she can only last as long in style as the people she represents, now spread over 80 plus years only.

Which is never to be an ending, for among that group there is a fair generational mix of young people able to force change by encouragement. Which might drop the scales on political eyes. Allowing her to now see what she has been newly told is good for her.

Part of her learning curve will involve her to take a closer look at her own moral fibre. Not in dread but wide eyed. Because although a servant of humanity, almost more so than religions. She let her guard slip by not really heeding the supposed morality of what religions should have implanted in us already.

Before I move to my list number four, which is theory in the false name of science. A bright star, enough so to bedazzle politics. For in progress, she seemed better able to ignore God than give him credit for setting all God particles with motion.

Being a situation, she cannot give politics an answer to, but in seeming politics never asked science the question.

FOUR   Science to be a topic and subject at the same time is a good equation. But in either case she is nothing unless to be adorned by any section of humanity who becomes excited by her.

Though she has brought us all very much by enlightenment. We need to put her in her place generously, so she can play her own hand. Rather than be used by some to endorse their standing for whatever means.

If we show we realise science our topic is the subject of explaining our surroundings, that's fine. What we must guard against is not to assume what she cannot explain just now, she will expose to us later.

Which asks the questions all relating to humanity only. Why does science think she needs to explain things to us, that are essentially unexplainable? Unless most of our scientific community, who generally are now formed from within our political groups.

Which only has relevance if some from within either community, science and politics. Display or express their opinions to dispel the core concepts of most religions who have already expressed their attachment to the concept of God. Even when some end their own argument by further following the ideal, God is.

For me an acknowledgement that we do not know all the answers nor may we ever. Because the full explanation of time is not opened to be explained under our present mind set. All we might get away with is to set the new situation. Whereby there is a future beyond what can be explained mathematically.

Why we must set science to be in a lower class of reality than how our religions operate. Is born from the solid ground of the end product of how matter interaction might work or actually works.

Almost exemplified by how people like me of any community, scientific, religious or political. Manage to break all the rules by following the nature of our pasts and what they might or must lead to.

Which is the uncomplicated theory of God previously expressed through or from the outlook of most religions. Then followed up politically and scientifically. Which from most scientific perspectives was to deliver us self-doubt about God mathematically.

It was indeed in that voice we were led and still are cajoled, not to believe in the concept of God. Because he cannot be put into any equation to any style except now to belong to the unreal concept of spontaneity. Which has to be a mathematical term by any standard, but particularly those we use to explain how spontaneous cannot work, but God particles with motion can.

If to consider for or against mathematics is to be a, even the core construct of how we explain science or how science can be explained. Then all to do is time the anomaly to when and how it became relevant in science. After it had been running in its better role of managing the arithmetic of numbers for thousands of years.

Knowing now we can expect all things to eventually be properly formulated, even by using the unfinished style of how we developed the stalwart of formula, mathematics. By no more than extrapolation to the era of the Big Bang theory.

We must expect to be able and square science away in her own style, but now soaked in human references above all other considerations. Even when we know she will never be able and match our progress about the realisation God is. And the events that still lead to proof of that proposition.

Which came only now, in this modern era over the past 10 years or since 2012, now realised. When in the name of humanity, we were able to confirm the conclusions we first nearly came to four or five thousand years ago about God.

With this section of my conclusions numbered four, mainly about science. I have been fair in my assessment for all our sakes. For it is wrong for any of us to look for reasons of any make or kind to deter what the effect of time gave up in any case.

Which produced one asking only, but in many different styles. To become the focal point of all reasoning in all time. Which when now examined in the negative positively. We can all draw our own conclusions providing we reach to accept more is available to happen to each person post life in the only way possible.

Which will emanate from reasons and sources beyond the reaches of any thought of human experience even like religions. But not politics or science in their assumed role to be our mentor even partner.

Because together they seem to have forgotten, one is how we operate while the other is why we operate. And can be used under those headings to indicate in reflection they are the only means we need to continue. Leaving religion on the shelf.

Perhaps not least because religions have in part sold themselves short by order of control. When some in the query of their own delivery, seem prepared to destroy other suggestions to their style of how some assume to operate for God on their own say so.

Which though used by me before as anecdotal relief. By now suggesting our UN can properly adjust that wrongdoing. We cannot us her to set better scientific projections, for in open display, science only works for politics.

Being a place of its best quality to be able and explain how we of politics can better use the wonders, magic and tricks science sometimes uses to set politics only in role. For when science releases her physical wonders she is at her limit.

She has no mandate to wander and roam the corridors of spiritual excellence casting aspersions. Just because she on her own account cannot rationalise the concept of God or God is. But uses the hollow bones of politics to try and make her case, which is not a fault of science or her multi talents. Only some of her operators, who may align themselves to politics for both advantage.

So not to influence science in any way politically, even religiously. But it might serve science well if she, even in theory. Adds my suggested open bracket, question mark, close bracket, (?), symbol. To theoretically add to any new, even existing formula ratios, to indicate they must leave options open.

Whereby she, science closes no doors, even if experiments are negative at first. For when mandated to try, try and try again she will show her true colours of at least leaving all doors open by closing none.

When science grasps that realisation. Her best view might restart her own acceptance of why the Big Bang Theory is off key. But shown to be correct mathematically by the indifferent standard of accepting formula nobody can decipher.

Whereas now, science in full regalia has my puny theory to start from anew. Set by scientific events to have occurred 10 short years ago. When she proved of the God particle. Which was a positive result.

Allowing me not of any distinction. For I am we, of the same species, humanity, not of any distinction. Until we accept and realise how we alone in the entire universe fell to the concept of God and God is, to be a means to soothe all our ills.

But in the meantime, to prove that issue by referring or rereading the positive of a real experiment which could even be claimed to be negative, I/we can assert, once the smallest piece of matter the God particle had been proved of in form and reality. We had a story.

Which runs in the name, my "The God Particle Theory". Now offered scientifically proved. For when we found one, we found all. That's as simple as it gets. But to now realise the state and the number of the all, is already known. Except from about 800 million years ago. When new numbers were formed.

For me to now utter as done before. The space/room to accommodate all the God particles already there, at the time of our real singularity. Was strewn in equal proportion and of equal construction spread in lattice field sponge form. Which means they were set in simple three- dimensional array.

Which is only provable by effect, like how our universe is in three-dimensional display. But before it got as it is today. It like us had to form under known of instances and through known circumstances.

Which allows us, in this case me, to set what must have been the standards for progress in the form of movement to work or more importantly. begin. Which can only produce connotations in the lines of to consider why, how, reason or purpose or because. Which by return must have a scientific explanation. Which is not to have been spontaneous.

Therefore, even if to disprove that theory when to offer my own. There is no alternative for us of humanity. But to set the only formula possible for any unexplainable scientific feature to have occurred. So, in being, if the only first matter to be, was in display as suggested. Then at core it only needed one motive. But set under extraordinary circumstances.

Which could only now again be realised post 2012, post about 100 years ago when the Big Bang first showed its face. Post four or five thousand years ago when we first rationalised the concept of God.

Plus from when we first came to God perhaps 60.000 years ago in Great Spirit form. We set seeds of content which drew us to be big enough not only by stature but by imagination which can be successfully accused of to be the forbearer of thought even pure thought.

Which now by undeterminable time scales, we have come to be able and fit the only possible way or reason so far. Whereby anybody was old enough to mention how God could have started the whole process of time.

When he set his own configuration of God particles with motion. Being a complete mystery to him. But in line to be the only way the immensity of God might ever be recognised. For when he ruled pre 13.8 billion ago. He did not know of his kingdom or what it could ever become for in effect he knew nothing.

Unless even without any kind of motive, perhaps for the tenth time. By releasing the matter of matter which was always there in any case. Being now a scientific fact. By giving the virtually nothing of diminutive matter, motion. To lead to the series of events leading to the writing of books and the presentation of ideas to be started.

Which in stage, almost lost the plot scientifically, when she as an extra element in man's toolbox. Began to think she made the box of tricks we of humanity had already found, we had been looking for over the past 60.000 years at least. When our truth was to call God by name without his cover, which meant we could call God anything.

What we did without realising it on most counts. Was to come to God by our own excellence of mind in error of thought? But we did make a good show, because on those terms so far. We outmanoeuvred how science must work and can only work from now on and ever before.

For when science formed over the same period of time from the year dot 13.8 billion years ago, until tomorrow. On her own account without reference, she set as they happened or occurred, the true formula of how things worked or more precisely interacted.

Right from when the first two God particles interacted, through to when the first atomic element formed, then in number by time of when the second and third. Right up to when 118 elements were countable. Which could have been a long time ago.

Because in scientific reality from about 800 million years ago. A new or different form of God particle interaction appeared or formed. Not now particularly elementary, for this type seemed to use evolution differently.

Whereby in or on lifetime scales of existence, plus for the obvious of reacting to their immediate circumstances. Evolution in the form of allowing, almost helped some of these lifeforms newly evolve, but to maintain recent links in their existing form. Which seemed to run well for most of any period of time when true lifeforms in the name flora and fauna coexisted.

Until from about three million years ago when a lead was cut for homo sapiens to appear. Who from in their day of very recent duration, mixed up the whole pot of what evolution had been doing for as long as time itself, if evolving meant the means to change?

All of which rounds the circle in one main respect only. For by now, when humanity emerged. Evolution in form but of unintentional means let loose a unique product. Which at the same time to be different in style by skin colour or other physical features of no particular account.

Often endorsed by circumstances of habitat or diet or geography or climate. Which assured some of us would be affected by how we ate or slept or dressed. But not by how we in our evolved groups thought.

For now, in the first time in the history of the entire universe scientifically. We had a normally formed group or element, who outstood the previous standard of all other happenings and events. Which led to the matter of change between God particles in action or not in action, only the action of thought.

Not only did we have a unique combination of God particle interaction to have formed us, humanity. Even if we were at first formed to be black of skin because of the very circumstances just mentioned.

Our situation from then ago allowed chance and evolution to change us in appearance in conformity to how evolution worked. But not to be different. For in the forms, we are now in, circa 2022. Is almost how we will remain; except we can still alter bit by bit evolutionary. Which is normal to how all other creature species are still evolving.

Except with us of humanity, being the only to have shown signs we understand the concept of God making us extra special. Derived at in our own way by how we can reason through our unique ability to think beyond the horizon of tomorrow,

Shown by how we have reasoned the fact of God without having to understand the principle. Sometimes clouded by the anomaly of science. A medium we chose to aid us in our search to understand. Yet nearly allowed her to destroy by ridicule, the fact of our species uniqueness shown by how we alone came to the idea of God.

Perhaps based on two assumptions. One, science and all her elements are right. Two, the human idea of mixing God with science cannot be set experimentally. Therefore, God is not an element to science, there is no equation for its/his involvement with science in general.

Plus, not three, but by inference, science in form, which has no form without humanity involved. Is now the spontaneous reason for all existences, because she through some of her commentators. Is the only means of enlightenment we can have about the universe.

Though crude assertion, the above scenario, is set against some individuals in various fields of science. Who might think to show their indifference to our thinking about God and religion. Based on no more than science has so far been unable to find God among the 118 elements we through her know of.

Alas, because of her need to be able and quantify experimentally. When she cannot see the image of God in plain sight. By return, that concept cannot be used in any scientific reasoning, for science is the order of all things.

Therefore, when she enters the theory of science in any form. She is compelled to use her own created catalyst mathematics. Her means to explain anything and everything. Which as we know it works well to cloud the desires of science in all her guises.

Even when we conveniently put to one side the obvious of what science is. A collection of elementary products having created their own codes of conduct to define their own structure as end products. Which needs no further soul searching.

Because from now on. In simplicity, all science can ever be, is a collection of numbered objects. That can interact under a given number of circumstances to give off a given number of results.

Although humanity is part of that or those equations being composite of the same elementary mixing. Because we came to God on our own account, we can run the corridors of science and pure science. Therefore, we of humanity hold the last word scientifically.

Which stands on that premise, our discovery of God un-scientifically is a fact. So, in consequence apart to how we are already operating science from within her own boundaries. We can extend her role via her most senior scientists.

To offer for our consideration beyond all else, because of the latent power science holds. On our say so, she will be responsible for how we the minions of humanity in simple verse, will be able and understand the concept of God. Now presented to us by science, mathematically.

Almost to be set in formula, for when God is better introduced scientifically through our previous thought of ideas about heaven one and heaven two. She will see in clarity, why we or she in science must now adjust to fit into or alongside most new equations. My open bracket, question mark, close bracket, (?) symbol for God.

Which is complimented by our free understanding soon. When we can all expect to die under my/our religious and political plan of to reach "Natural Body Death from old age". Whimsically tied in to the ideal, most of us will have some understanding of what that means for those of us alive and living today. While within our eighty plus year lifespan.

A time period so vital in the history of the universe. Because in it, we can assimilate what all our ancestors were trying to do for us throughout history. Which in simple plan was to account for time everlasting. Not least because of our generational life plan existence.

Which is a true venture that can be realised almost scientifically. When to consider for the past 800 million years. Only one creature species aspired, which was not proof but drove expectation. Not for any reason but God's.

For when we strip everything to bare bones. It is only we of humanity who are capable to pass the baton to God. But on his terms, which we almost gave him in any case.

For when God set all God particles with motion. He had no idea of what might occur, except something. Which it did but out of sync. To only come into focus when we realised if from the year 2012. God's plan not only covered the past, but it was also always open to cover the future. Now fully on Gods terms, even after being directed by us.

Led by how we displayed our species singular projected understanding, even as early as 60.000 years ago by connecting to the Great spirit through imagining. Even though to consider we might have an afterlife future by the Great spirits guidance.

Then from about four or five thousand years ago when we changed our flag to call the great spirit God. Now capable to deal with us post life in heaven and hell.

But on who's terms except ours, for is God sure, which must read no, for no other reason than the obvious. God relies on us, perhaps because of all the plans he could have set for himself. They would have betrayed his only ever desire to wait and see what might occur until heaven one and heaven two came along to cement the future in place anew.

Which is a better story than science could ever manipulate. How could she alone set a plan of continuance which like herself would be finite. Shown by how in expression, science in her style to explain almost everything while at the same time presents her theory of how everything will eventually end. When by through scientific projected study. All matter interaction will have turned full circle to have spent or burnt up to regress and reform to a lump of matter the size of a pea. Ready again to spontaneously Big Bang.

To avoid closing any discussion with a question mark, but in the case of my numbered four item headed science. I leave her now to her own devises for a bit. I also leave God to his own devises, which are universal in all aeras.

Without to tarnish the good will so many people spread over other human beings. Some of my last offerings are now laid before us all. So, we can be sure of what is going to be our fate, good over bad. Which reads positive over negative.

I will further present my conclusions in two short passages without comment, but in style to carry the reality of time, which as a medium will cover all our needs.

ONE   All my writings so far have been real, so too is God. I make no case for him except when he operates heaven one and heaven two. Which will be done on one basis only. To enhance the future efforts of humanity. This time as God's agents of time, for effectively we gave God motivation.

Therefore, not by return, God will use our wiles to help him help us to satisfy him about why it was his own good idea to start at the beginning. When he alone set God particles with motion. For there was no before that operation except God.

By now having been able and set heaven one and heaven two from our suggestion while allowing time to run its own course for us on earth. God will have shown how he found it easier to connect with us than any other species if throughout the universe.

Fortunately, God does not have to make a case for us. But in due, he does acknowledge he now looks like each and every one of us physically. Which is part of his magic beyond sorcery. For by that new connection God no longer needs to bellow and shout his case.

Another part of his magic to show his metal, also revolves around us in our species form. In relation to why we picked it for him to manage heaven one and heaven two at the same time over new time eras.

Which was our doing. For when we came to our magic of now realising, we have at last decided not to kill one another for any reason. By internationally declaring we have now set the one standard of to expect to die by "Natural Body Death from old age" only.

Plus, under the same conditions and circumstances, we set in secular and spiritual declaration. To follow the new bearing just installed via international political consent to introduce by modernisation. My additional maxim to promote only "The Rights of Humanity". To have a plural connotation instead of supporting the singular by their demand.

With those two new additions operating now in our vital 80 plus year lifecycle. We might not need much more heavy legislation except to cover the past. Which always only ends yesterday, until we reach heaven one and or heaven two.

Which will become the biggest equation science could ever launch, for the answers generated here will far outreach any imagination. Which is why it will be up to us of the species humanity to direct God of who is to go into heaven one or two. But now God can direct what for by learning our story.

Where God scores uncountable points over us, the same people image per image he is. Comes from the small fact. Although he has been aware of and followed each and every one of us as we generationally grew, aged and died. He will use our council to treat others as he saw them. But not always by our desire no matter how much we crave his indulgence.

For by moving into heaven one or two, we now become wards of God at our discretion, which must reflect his opinion of how we taught him. Of which we must satisfy ourselves we gave God the best we could. So he in our wisdom could now magnify that to be of his stature.

Which amounts to what he may have always been looking to find, when he gave God particles the activity of motion. To check what might occur for his sake, which has allowed us think in better terms of we over the divisive term me.

My next short passage numbered two, which follows one in repetition, will only cover new ground or at best old ground wearing different shoes. But to maintain our integrity I might split this rendition two, into as many segments as we might need to make my point.

TWO   Has to be about humanity pure and simple. What I now write stands on the burning coals underfoot, which either damage almost beyond repair or have no impact. Because in either case the emotional range used are of our individual construction. Sometimes beyond our ability to see what we are doing or what just happened or is not happening.

Another first we are to understand, is to reacquaint us with the obvious, set beyond argument. I now run these pictures of humanity in the best light possible, which casts deep dark shadows. Unless we accept the change offered by these pages. Whereby beyond flat personal desire, I have given it that we are all in God's image or better God is in our image by all of us.

Although a demeaning observation for many good of heart bigots and racists. My tone is to inject if a person is to believe in God and heaven is for us, with hell for other God believers who do not look like us or as we see do not behave like us. Where is the measure of their difference to us so we draw such conclusions?

Which is not rhetorical, because bias has no mirror of reflection if my mind is already made up. Unless perhaps now when to consider we are all of the same opinion to die of old age naturally. Set by joint effort codes of conduct. Because we can now trust God to judge for us instead of we for him.

By handing the reins to God, what we can hope for is his understanding that we already feel we had done the hard work, because it is we who set the platform of heaven one and two for God to work from. A deal we do not need to remind God of too often in the future, because he will already have taken over in heaven. Which although his full real domain, he will still have to be instructed by us.

But before the final decision, because from within our 80 plus year lifespan, some of our younger generations are already learning from us. By joint effort with them we can set the record straight to help God along.

Especially now that he knows that we know, which is a sheer delight to God. Afterall what better story could he have imagined on his own. When all he ever did so far was to give God particles motion, what else was there to do long ago. Except perhaps wait and see what would or could grow from those seeds.

Which is why I have to present my ideas in segment form so God will have no difficulty in being able to follow our directions. Because we started in the right place at the right times, even if it took us alone, 13.8 billion years to flick the switch God left for time to start. Even not to know the form of that situation.

One thing we must do post haste to rationalise the full potential of God, is part of what we have already been doing over the past four or five thousand years as best we could in all cases.

So not to confuse the surety of God, plus because of driven history, particularly human history. My focus of our general 80 plus year lifecycle is honest but deliberate. For it is the only time frame ever we could have discovered God in concept. Let alone his involvement in the future only. In the future only, for that is God's only domain.

All we now have to do from within our eighty plus year lifespan is set the proper situation whereby our young and offspring can better stimulate God than we have. But to remind ourselves we have done pretty good so far.

Because humanity is so unique in the entire universe my intention is not to burn our bridges of what we have so far achieved. Which is why we must pay court to God in the future which is to help him maintain his new interest in the only species so far to be of interest to him.

Taking on our collective human past of no more than about four or five thousand years can be negated if God was not involved. Wherein stood a collection of creature species who did not have a clue to why they were here there or anywhere. Except to propagate driven by unknown forces. If to be named, they were the twins of evolution and instinct. There I begin and end.

From my past notes we might agree God if through religion was a symbol of change. Which in effect created the biggest fantasy of now, then ago. That we would be able and influence the future by our conduct of now, then ago or yesterday.

Which as a product of thought was an unfinished rhapsody, but good enough for us to hum the tune of what could be. Whereby when we acclimatised with the idea of God. We misguidedly assumed he had some sort of bearing on our conduct of then ago even up to yesterday.

Not least because we could not really account for our own behaviour or more so the bad behaviour of others. Which allowed us credit God with the ability to punish all wrong doers, but not in front of us, could that work. Perhaps it could if God directed some of us in his name to act as executors of his will.

Without a set ratio, my view, which often follows new ground in our thought patterns. Can be easier to follow, if we pay less heed to what the past was supposed to produce, even to include God. So, we can set a new proper standard of how the past did affect us. But now on Gods lines in the future.

Which is not to deny the past, the point being, God had no input into the past, after all he is God. But as we did include God's involvement with some of us and at the same time some of us anti God people. Who might have turned on God to side with the imagination of his cur from hell. Is another reason to claim the past was our ground only. But had futuristic connotations. Now executed by God in heaven one and heaven two.

All we should be doing about the past in relation to us all of humanity, is set it for God to judge our conduct then ago. Post "Natural Body Death from old age". So now in heaven, why God should listen to any person, is because he is God and we all released him from his own lack of knowledge he never had, until after 13.8 billion years of waiting. Humanity gave God purpose on his terms.

Therefore, to balance God's books without conflict, plus in knowing after we taught him. He knew of every past action by everybody in the human range. For he was capable to watch the reactive range of all God particle interaction always. Even in 2012 when humanity proved for us, God's own God particle interactive capabilities and limit.

Creating the mythical concept, the future was yet to begin, which it already has in heaven one and heaven two. Except heaven has no history. Unless God listens to our earnest plea to associate our human pasts to be the best pre reference of how heaven one and two work over the former ideas of heaven and hell.

Another segment on the same theme follows thus. Even when I suggest the past may not count, my theory was and still is to heighten our human emotional ranges, which God knows little about.

My dismissal of the past in God's name and at the same time my elevation of him in how we direct him to judge us on our past actions. Has been done so we can relate to God and he to us, but in real life, which means in real time. Which on his lines is only the future?

Therefore, it is vital we of humanity get it right, which we will in my next segment after we absorb this story. If God was an active past person by type, although he looks just like every single individual we are. He has not been able and absorb our emotions for what might have occurred to us individually or collectively while we lived or died under the most brutal of circumstances.

Remember God had no route to anything that happened over the 13.8 billion years until we of humanity came along. So, when I suggest he was not involved with us in the past, that works. Is there a definable sign any of our billions of universal galaxies showed or drew a special interest from God, I wonder?

On entering heaven through "NBDfoa", apart to the realisation we are at last here. Which is not my idea but ours. For when humanity came to that concept if from as early as 60.000 years ago. We created the universe, if not for us, but God. So, in consequence it is up to us to set the greenhouse to encourage the growth of better thoughts than those that reject or neglect.

So here goes again, for God in heaven to be able and do his job by desire, for in a long time of waiting, he will have to follow the plan that formed without his input. But were nice enough to be pleasing in any order of presentation, because at base none ordered harm or hurt for or against each other. Even though harm or hurt might have been delivered or felt in the past.

Because they are carried in the full emotional range shared by humanity, they must be considered by God for first our sake, then his. Because when he adds his input and understanding to our leads, he will see in better focus how it is us who are trying to set his standards above our own which carry bias more than we should.

Though our domain, now post natural body death, alas an undisputable fact. None of us will be able and avoid God's judgement which in effect is ours. But now never operated in spite or envy or fear or terror. For those tortures occurred out of God's presence but in the past only.

Which allows we the sufferers, can lay our case before God, so that he can decide on heaven one or heaven two. Which at best and worst are not to be repetitive in kind to counter what went on before God could be or was involved.

All that we can hope for in heaven one and heaven two is for God's full involvement by our direction. Which in the face of Gods image of us, we or God can no longer lie or deceive, but in the best of all cases. We can imagine heaven one can be the master room of where the best memories of the past can meet again in the harmony of comfort worthy of Gods gratitude to us all of humanity.

We, who released God to do his own thing, guided by us from our honesty of presentation humbled by how we set him to operate us in heaven one and heaven two.

Which might need us in this segment to turn one of our last stones over to reveal what might lie underneath. Which cannot reveal the end but might reveal the beginning.

One of the last problems we might have to tackle before we reach clear water, stands on the firm ground of our human diversity. Covered and enhanced by the fact we carry over two hundred different flags in the name of our unity.

All of which can be neutralised under the very real acceptance of adopting my suggested coup, of allowing, even forcing our United Nations, clarion my new maxim "The Rights of Humanity". To be the foundation stone of all new political legislation with already built-in safeguards.

For now, when we call humanity, we do not call to the diversity of humanity. We call to all, which is the individual but not in the singular. For to run with old habits is far too often to run in the past. Which is not an option when the future is going to be the path to the future.

Leaving us with few options but huge scope. Because now that we have established the most important historical timeslot is now leading to the future. Our main task to cement that concept to reality stands with firm thought.

The only real ammunition we need to make better progress than we have so far achieved, is self belief. Which will emanate when we come to realise, we each might only have 80 plus years of living, before we can gain the real benefit of what heaven one can deliver or what heaven two can delay.

So, to begin in proper order, if we sit back in repose, not for self, but each other as well. Then to focus, when we each die within the hoped for 80 plus year life cycle range. We will in all cases go to be judged if that is the word, in heaven one or heaven two. Not by our conscience but the holder of our consciousness, God.

An almost physical representation of each and every one of us. Because when we came to the idea of God there was no scientific or moral, even reason of why we should. Even though this universe of ours had been running for billions of years without explanation. Yet was so wonderous that its existence could only ever be explained by a product of chemical and scientific interaction, unfathomable in scale, we of humanity.

Who now in our, my penultimate chapter and verse, dare give this extra rendition? Because we of no particular claim, are the only force in the entire universe who can name its cause, but to be sure, that claim stands, and to cover all angles. We must now enter our full credentials, which almost follow thus.

Diversity and division are like the left and right hand. Both vital in use and definition, but in all cases different. Because they are constructed as opposites. Which from within the depths of human interaction, means they are of the same function but different.

Two hands can read 10.000 religions, which on the face of it shows no form of clarity if some of us add to that mix by assuming we are right or left handed or of one religion or another. Being small diversions, which although not diverse show division. Which is not the foundation stone if we are to naturally show signs, we are equally aware of God's presence or existence.

Which could be deferred because of our presentation to God of what humanity is, leaving him to ignore all we have achieved and set his interest elsewhere. Which becomes another example of what he had been doing for the past 13.8 billion years.

Therefore, to untie the enigma of why. All for us to do singly, collectively. Is lay our hand on the table so God will never be able to trump our cards to claim our stake money, which was always our ability to think outside the box. To think in ranges no other creature species could or had shown signs to be able to.

With us being cleaver enough to understand and in some cases answer God's needs. By giving him the insight to be able and record when he heard a plea, or a sound of enquiry made at any time in the history of time, it was always from the same species. The one we call humanity. So in consequence when God replied, even in kind, vocally.

He was always replying to the same image he heard, but now through our direction, God by self creation, set his own image to be like us. Effectively when fast forwarded, God's image of today is the same as we are. without diversity to be of any consequence to our differences.

Which we have to self rationalise, to cover how we can be different without the need to be diverse. Not least because when our 80 plus years are done. Among other things God's real ability to be skin colour blind really kicks in.

For then now, still relying on our advice on how to treat some of those who created emotional turmoil while we lived, to be sometimes set in heaven two, then why. We must give God good reason to trust our decision making, which can only ever be suggestions.

Meaning we must create on our own account, why God can trust us in heaven when we did not trust one another while we were in life.

Strangely enough a matter we only really came to post 2012. For no other reason than that time mark allowed not just some of us, but all of us. Draw new conclusions of how we mismanaged the past, sometimes under the best intentions.

For when we tried to create forms of balance and equilibrium even human equality, our medicine was in the wrong dosage. When delivered in verse to be human rights along with religious tolerance.

Some of us overdosed without the proper concern of what we were doing except to take the medicine we, some, thought they were entitled to. Never to have realised the more medicine, the sicker the patient.

Which is not always the full story until we can reflect to what we were like in the past generationally, which is not a sign of how we were in the past ten years. Which becomes a pivot to build the future post "NBDfoa" upon, but now in God's hands.

But first again, we must give our young and next generations something to suit God's frame of mind on our terms, so when he decides, all the decisions are his. But now only with the reflection of how we interacted generations ago and more recently. For the two pasts had different emphasis.

Continually highlighted by the under tone of race and racism. Old die-hard holdings we always seem to drag out now and again when we get bored accepting our own failing. Alas in most case our modern standards of racism are completely misaligned to be mostly concerned with our skin colour tones.

When in fact racism is practiced in every facet of human interactive conduct. Never to forget skin tones have nothing to do with who we are now. They only go to show we are in fact the most agile single species ever. Because from within the range of any skin colour group, we all came to understand about the concept of God.

That is perhaps why God is skin colour blind, for at first, he only knew of us by sound. I wonder if that is a reason to be racist, the sounds we make. Which is not a slight but the beginning of the means of how we will have to understand why the concept of racism is used to blight normal human progress, for who knows what reasons.

Though many great people including us, have tried to counter the worst aspects of racism, and failed. Not because they/we did not try hard enough, but in part because many could not relate to the facts. Although we are the one species on God's scale, because we discovered God for his sake alone.

When some of us took that realisation onboard, naturally we wrote our own notes Which not unlike these I have been writing, began me or my or I. To have been recorded in my style of presentation, which was assumed to be unbiased by us, but normality took over.

Whereby we as the individual, are instinctively inclined to follow the naturally installed pattern of finding or setting a/our pecking order. Being an undividable pact, we made with nature, through evolution and evolving.

Such early codes of conduct we practiced on those very lines above, put us on the wrong path. Even when we came to consider the Great spirit pattern of existence, which resulted in the theory of an afterlife in completion. Whereby little changed, was when we first came to the pure notion of what was eventually to turn into racism full bore.

Which was never based on skin colour alone but tied to national or tribal or clan conditions, loosely based on the structure of what the pecking order alluded to. Which was class and status, for in most nomadic groups at such times. The order of the day was survival. Plus, in most cases of interaction very historically, we were not different by any degree to disagree, except perhaps unless if we met at a place of abundant fruit or berries, we could gather, until the hunt.

True skin colour racism is almost a myth, though we seem to have a history of it by division. Which was cast by adding the wrong ingredients at the wrong time under the wrong understanding.

What we did have, do have and can't release ourselves from in all societies in all countries, in all religions, under all political systems. Is our innate ability to compete, which can be felt if we imagine the drive our pecking order set upon us. Which was almost that of to survive above all else. A tied objective of following pure instinct.

When carried in early days, such emotions drove some of us to be extreme to the extent when we did compete internally. We approached our dilemma on a no holes bared with no prisoners taken attitude, we competed to always win. Which was still mostly applied internally among our own society.

Competition matured to be part of our culture, which could have been classed to be heavy. For when it matured, it turned to be hostile, running to win is good, to lose is bad or worse to lose is less. All of which worked to levels of control if competitive competition was to mind.

When our nation states formed to be large or small, but in division to be north or south or east or west. Plus, to include regional peoples in such described areas, who self acclaimed their individuality by descent. Was born true or old style or proper racism, which meant competition in the positive.

Now personified on the fields of sport nationally and internationally. Whereby often in true good style without malice. When teams compete the racism of support can sometimes overflow to the good or bad of how true emotions are spent.

Alas different sports draw different reactions from different sets of fans or supporters. When if in one sport the losing fans show animosity to the winning team and or their supporters. Whereas in another sport the losing supporters enjoy a social connection with the winning team fans or supporters. No link is made except in all cases of reaction, racism of sorts, is the outcome and always has been.

Which has always been the design of all internal and international sports. To see or test who is the best. To be a pecking order study and to be racist in combination, north, south, east or west. Which never was a bad thing, for the first measure of racism was part of the human psyche, to compete to compare in order to improve.

Although some very poignant historical events seemed to ooze racism, they were not verifiable. Because their makeup combined the full combination of how we allowed our religious and political status be declared under any rules set by individuals from within any so structure, who thought they had a say also.

Which could have been fair until we define the true colour of racism to be a hoax. Whereby the matter of modern racism is often applied by some people of any particular mix of character, who could wish to gain advantage from their own situation.

Fortunately, when we introduce in standard, above all life-time religious and political expectations. My maxim "The Rights of Humanity" and my primary objective of all religions to fixate on "Natural Body Death from old age". Along with all political ideologies to follow in quick pursuit both adoptions. We might close the door on racism full time.

For now, as a stop gap the way some seem to ply racism is a black and white reflection of how not to contribute to the extreme important idea. Humanity in us all can take comfort, especially with an 80 odd year background to support our true and real link with God, will be met, when we show God, he has nothing to worry about.

At last, from now, because we have at first began to tackle all our ghosts at the same time. Which is not an end game play, for that only comes when we reach heaven one or heaven two, which is not an end game play yet.

When our real task is to marry 13.8 billion years of universal existence with how it could have happened or occurred. But only driven by human ingenuity on God's behalf, for God knew little of what would or did happen in any time frame. Even when he was compelled to show interest in us.

Not least because at times over the past four or five thousand years, things occurred to draw his interest above when he felt his real name was only the Great spirit. So, in consequence along with how we brought him along. One of the last or best things we might have to do is show God how we have conquered the sordid feature of how racism in the fields of humanity might deter him of showing his own excellence.

Therefore, in full damnation we of humanity 21st century style, post all 2012 scientific revelations. State now, all forms of racism, bigotry, bullying, intimidation, indifference spread as means to discredit. Are products of fear and doubt. Self-fear, in your/my own ability to be able and feel God while in his presence and he in ours. For the twain are true.

Laid down by people such as you and me, who were not sure of our standards, but offer our opinions just in case. In the real belief and hope we have been able and help God. For under the blue sky, we have not held back in our approach by giving up our secrets to God's own use when we reach him in heaven. To find our station in heaven one or two.

Not that we can decide, for when we, uninvitedly. Sought to understand God for his sake more than ours. We had to travel new ground always bypassed by the flurry of new knowledge, passed on or left on open ground to the annuls of scientific study for its own sake. Without surrendering anything to God. Who has had to rely on the common force of humanity to raise him in station, so he now knows of we who discovered he?

Fear as a key opens no doors but closes many, for if fear was to encourage the negativity of racism of bigotry of extremism of fanaticism of radicalisation, then she has no voice. For their noise is intimidation.

Although some of our objectives must be to absorb some elements of scientific proof for God's sake at least. When we come to mark our exam results, those can only be done in Gods own place of refuge and comfort. Heaven per se is that new area of calm. For there is the only place we can imagine God feels comfortable, if ever to be involved with us here on Earth.

Because in heaven, God can be fully aware what occurred on earth historically to draw his interest in the first place. So, on those grounds again. I set a different segment of my fresh thoughts to arm God in his pursuit to understand how he should follow our good conscience.

When we direct him to pass judgement on others, set by the unbiased emotional strain some of us were put under by yours truly, other human beings, even homo sapiens. For those titles in their proper use determine we are species. Then on my say so we are the unique species in the universe.

Then to expose in better light why we are not racist but accuse each other of being so, because of our political failings only. Which when used through human rights taint us to be racist by skin colour more than any other cause.

Not to make a case for or against, but modern racism of our understanding stems from failed political enterprise. When in part they, all types and systems, agreed to promote liberal autocracy as a backdrop for social morality.

For when first introduced around the league of nations era. Our ideas were to dismantle the only standard of human achievement we could measure which was entombed in our class structure, co-existing with our structured societies measured from the top down.

In other words, we at such times were endemically racist by style, which meant competition, which meant the rules of engagement to play. Were delivered from the top down by the people at the top. On the same terms we found to have been operating, for at least four or five thousand years and possibly as long ago as 60.000 years earlier.

Unfortunately, under our guidance almost without blame. Because of how national progress was obtained by exploitation on several levels. By not noticing or paying heed to. Some nation states often in progressive industrial mode. Almost without notice created our malady, which grew to be skin colour racism over and above the other style of being racist, which meant to compete or be in competition of sorts.

Modern skin colour racism has produced its own blight, perhaps for all the wrong reasons or from our political lack to understand how to remedy the stain on our morality we keep force feeding.

By at first on a white or from a yellow or from a brown or from a black skin perspective. We all practiced group style racism on the lines I mentioned to be competitive, not just in sport but procurement also.

Alas at such times when we were local to our environment, the tinge of being racist just ambled along. It is only in modern verse, and I mean modern times, we politically more than by any other means. Have exacerbated our born right to be evolutionary different.

By how we overcompensate by giving with one hand and taking away with the other to the same elements of humanity. From, on the lower levels of society. Because we legislate from the top down.

Therefore, in transition it is only we of the lower tiers of society who are to blame for all errors, sometimes even religiously. Which is never an issue unless we are driven from the concept of God. Not by our peers but those who assume to be our peers. Sometimes dressed in their well-fed coats of celebrity.

Who do not seem to follow their own compass, which points to an eighty plus year lifecycle in any case and all cases. Which points to the theory of God in heaven one and heaven two. Which would not need to matter if that was it. But it's not.

For to be God worthy is an answer to all that our ancestors and forebearers left for us to enhance. Shown in relief when to consider the ungodly proved scientific fact. The universe has been evolving for 13.8 billion years. To eventually, from about 800 million years ago, evolve a different range of lifeform elements. Starting the roll call of creature species.

Who in turn created our own lecture room, whereby we gave credence to most of what we could see and some of what we could imagine. Through new mediums we called science. There to explain as best they could, features like the night sky and how to make a cup of tea properly.

Although left to her own devises, science did not always deliver, especially if she was misread by some of her wardens. Who if to have followed their tool of mathematics pure, by its code of not to always know or worse to be assumed she did always know and set the wrong direction unnoticed?

Which is not my true observation but is my range of doubt to her ability to be anything else but be spontaneous by habit and func-tion. Which I balance against my belief of God and the structure of the universe which evolved by appointment of sorts.

From where we must try and set equilibrium spread among the only source to have been able and name the universe proper. From the single perspective, we in the name species are the same unique species, who released not the genie of God but God's genie in us to set God's course.

Which does not need to traverse any rapids on the way. Leaving us in the urgency of now to aid God in his task. Which is why we must dispel our overt way of how we tackle skin colour racism in the wrong context and from the wrong perspective.

By at first wrongly classifying the way we assumed how we could remove the worst elements of what skin colour racism produces, which is not the pure racism of competition and to be different by circumstances alone.

Although such bad connections need to be controlled even policed in the proper and fair light of natural justice. We must protect against over policing the venue when there are only a few players in all cases.

Therefore, when we set rules and standards, they can only reflect the neutrality of all law enforcement agencies which might get involved or who might be drawn into the minutia of how we wear our skin in any case.

Not by who said what or why, but skin colour racism only exists to satisfy the wants and wishes of the prig, the bigot the antagonist. Then often the timid the bully the coward the braggart. The me before we merchants of Venice. Set to draw their dividend of interest based on the loose ground they/I deserve it.

Often based on the fable, my/our/your skin colour was responsible for my/our plight. Therefore, if to play the hand of greed over natural justice, I deserve my pound of flesh for what I was made suffer by racists even historically. Assumed only now, modern verse to have been caused by the claimed superiority of one skin colour over another.

Which in real terms is a fact, but it depends on who calls the tune either, human rights style in the singular. Or in "The Rights of Humanity" style, which is the plural of me/I, never without its real connotation. To set the condition of the plural we, to be of equal standing over or from within everything we are involved in or with.

Of course, to temper, my offering of "the Rights of Humanity". I set it in Open City status. Not so to leave it so any first-round considerations can be prosecuted in separate claim. Like if a religious group or a political group or peoples of any skin colour shade claimed me over we.

Our/their, the rights of humanity, are not to depict we can seek retribution or reward or compensation for past error of judgements. Set upon us because? Then list an endless claim of what for or why reasons of how the past let us down if directed by people we did not agree with or who exploited, by who's code.

Which of course has a broad base of reconciliation to be mooned over. But must not be used like a whip, whereby now it is our turn to lash the ancestors of those we feel we were aggrieved by, without further thought.

My "The Rights of Humanity" is to be set with a broad base but must hold the matter of my/our intentions to encompass modern life conducted in its present range of to be 80 plus years long.

Rather than to encourage individual parties to pick and nibble at, and too often line their own pockets with the capital of money, even though so many use it in the fields of waste. Almost pretending what they get or got is what they need.

Which is only a moral consideration. Which is not to be turned by whomsoever. In call to have been of specific significance historically, to now mar the future. When old style human rights are sometimes used to cloud the arguments of, we, by skin colour or I by personality. Were abused and now need compensation for the historical suffering we underwent.

Which can only ever be a point of view, for the future in not to be a reflection of the past, but its maturity. Therefore, when we do look back at the reasons of why and how some people gained their vast wealth in the past from what can now be construed to have been exploitation and worse.

All to do to be aware, is mind, such feats now carry the name to be entrepreneurial or to support the arts or in the name of common celebrity. Who seem to draw on the society we all live in, to the extent some are able and line their advantage with the interest money in the form of the dividend money creates for itself?

Which is never to be a direct condemnation of any type of reason of cause of skin colour of circumstance from the past and now? When human rights had been best used to be a me, a singular concept. Who can complain? Unless by being the singular gives the impression, I operate from the top down. Therefore, as I speak, I speak in command.

Perhaps the best we can deliver to ourselves any time soon, is the future of tomorrow is a better option to introduce change. Which might have a better chance of success if we learn to prioritise futuristically instead of trying to work the past wrongly again.

My clues about heaven one and two, not new ideas, only of the future. Can be used if we heed our own advice. Which is almost a nonstarter, because some people will only see my argument to be some sort of placebo. Something we can take on board to ignore the past and its effect as it should be.

That of course is our joint human right but is not part of "The Rights of Humanity". Which is now set firmly in the future only. Because that is where it will first appear. Which again sets our attitude to be of better concern to the prospects of our young. Who like us of the future, with us in our their 80 plus year lifecycle,

Who will eventually have less of the mire of sorrow, history left us older ones to deal with. Almost now tackled with relish, not least because when we came to the ideas of God without foundations from about four or five thousand years ago. We have now been able and establish God's surety.

Now carried by 10.000 world religions under the full range of how this single species humanity, appears in our many guises of to be different but the same. By skin colour, culture, and big time, our ideals. For together separately, we came to the theory of God in concept, long before we came the theory of science.

Which is a spent realisation, for science has an end story tale to be added to its formula mix whereas God's story is yet to begin. Providing we get it right by not overplaying God's hand or involvement, how could we, or worse. Never to underplay God's role by allowing any form of personal descent call not to believe in the concept of God. Lay their separate foundations under the wing of using Liberal autocracy.

My almost last segment of how I compiled my full belief in the network of how God will work in heaven one and heaven two is rock solid. The little left to say in this world penultimate literary offering about God's function. Can only pick up our story in heaven one and heaven two.

But first, all will have to contend with the story of God. Who when he looks into the mirror of life counted while we all lived under any circumstances and in any physical life form phase or of any generation. All he can ever see is a reflection of himself, which is we. Not by our invention or desire, nor by appointment.

The function of looking at his reflection is answered when he found if by sound only. A noise to be of interest to him other than to continually hear how galaxy were forming by clattering combined and congealed lumps of God particle interaction together.

Our sound in the form why, already out noised all other big bangs. For ours was based on to seek understanding already knowing we won't understand the answer, but we still had to ask the question. With the Good thing being we of humanity had been awarded the image of God in likeness.

Because we are the only species, out of 800 million years of the existence of all creature species so far. Who were able and take us back a further 13 billion years when God gave God particles motion? In what must have been an almost fruitless expectation of to wait and see what might be delivered. From or through how the wait could be measured if it was ever to be timeable.

If humanity is ever to realise God's plan, then the best we can do for him and us, is set the rational means whereby we can continue the future to account for the past at least in payment. For to stand with God is a pretty good reward for helping God understand himself.

Which is why from another line of approach we should clear to accept skin colour, never was a racial identity clause, but competition is. When now taken by other examples. In the full and proper name of science and how to use it in proof.

For it was through science and the study of what DNA profiling delivered. We are able and state almost categorically. Humanity, pre species turnout, we were all more to be black of skin when to have first evolved over about, leading from three million years ago.

But not just that, for when we carried that DNA footprint from whatever exact second of time, we evolved into it. For appointment, has never been part of our character, therefore when we do realise, we can change or evolve further. Like to change our skin colour tones, along with other features, like hair density plus other discernible minor change.

Once we came to our God philosophy outlook, based on no other reason than when we saw the night sky. We wondered how it worked at first. But then grew, without the aid of evolution to wonder why the night sky was there.

Something, because of how we already out evolved evolution. Leads that we are the only species to be able and extend any scope of reality or non-reality. To express the only way how the universe could have begun. Plus, the only reason for it.

But best of all, in knowing we are here, certainly for the duration of our personal living until "Naturel Body Death from old age" arrives. Plus, to tie in with the proposed obvious, God is his own mark. Even if to be used by us, which was no plan only reason.

It is for us to tie up all the loose ends when found, providing they form a viable plan to fit the theory of everything together. Which must start at the beginning.

So, with the room/space already there, filled with evenly distributed God particles. Locked into total dark, total cold, total inactivity. Without giving the game away from any source or reason or idea or thought, for nothing was available. Which only means no explanation was available.

Which can only be spread when to consider, under such conditions, the greatest of all scientific experiments was proposed to be set. In so, if I, which is not me or us. but the source.

Which in effect had to be nothing else but God. Who contained all wonder in any case, but did not know the dynamic of how or why? But remained aware he/it was always somehow connected. But now again or for the first time in any case. Set his own plan to wait and see what occurred. Which peaked when we of humanity showed up.

Following all the best guides we have created for ourselves to try and understand the immensity of God, is why without prompt. Most of our world religions set it in creed and tenant and doctrine and control. God was eventually to ply his skill to our needs and desires.

But we were also wise enough to have gathered by example, God's work would be done in God's place of heaven or paradise. Whereas if we were not up to God's standards we would languish at God's pleasure in hell. To be a dastardly place of punishment for not following God's laws set by us.

Unfortunately, the phycology of thinking heaven and hell became too divisive historically. For by setting the ideal of having a nice place or a bad place at our disposal. Led many of us to begin and criticise each other on all levels of interaction.

Whereby we now felt or seemed to show by the variation of social, moral, political even religious interaction. We, whom so ever, were different to the order of being good or bad, but on whose ledger. Which is almost life in the raw, and now needs little attention.

Which can begin big style when we accept from now on. Under the application of the plural concept of "the Rights of Humanity". Of the bi religious and political concept of each person in any quarter. Can now expect "Natural Body Death from old age". In full expectation of not to have suffered slavery, torture, intimidation, bullying, cruelty even to have been ignored or murdered.

Which without force is the least we can accept as a starting point to create a neutral thinking platform, for our attending young generations to expand. To be made easier for them when we also offer them a better study in the realisation of God.

Who will eventually attend everybody in soul form, post natural body death? But in the better recognised heaven one and heaven two. The same and only place God will be able and communicate with each and every one of us in his voice. While looking like each and every one he communicates with, but crucially following our direction.

Being the norm, but one of the best ways we can show God of our sincerity in being the main species to have aspired in the spiritual form of its excellence. Plus, to help God, who never had any problems in another field, being that of to identify with us.

What we must do, for when we direct God about his treatment of our conduct while we lived. Is help him to be able and balance his own books, when he was able and witness all events in all times. But was never sure as to why.

For even when we were in action throughout history and God witnessed every second. He did not know what was good or bad. Evil or tender, rough or smooth or bland or nondescript against huge emotional outbursts or repression. Of course, God knew of, but not the real significance.

Which is why I have given God licence to follow our leads at least in heaven. Where he by our sincere commitment, and his own records. Can set each person by person as they/we arrive post natural body death. To his determination of heaven one or heaven two, set by how we expressed our true emotional values.

All of which will hinge on one vital range of how we of humanity continually misfire on how we can best bond to show we are the only species to move in Gods own thought fields.

Our planet Earth with over 200 flagged nations, over 10.000 world religions, over 60.000 years of measured progression. All leading to the one conclusion without comparison. We the species of humanity are unique. If for the only reason we came to discover the aspect of deity.

Hid in 13.8 billion years of chemical interaction often with atomic relevance included, we of humanity are the only witness to the night sky for its own sake.

Already knowing the why without all the details, fits into the full story of God to have started the whole show. But in context was not sure why, which might account for the long wait he has had until our year of 2012. When we of humanity again discovered how he started the story of the night sky as his secondary prize.

Until new elements in the name creature species were formed, capable to share the exact same thoughts about God in his 10.000 definitions. Our newness of humanity, who in name are specie. Unique only as the species humanity against all other creature species. Because we come to understand God for his sake and nothing else.

But from within that, our recognition. We set the tone, God could also discover why he set all the God particles already lattice field set, with motion. Which interacted in the only ways possible. To eventually over interact and create a process which cannot be reversed.

Unlike when we recovered 'a' God particle in the Large Hadron Collider in 2012 under CERN sponsorship. Which was only an example of how matter could be disassembled into what was its creative component. Through when applying motion to matter in a hushed dark cold environment, whenever.

Although to be ambiguous, if to think is an element, what then are the components of thought or to think. Which when spun cannot mean to think of God needs component recognition. Like for instance, God is the 119th element or in time the 145th or last element imaginable. Which is more thought. Or more so via theoretical science or physics. When to think in the name parallel universe or wormholes or other imaginings. Which when entered in theory are acceptable whereas God might not be.

Without thinking, is perhaps a serious reason of why some of us are regressing to deny God. Not for his sake but ours, not least because when we deny God in concept, we also deny any prospect of the future. Which is a double fable.

For without God our universe has been trundling along for 13.8 billion years on the strength of 118 recordable elements having formed on their own account. Plus, in 800 million years of that time span, has also produced a different range type of living creature species.

Although chemically constructed at core, carrying part of the known of element range in their make up also. Practically all set to preform to suit their environment when met. To the extent some in all ranges further evolved to suit current changes to their conditions.

Until yours truly, who also are the only form of evolved species to adopt to the combined living conditions enjoyed by the collective mass of the millions of other creature species involved.

Which creates no particular wave structures or lay lines. But does give sign our species of humanity has found or developed talents or skills that were not in the book. We have been more cavalier than other groups tied to pure flat instinct.

Which is only of merit. if we can benefit others as we deserve, for what we have done in finding God and releasing him to do his own thing, if at first under our guidance. Which could turn on how we present before God how we should have already settled our skin colour racial issues ongoing. Because when we tried to tackle them in the past, we never realised they were not skin coloured, they were competition issues.

This must be tackled on a species basis. Which includes every member of that one group humanity. But will pivot on our skin colour differences, by choice of the grunt, the bigot, the saint the sinner. Those who dare opine, those who seek the solitude of self-quiet, the braggart the bully. But none who deny God or the concept of God.

For with your hands uncommitted to try and improve, we need no help, except for you to listen and learn. So that in good time you will receives God's sole choice of to put you in heaven one or two when your 80 plus years are done. Courtesy of how others in we have tried to set God on his own path of applying common decency to those of us who tried to count giving before receiving.

To now refocus on our 80 plus year life range internationally, which alludes to our political standing. Is a good place to remind ourselves we are of the species humanity? A single defined group spread throughout the world, who know we are different by various features, one of which is our skin colour tones.

Therefore, how do I reconcile that feature politically, if I do not move in the direction of reconciliation? How then should that feature be reconciled, which as an open and real question needing the attention of the sort to open doors rather than close any.

On all political lines, now that we have set the primary standard all involved politically are to expect "Natural Body Death from old age". We have just closed the doors of discontent in theory, which is a good thing. For 80 plus years of living does not equate to any type of skin colour tone except all.

On the religious fronts, everything should be the same except are they. Even though religions in theory are more inclined to be universal. Many are selective, which is part of the reason of why we have 10.000 covering far less in the number of specific skin colour tones we have. Even when run from the four main branches to be Black, Brown, Yellow or White.

Although four into ten thousand runs at about two point five thousand each. No such figures are tangible or readable, but that is the case. Therefore, when we now think religion, we must think God first.

Which is a better way to associate God and humanity in real reality than try and account for why or how skin colour makes any difference religiously. When we can solve such problematic equations politically anyhow.

In simple form when we look at another political option of going to the Olympic games. To be seen and noted in full technicolour. To always be counted as the same event even when to be split as the Winter Olympics as its own entity.

But never in comparison with the normal or more widely accepted different larger event Summer Olympics. Except in how they differ, which has nothing to do with the weather.

All of which becomes self explanatory when to consider the competitors involved in any of the events, winter or summer. Are all drawn from the mass of our total of separately flagged nations throughout the world. On the one basis of to compete which is the capital of what racism is without knowing it.

Were, I to have stated in simple honesty, competition is the root of true racism. Under my imagined terms of to explain that cliché by my use of the term, to apply Liberal Autocracy. How close have I got to be racist or in meaning how racist am I when Liberal Autocracy is applied against me.

Even to be my own invention in term of phrase to indicate how a formed structure of human behaviour can become mislaid by the ignorance of only operating it from the top down. Which by form leads not to the advent of community. But in how we can force competition into skin colour racism.

Because instead of creating the deserved harmony of what the human species above all other creature species had achieved. Held together by our universal acceptance of to have separately come to the/our, God is concept or to accept the idea of God at least, leading to at best.

Which as a story is complete, because when to realise in simplicity, which will never be boring? Humanity, who second hand created the story of the universe by understanding alone. Can now concentrate on to put those ideas into the simple formula of acceptance and better understanding.

In such ways to avoid constant reappraisal set again by humanity, when we choose to be different by race, by religion and by politics. But much worse, when we sub-divide such divisions if all are listed. To have and hold separate connotations for one against the other or one to be better than the other.

Which at last can be contained by those of us alive today, living our 80 plus years until "Natural Body Death form old age" calls. Who can decide in agreement or not to add our Dublin City accords, which are there to combine rather than separate?

Because when introduced within our living era, they can refocus us into the future as it might be. Instead of back to the past as we thought it was. Without really bothering to find out why or how, because we had made up our own minds anyhow.

Though we must find the proper legislation to be able and hold common ground. What we must not do is only legislate from the top down. For in that design the best we will always do is only half legislate. Mostly on the terms of applying Liberal Autocracy on the good old assumption of what I say you must do.

Perhaps if we constantly remind ourselves, no matter what of the past, except to tidy it up. Our future will from hence. Post "Natural Body Death from old age", will be set in haven one or heaven two.

Alas without complaint, for those are Gods rules set by us, humanity one and all. Even reluctant believers in God. Who cannot hide behind the shadow of what God is supposed to look like. For God looks in perfect image to each and every person in the human species genre.

People such as me and you who think what we think whether we like it or not. But people who think, who think. On greater scales than the richest of men, the powerful of men the Godliest of men for all in title are we.

So, in the first final contest what we should be fair in doing, is to self rationalise why some of us set to be different in class more so by skin colour tones, than for other reasons if they go unmeasured.

To use one of our balance cups in two parts. I use the example of our best means of how we of humanity expose our likeness more than our differences. Which is a byword for the fact we are the one species supreme. Because we came to 10.000 world religions with most owing to the one theory of God.

Yet are in denial, because in some instances we cannot reconcile the fact of our skin colour differences to have no bearing on who we are collectively. While at the same time cannot see we promote our ready differences under the terms of competition. Which is not planned.

But when ripe, we read it the wrong way, often under historical plans which set our differences were by our skin colour tones, which was never real. But suited some financial situations which prevailed ago. Thus, allowing some of us use the exploitation of skin colour tones to set racial standards which are not there or never were. But were made so?

Alas leading up to these present times whereby when we say race or racism, we read black, brown, yellow, white or mixed shades of the same skin to refer to race instead of we, the species humanity.

So not to upset the apple cart, all for us to do in good style. Is maintain our racial differences in the proper harmony we have been doing almost for centuries in real time. Which when properly viewed in or from a competitive perspective.

We will have delivered a way to neutralise one of our many failings. Our ability to divide the same people by the colour of their/our skin to be a racial matter when it is not. Shown time and time again when we, if by how when we are in competition, compete.

Even if when this is done on national scales. Whereby in normal perpetuity, internal sports leagues, of whatever inclination compete. Sometimes further set by how some countries have set their own particular trait of what they compete over.

But always maintain the general standard of placing each group when the season is over. Into the order of merit of where they finished in the league or table of competitors. With the general tone, the order of merit stands to be Gold for first, silver for second then bronze for third. Which is only symbolic for the good reasons of definition.

By mentioning national competition in the way done above. Can we draw any conclusions about the racist aspect of competition on national scales only? If in the theory of nationalism historically. Peoples could almost be set to fall into different national groups by skin colour alone.

A single feature of how humanity developed historically. Set in DNA relief of how all human ancestors were almost certainly black of skin. When we first developed as the biped species in Africa from about three million years ago.

Being a natural feature driven by at first the circumstances of birth. Even if only directed by imagination. Given light today by how we can see by direct link, from where it can be noted. We have been able and connect our DNA connection with its own history of at first appearing in East Africa.

A place where natural birth still produces people as our ancestors, dressed in their/our black skin décor, set by the circumstances of today as then ago, when ago.

Which even as a broken chain needs no further exact study when to realise our skin colour make up of today worldwide. Has produced the national or otherwise combinations of skin coloured people under the one definition to be species.

Which in accord has often failed its/us, when some of us try to understand a reason for our differences when there are none. Unless we are bound to follow historical representations of how some of us were better than others if assumed. By how we were led to believe the scale of skin by colour was a passport to our worth or value, commercially, then socially, then morally.

Then politically, but in theory, not religiously. For religions were often locked into their own policy of attending God by his desire. Which as stated before was supposed to show no bias on any levels of status.

Because most religions as one, often claimed to have been appointed to suit the group or standard the group concerned, felt they had reached. In being made up of a collective tribal format, appointed. Which in term when it/they developed historically, they/ we became the same nationals we now are.

But were unaware of how and when we got where we are today circa 2022. Whereby we had come to force feed the present with skin colour racism. Because we do not have an alternative, and it seems easier to stick with old prejudices than try to understand the error of their ways.

Therefore, with cause and reason, to dispel the banality of why some of us think black and white about skin colour. If we address the subject in its proper name of humanity, which is the forename of our creature species definition.

We have no where else to turn except focus on what it means, when we realise history as a lost dream which was always a nightmare. Is not ours to work with, but the future is. Set in plan only from the perspective of being alive and living today. Even if only marked by an expectation of lasting for 80 plus years.

But in mind to connect with the reality of God and his plan set by us, to tend the future on terms equal to the expectations for the single species community, of humanity. Especially now when we can assure God, we are the one species combined in unity. Expressed by how we alone in the universe had named the universe.

Who are now ready to show God our good intentions of turning the matter of how and why some of us assume we differ by class and type. Expressed by how we can view our skin colour to have a bearing on who is better, perhaps carried by our historical nightmares.

Like if when it seemed easier to follow orders from above, when to serve those above, but in their surety, we would be served from those below. Being a factor, we moulded by the circumstances we thought by.

Being a trigger of how we were eventually to develop under our own impetus, once we came to visions of the Great spirit. Our means to carry us into the future, providing we were to hold our station of how society worked or so we thought.

Which we compromised by the simplicity of assuming, because of circumstances we did not then understand. We, whomsoever, set the marker for those below us to be less worthy if by sign to be of different skin colours. Which was to our classification only.

But sometimes led by those above us, who were in better positions to exploit any situation they in we came across. Often set against their/our standards and acceptances and or circumstances. Which allowed we could use in any way, what we came across and classed to be different to us by any measure, even skin colour tones.

Almost becoming history in the raw under the name of skin colour exploitation, which never was racism, but was competition. But in modern verse, if under the wing of liberal autocracy, has almost become our nemesis.

For to misuse any form of compromise which always clouded the past. Then attempt to carry it into the future. Can never work, because past standards so far, were never up to the task to be worked on generationally.

Which is perhaps why we are still in crisis and have been unable to recognise why. Because we are not the same generation, we thought we once were, on several different levels. Which leads me to try and not repeat our mistakes or worse, compound them in modernity.

By assuming we are sophisticated enough to make a difference. Not by causing action, but to follow the old trail of allowing the matter of individual choice. Through the offices of human rights and religious tolerance take hold anew.

By applying the untested reason of my definition of why we need change, when we already operate Liberal autocracy. To police change by reinstating individual choice in the matter of human rights and self-applying religious tolerance.

So, in essence, a person of any ilk, by my suggestion, can assume the right to always speak for self in clause to speak for others. For Liberal autocracy speaks for all by me/you and us. which is not the correct representation we need to present the case for we/us. Which is the plural of humanity.

The plural for how, lost our way humanity, can set all records strait through our young. Who even of now with others of us in our 80 plus year lifespan range. Will be able and interest God further.

Because they will have shown God, we are better in style than he thought we might turn out to be when he first heard sounds from the only species in 800 million years to ask questions beyond the reaches of what pure instinct had delivered to all creature species.

For the best we can do by suggestion for our young, is to acquaint them in better style of how we should tackle perhaps our biggest blot on our copy book. Our made problem of how we allowed skin colour racism take hold when it is not even a factor against the welfare of humanity. But it in theory as a subject or topic has put up its own smoke screen, perhaps unknowingly but not without consequences.

It could be difficult for us to lead our young if we follow our style of delivery most applied from the top down. But when they realise organisation has to have a format, they will be able and direct such plans by no more than showing us/all, their new ideas.

Organisation must be delivered on the basis or our sameness and not our manufactured differences. Which now can only work post haste by using the knowledge we of humanity have accumulated in 80 years of living.

Which is the new timeframe period where we can work our problems to have been of no real consequence. Unless we drag them along with us even unto death. So, when we come to heaven one or two. We challenge God in ways he has no interest in, because we had already set the playing field while we lived to give God clear ground to award points for our innings.

Therefore, by the good fortune of us to include our young to be able and improve our situation. We might keep God on side providing we solve our skin colour racism blight. By the more than easy means to show God. We understand now, why it is a no-no to mainly use skin colour as a means to differentiate between the same species of humanity and humanity.

Never on a one-to-one basis, but to only use a reflection of history, about in all cases of skin colour difference. Whether eventually created in time by how adaptation in the names of habitat, geography, climate, diet aided us to change by dress or culture. Leading to the uncomplicated situation. We of the same DNA, our species of humanity over time simply developed to be different by skin.

Which as a fact needs little further explanation, except perhaps? Not even to understand but take on board, howsoever we gained our skin tones historically. We still own them. But in the line of thought reasoning. To dispel the overworked negativity of skin colour racism, we can verify it when to consider we have always been racist by competing.

Which is a real human trait, look to how we have amassed 10.000 world religions in the same competition for the same God. By which we have now stabilised the means of any who sought to take God on full time to their own view. By acting for God on their say so alone.

Though we dare set aspects of our political control through our United Nations. By how we sanction our UN to now classify religions to be religious or not. Depending on how much they want to run God's affairs by their interpretation, if to kill or bring mayhem about in his name.

No form of skin colour racism or competitive racism can be measured from such acts. Nor can we measure forms of hate to abound, nor forms of anti-isms against specific religions be called. But similar might be accused, leaving it further for our young to unravel our dilemma in their better offering for future conduct for all.

So, in good measure, when we set these last few pages with the full intention of motive explained. Based on the surety, we are the one species in God's name to wear the same coat of skin, which denies any to use skin colour negativity racially, to any degree. But we can be competitively racist in its proper order.

To form that analysis and maintain forward motion with an assured future perspective in mind. I can equate why we may have formed skin colour racist attitudes without the need to date line any period of time. When we may have forced the conclusion, one skin colour was better than another.

Without any debate, we can assume by association our main skin colour groupings of to be black, brown, yellow or white. Were geographically inclined if created from their own historical background makeup.

Almost as obvious but not perhaps as clear. Whenever the trend of to be national was forced in equal status by each skin colour group. We in our tribal and or clan situations, when forming alliances. Fell to the crude almost animalistic or other creature species habit of following the path laid by evolution. Of to propagate above all else which held us apart.

But if our term was made more difficult because if drawn to the concept of the Great spirit, we were beginning to pull away from one aspect of evolution. To almost self-determine about the surety of the Great spirit, who now then ago, gave us our first insights into a future, which when seen by imagination. From within our skin colour groupings by area, who had by then come to notice of each other. Although the same, we were different by style, even in belief or the measure of or way of or intensity of. So, in consequence it is easy to follow each skin colour grouping set to be competitive before being skin colour racist.

Competition was a form of progress counting, which is easy to swallow when all combatants were of the same skin colour. Not as a rule of thumb, but if we did compete while of the one general skin colour. How wild might we get when we found we were of many, which is almost a modern realisation unfound.

Unfortunately, when to take a giant leap forward, we must be careful where we land so not to crush the vital contribution others have brought to the table. Which can be heartfelt, honest and vitally humanistic. Although good, we must not accept the purity of any idea offered including all of mine, are set to be right and proper.

How best to measure any idea, is of its intensity to we, over the usual of following me by dint of my human right and my religious tolerance code. Which can lead me to also deny God and religion any way round.

Although a general standard to behave so self-acclaimed, what such behaviour induces without penalty. Is for our right under my new proposed "The Rights of Humanity", to exclude people of doubt from policy making. Not self-doubt, but in show, people who cannot make up their own minds. Which is not a standard, but a code, whereby such peoples good will cannot be used against them.

Whereby if someone else was to tell them/us what to do in God's name, like murder and kill or of the same intensity vote yay or nay. To follow strange, imagined rules of the right to murder other religious groups or in the name of racial superiority, which is not. Or to ethnically cleanse for the good of those to be murdered.

Never to decide for others or attempt to classify others, but the best way we can serve each other is to already have in place. A core rule structure set by standards to ensure we can all face the future on the same terms. Which is to expect to reach "Natural Body Death from old age".

Plus, then to be held at Gods pleasure in gratitude for how we released him to understand his own attempt to motivate himself the only way possible on a wait and see basis.

Then to back that up, plus to avoid further confrontation, which never should have been there. Is to lay waste to the misconstrued idea of skin colour to be a race issue problem. Which by return will also destroy the myth of how skin colour tones have been used to stimulate racial tension on many counts, which now need focusing on.

I had mentioned both currently and historically, various forms of skin colour tension occurred and still occurs between the same skin colour mix of people. Like black on black tension, like white on white tension, like brown on brown tension then yellow on yellow tension. With the addition of inter tension between each group just mentioned. Which are pure examples of tension only.

For any previous inter tension between peoples of the same skin colour were factors of competition. Which needs no further explanation if we all still lived thousands of years ago, long before we came to realise our skin was different by colour.

Which again had been neutralised by us on the true understanding God was/is skin colour blind. Bearing the rational, when he looks into the mirror of history, onto the face of all creature species lifeforms.

He sees only two images, one of procreation, the other of who named the night sky and to have given it the method of reason and style of how it came about when receiving the only order of motion in disorder.

Who then went on to harry God for his own good by drawing his interest to their own query of why they/we are left to tidy up our own mess when now alive. While relying on God to justify in praise or condemnation our previous conduct in the good name of the species humanity.

Who before our living young take over the tiller. We can at least revisit our attempt to balance the nondescript way we had tried to tackle to insanity of how we managed to compromise the matter of our own skin colour.

Which can be undone, when to consider we all have a future whether we understand it or not, whether we like it or not. Which is not to be a form of coercion, but if to realise, and we should.

When we in line with all other creature species came to be, by the advent of time passing. Black of skin being our case. Our joint improvement was not determined by skin colour, but sheer tenacity. Improvement by us alone on the scale to out operate the way other creature species worked.

Was assured, when without prior awareness of why or how. We broke the mould of instinct, which was part of the form used by all other creature species bar none. So, when we changed that pattern uninvited. We were started on a trail which is not yet over by a distance.

So, in compliance with such a strange situation whereby we of humanity are the only group to be able and free God to his will by our lead. It is we who have to build the framework of how we can fit God to be with us on his terms alone, which he must learn from us.

Which is why I insist to include us all to be counted to our task. Not so by intimidation or bullying. But when I/we mention, we all must be included, it is for our sake. So, if we are right we have not left anyone behind. Which is not like following orders from above.

Our intention of total inclusion of all is to cement in block the idea we of humanity are unique enough, to have stimulated God's interest after waiting for 13.8 billion years for something to happen. After he gave all the God Particles, he could only have distributed in lattice field formation three dimensionally, motion. For what else was there for him to do?

Therefore, without prompt, when I include all, it is not done on their behalf, but ours. For we are all of equal stature in God's eyes. Which must be met head on, for when in heaven one or heaven two at Gods discretion.

It will not do for God to be led along to be told, I just came along for the ride. When in fact such people in not to want to be involved in their own history. Are not immune from it, no matter the consequences of.

Which when to realise God knows all human histories in any case. For us to insist as I/we must, there can be no self-claimed exclusions from past deeds while we each lived and interacted. For in being the individuals we are we cannot change the past, but we can alter it.

Although on some personal levels of how some of us might interpret the past one way or the other. When God pays our dividend, we can insist he takes charge from now on. Which gives him the key to how he can set whomsoever in heaven one and heaven two.

Because of our guidance, which has always been meaningful, honest, even just. But big time delivered with emotional gusto, set from negative and positive aspects of how some of us were affected while we lived in our normal drive to show we had something to offer any attendees who were interested in us historically and now.

Never to finish on an open page, not even to finish the saga of skin colour racism open ended. But in line to transmit to our younger generations we are also ready to learn. Plus, to blue ribbon stamp, our new attitude to racism of its only type. Which stems now only from our human ability to be competitive.

In order to liberate humanity in all phases, the last quarter of to do so, will be set by how we in collective harmony agree to differ but on the same principle of how we came together. By accepting the inevitability of "Natural Body Death from old age".

So not to bend the pin, when we settle skin colour racism to be a non-event. We will have doubled our chance of to set mere competition to be our new racism on acceptable terms which is a must.

But does not mean we need to count all types of competition in the same light. So, if we fixate onto, into the fields of sport primarily, we might be able and value our self-worth more then we realised we had. But in all cases, we are always the same species of humanity.

So, before we cross the threshold of being right and proper. In the right proportions we should mention the consequence of not setting racism to be a competitive experience only. Not least because of how Liberal autocracy has been misused to promote the wrong advantage of following skin colour racism.

Which had been allowed weave its own web of to claim harm and hurt against personal feelings, expressed from one perspective only. Alas falsely labelled if under what liberalism delivers.

Which like how the old hand of human rights could be set to the wishes of those best supported. Whereby if a party was to claim harm or hurt, then often to spare their blushes. Party A, who could have been our legislators. Perhaps in the cause of what they thought harmony should be. Sanctioned the payment of two types of dividend if to try and control further outbreaks of the same insolence.

Never to be able and realise the point of species integrity was set to the breaking point. When we allowed any part aspect of the whole be able and promote their need to be compensated for the harm and hurt some claimed for abuse that was not there.

Plus, not to realise further, if a person's claimed dignity was to have benefitted from any award. What was there to balance such an event, unless to be critical of others who although accused. Felt they were not in fault by their terms of reference.

Even if not to realise what some might have thought as banter, was offensive. But only now applied when inter skin colour shades were included on a racial calendar that does not exist.

But had been given light by the imagination of some of us, who had relied on or have applied Liberal autocracy as a fair way to promote the unevenness of inequality. Except to those accused of wrongdoing, being blamed when they thought they were right. Then under who's flag, ideal, religion or political settlement.

Which can be settled when my "The Rights of Humanity" is given sway to operate its own measure of Liberal autocracy. But this time by attending to the now obvious. We of humanity from complete historical wellbeing. Can now state categorically, species, our human species is not a byword for any claimed tone of skin colour.

We, from within our own historical understanding. If required, can now use the new maxim the rights of humanity to factionalise the understanding. When now in our 80 plus year lifespan, when we look across the table, all we can see is people. Human beings, we of species in each other.

We, covered in the same mixture of skin we always had, but now at last are not afraid to be aware of that spectacular realisation. Ask the same younger people who share our 80 plus year lifespan. For in them we will begin to see the honesty of character we should have better cultivated. But at least it's not too late.

Remember, although we of humanity set all the rules, we can be relied on to change them by understanding more than in retribution or in some cases its new name of compensation. Which is not a free pardon. But a reminder to those who would seek to gain from the flaw of how we set to protect some sections of our divided community.

Against how some of us applied to use our skin colour in blame or to claim. Whereby if under that guise we were offended, irrespective of the nature or type of the offence. Liberal autocracy wrongly assessed from the dated human rights readoption.

Gave for any to feel they were offended, to have been offended, which broke all the rules of honest morality. When the powers to be, if driven by Liberalism joined to the singular clause of what human rights was supposed to convey but did not.

Which left the door open for the collective individual in we by group also, to use any means to interpret why we felt abused or intimidated. Which in turn is a normal trait if the need was to right wrongs and not comment on the matter of being treated with the courtesy, we all deserve.

Unfortunately, or perhaps the reverse, but most of our problems of the past in terms of how we were always competitive by any means. Not least set in part by how competition meant success. Not from the negative of competing religiously or politically.

But in the positive of learning when to move by group to be able and gather the right crop or to have learnt about animal heard movements to suit other parts of our hunter gatherer existence. Led most of us to turn that competitive edge we might have had or gained by good luck. Into forms of superior protectionism.

Unfortunately highlighting in obscure ways of how simple acts tied to the art of survival. Were beginning to create more stringent forms of separatism. Which also in part highlighted how some of us took to the art of noticing we were different if by style, even to be hunter gatherers in the same style.

But were slower to recognise over time, we were different by skin colour. Until some of us even though we were all connected to the Great spirit concept one way or another. Began to count our differences to be skin colour based.

To then only in theory, begin and create the offset idea that skin colour had something to do with race. Which had become a new name for clan or tribe, almost religion, then probably nationality.

All factors to have suited how we were formed to think in the days of Empire and Imperial nationalism. Which have not really gone away but have left us in the modern situation of trying to cure past ills with the wrong medicine or delivered in the wrong dosage.

Therefore, on that basis and with more to come from all quarters. If we quash our almost juvenile stand on how we have associated skin colour to have high racial connotations. In terms of how we of the same species are different.

We should change that perception, often now by listening to our young who are far better disposed to value all people to be species connected. But do cede we are different mainly by our competitive nature. Which should be our new racism if we need the clause. Then how bright might daylight shine when we are all there on the same team of humanity.

Without having a defined plan except the certainty of God, which is not our plan nor is it God's in any way either of us can imagine. Which is why we can settle on the one plan of how the whole thing started. Without having to come up with the answers of how things might end and the circumstances thereof.

Although we were given our best first lead in the year 2012 when we, in capital letters, first rediscovered the God particle in being a bit of matter at its smallest in size. All was not lost but began. Which in single rotation form ended or reached the pinnacle so far which is humanity.

Allowing in kind regard, why we of any team or side or group or clan, tribe or national. Should set a story line to grow to make sense of what 13.8 billion years of time were for. Which can only work if we become aware of one main feature.

We are the one species of humanity and in consequence of how we failed the past by not to really understand its form. That factor can be side stepped in good order if we now set to understand the future on our plane, which is now. Then on God's plane when he takes over because of how we taught him.

Therefore, in consequence to measure how we can dispel the distraction of thinking racism holds its roots in our different skin colours. I set these facts as one of our new/old ways we all can use to come to the same conclusion.

But in caution, to combine my singular prophecy about our species integrity. It is not essential but vital, each of us are to understand, we are not in comparison with other creature species. For they unlike us are tied to the restraints of instinct delivered by evolution.

Whereas we broke those shackles when we saw an image of the future through how we were able and imagine the concept of God. Then to fit those images through our unique ability to think over and above, at first our ability to understand what we thought and why. Then how to fit our ideas into shape.

Only to be exposed in real time, in real time, by those of us alive today. Who can stand line abreast to solve the errors of the past by not reliving them in the present? Which is why I have turned skin colour racism to be a non-issue event.

But to account of why many of us feel we are different if only by self appraisal. I openly offer in term how we can be racist by being different in any case. But tied in bondage to the reason for our differences irrespective of our skin colour tones.

My clause of being competitive while being of the one species group humanity. Now fits to be our racial standard. For it by description defines what racism was assumed to display. One groups superiority over any other group for any so reason. Which had been used in the past so that one group could exploit another to their own ends.

Which by tone usually centred on the colour of a person's skin. For what only ever could have been invented reasons to suit prevailing situations. Which is a blight on all groups entitled to be of and represent humanity in name, to be the only species to have named the universe and to appreciate the night sky with equal relish.

To say nothing of the fact that in full combination, every skin colour type from when in all reality we all shared the one tone to be black of skin. Also expanded to herald the same, our image of God, 10.000 different ways.

With most heeding to the style of how our community had developed under the circumstances of geography, habitat, climate, diet and other prevailing reasons and how they had borne down on us. Which was always the unseen norm for us all, enough so to drive a wedge between the same people of different skin colours.

Almost an impossible situation to reform or even understand when including historical perspectives. For the hand that history dealt was always one sided, in knowing to suit the human rights of the recorder of the incidences. Howsoever read or presented or understood one way.

Although a right to correct such wrongs from ago. No unit, group, class or style of person in any religious, political or skin colour classification. Can expect the burden of settlement for any claim or story told. To fall upon the future which is now.

Which is the time carried by all alive today. We in our 80 plus year life range. Who's only responsibility is to the collective of self, shared as the new "The Rights of Humanity". To be a special time of reflection locked into and controlled by the collective of humanity.

Who might be able and look upon new horizons if to grasp this hand of reconciliation offered by the open mind of humanity to the one species of humanity, we who still wonder at the night sky in all its glory and in all its mystery?

A big stone to turn over and check its details, comes when we now bury the negativity by my reasoning of what skin colour racism brought to the table. Which is nothing but the grief the idea brought upon the same people we always are, plus then ago, were.

Never to ignore such a contrast of opinion. But to remind we, the errors of the past cannot be solved by going back to create the same errors of now. Which is to still divide rather than unite. For how to pay the dividend of compensation is not tangible if the idea stimulates the ready means for those in demand to pay. Want compensation for their hurt also.

Which calls for us to be shown how best until new lines are found, of how we can rest the old idea of what was deemed to be skin colour racism. Done in quick style when we change its name to competition racism. Which is the real byword for racism in any case.

Hardly ever to notice we have always held to be competitive in the best ways possible. Which have led to our species humanity, to become the foremost of all other creature species groups. Because we at first like all came to bloom, but instead of germinating to only propagate, we eventually out evolved evolution.

Becoming the only species ever to eventually realise, not only did we have ancestors, but we had a beginning also, if driven by a non-evolutionary urge. Which delivered us too today. To be a place whereby when we give up the reason of why we are different within the same species. We will find it easier to be able and understand God's motives before he did.

Competition to be the new black as racism, is easier to follow when we examine a human only way in how we compete, largely done on the fields and arenas of sport. If through events such as the Olympic games.

Now, I assume we are old enough to be able and realise, when we compete, it is done under the almost extreme example of hostility. Which might be the cure we have all been looking for. Not least because under such conditions, very often our emotions are raised to the extreme of pleasure and to include sorrowful failure also, but.

Most sporting competition comprises of great effort in all fields. And allied to that prospect but not calculated, is how in the general name of expediency. Final place results are awarded with medals of Gold for first place for the winner or winning team. Silver for second place and Bronze for third place.

Without special merit, our Olympic games of competition. Comprises of most of our world nations competing, each carrying national flags in banner form to determine their nationality. Which is fine and fair, for when a prize of first, second and third have been awarded after a particular event.

The three national flags are raised to herald the quality of the competitor and the commitment of their nation. Being a nice visual way we all can see the result of an event and to whom.

Not to sell anybody short but a very nice thing about the Olympic games is how it usually follows the three winners, who's flags had been displayed. Congratulate each other, plus in recognition in some cases of normal competition. Hundreds of competitors from as many nations competed at the same event.

Although there could have been religious or political tension between some nation states. In most cases of sporting competition all the athletes and or competitors in the same mix of sport.

Openly respect one another, often shown by the commitment to their task they have chosen to compete in. Which is a binding to show how joint commitment even without contact while training, can win through to join the essence of people over national rating. Which is us.

A wonderful aspect of sport competition the five ringed emblem of the Olympic flag conveys to all. Is the true aspect of the competitiveness of competition, almost set on a no holds barred configuration? Whereby under many different flags, the competitors, each to carry their own skin in complete normality. Without any consideration, except to eventually hold up their national flag in pride if they can.

Who display no form of skin colour racism, which must be left in the past providing some are not induced to wave their flag in the face of a different skin coloured competitor just defeated. Claiming ancestral racism of the now old-time skin colour superiority pattern.

Recognising the hurt many people still hold, even carry about incidences of being insulted or being morally abused or belittled by the bigot the bully the braggart. We all must try to override the storm until the air is stilled. Which is not to forgive and forget.

What we are looking to do until the cavalry arrives, which is we in any case. Is shine the mirror of insult back into the face of those so shallow of mind and in self sorrow even if they have been abused in the same context as they are accused of to issue.

Might be, never to surrender, but offer better terms of agreement. Even if out of our hands.

But always on the full grounds we like those who abuse, and torment, are the same species.

Carried no better than to quote the simple phrase, we are the single species of humanity. Born of the same black skin to then remain so, plus in times long ago to alter into shades of brown, of yellow of white along with mixes of the same.

Which denotes our skin colour range is not a racial issue, but competition could be. For that can be shown to throw up the means of why we are different by result, for competition is to oppose. And racism opposes.

Our best counter that skin colour racism is not viable by the best codes of human morality. Can be judged in the name of our human species, who when having just competed in another four yearly round of Olympic sport competition events.

Which will show a series of results relating to one species only, humanity. Allowing each of us draw our conclusions to what happened or what occurred.

Which I give to be almost as follows, in the caution to contain skin colour racism and all its worst connotations. For if the idea at its worst end to be skin colour racist is applied by either side even among groups of the same skin colour as mentioned. No lines can be drawn either way to curtail or change direction until one side in not capable to continue.

Not on a point plus basis, my call to allow competition racism, is a matter of diplomacy. Whereby as we know from within our collection of over two hundred flagged nations. Some people delight in their nationalism, which can be a very heavy burden if their fervour needs topping up from time to time.

Which can be taken on in full if we, they are included in an Olympic result readout, whether they were involved or not. Which for brevity can be measured on the number of Gold medal winners of all competitions only. Knowing I can make my case under those circumstances, I precede in general caution, so not to alarm people into claiming victimisation.

By being able and think species first, which is our common ground whether we like it or not. What then can we draw from the number of gold medals awarded to the winners of all the listed events we may have racially competed in.

Never to be an ailment, only a cure, but however we try to stack the pile to suit some of our old thought of issues about skin colour racism. None work on the flat dead thinking about superiority or skin colour superiority. But all count, for when we list the academy of winners, even nationally.

All to be found as the winner, is humanity; the black, brown, yellow and white skin coloured humanity. The intermixed skin coloured humanity, who first of all competed racially, in all the listed forms of sport organisations like our Olympic committee chose to offer us all so we could compete.

With no other objective, known of or not, understood or not. Of to bring all the nationals throughout the world together to honestly compete. To the best of the ability found within any national group. On the grounds of my national group is part of the international field of unity expressed on the fields of competition.

Which shows the limit of how racism must be carried from now on, on two main counts. One, its form is only to astatically please through competition. Two, that idea can help bury the unreal skin colour factor of how some people live by that code to be racist without now being able to support their theory.

Having nowhere else to turn when to realise the value of gold in so far as Olympic winners are concerned. When spread among the black, brown, white and yellow skin coloured winners. They are not even nationals of the Olympic kind, but in competition for their flags, which also have no racial connotations internationally.

Therefor when the last gold has been awarded, the final list of winners will be humanity. Shown in full skin colour spread to be read thus. We, I, me of my national team, by competing with any number of nationals in our sport range to win.

Shows but one result, humanity is the winner. For even though we are racially competitive when we do compete. Over time and in good order, measured four yearly by this competition or annually or two yearly in other sets of competing.

In every case, our gold medal winner is always humanity. For by a strange quirk of practically all forms of international competition. Not by scale, we do have the same range of winners always to be black, brown, white and yellow of skin, which we now recognise as humanity or the species humanity.

Without any form of impartiality, if the need was ever to test old forgotten theories about skin colour superiority. Though some can claim their skin colour tone, which incidentally wins more often at a particular sport. Therefore, that by result shows they/we are superior, why not.

Except factuality is not a case of proof, unless all the components are balanced in the correct order of delivery. All said about any group who excel at their sporting task, revolves around the overall excellence of the species humanity in all cases.

Whereby each skin colour group while operating in the only way we can. By continually improving our collective standards, share the honour to have been the only species to have drawn God's interest in the past. No matter were we to have been black, brown, yellow or white of skin.

Which was to compound the fact, God is and always was skin colour blind. For when he answered to the noises of query, he heard any time realistically over the past 60.000 years. He heard the sound of one species only, the only to sound in his direction, humanity.

Perhaps when he responded again over the past four or five thousand years to the same sounds in essence. He did not need to see who made them, because they had the same footprint than before in asking of how or why even what for?

Which unbeknown to us of humanity, was enough for God in all cases. For if he was to maintain his interest in us as he has. He already knew of our individual life span range in any case. But because we had stirred his interest time and again, he allowed the time for his wait and see idea/plan to kick in.

Which was a time slot to be spent to wait and see if when his plan was found. How could it be made work if the lifespan of any creature species extended from 24 hours in some ranges of the insect world. To thousands of years which spans all flora and fauna offerings so far, except perhaps humanity.

Who, although we are generationally thousands of years old. Our main point of interest is so up to date. To have drawn God's interest to us again for what we can offer in the present time of now while we live. Until "Natural Body Death from old age ", kicks in,

Which becomes God's own future, so that 13.8 billion years does not run out of expectation. A time slot never to run out of time now that we have set God's purpose to relish what he has achieved.

Which is the future. For in waiting for something to occur after all the mixing of what God particle conglomerates. By mixing with other God particle conglomerates, produced as far as they could in 13 billion years. Then to wait a further 800 million years of the same action but from then in creature species recognition.

All to do was guess how things could change so that Gods head could be turned enough now. So, his interest was not only what he heard in the past. But how he could manage the future now that we brought him here.

Though we quite naturally brought God to now. It will become interesting for us all, which is all of us. To be able and see if we did get it right by now setting God to control the future almost in the same way we controlled the past.

But now in his hands and with our help. All to do as far as we dare look, is hope when God takes the reins eventually the future and the past might blend magically. Led by how our young learnt from us, to be also able and better lead God in Heaven one and two.

So, their young, who will have learnt from them through us, to eventually set God in plan to only ever have to run heaven one. Because of how we future generationally, never gave up on God or the Concept of God.

SECTION 2 AFTERWORD

To have 'stood on the shoulders of God' has for me been a wonderful experience ongoing. Whereby I have been able and look into my own history. Which although hiding a few skeletons, has not brought me to fear what the future offers.

All I have learnt to expect, is at some time by how so ever. We, of humanity in the singular, of the plural, will be accountable for how we behaved in the past. Which is no form of threat. For that realisation to come, is out of our hands. But is not past.

All I would hope to do from now on is paint a canvas of humanity, worthy enough so none of us would need to worry about how we are depicted. Which is not to set a style of behaviour numerically listed, so we can compare our grades set from the wrong perspectives.

Which in all cases will be studied in the how and why any living or dead creature species type? Has been unable and conquer the one question of time always. What now?

Which has never been to bring us to God or he to us. All we would hope to achieve on a timeline basis. Is set a straight line from the year dot, to yesterday, thirteen point eight billion years later. Which must include the concept of God.

Which must be a scientific realisation. For right or wrong, science has given us a set of tables and graphs and rules translated into formula, ratios, data, and a huge collection of speculative exercises in theory. To follow, then to try and understand the un-understandable.

Which is not a condemnation, but an experiment in the real aim of what science was built for. To be a matter of our species concern of how we of humanity are the last first vestige of what time was to deliver in reality.

To be the only ever species so far, to attempt and give reason and cause to the matter of the fact of what the night sky is for? Which can only ever be answered one way, which is/was and always will be scientifically. Until science runs out of options, when to realise she in study can only take on what is before her.

Whereby a given number of elements under a given number of circumstances act or react together to give off a given number of results. Which by result allows we of humanity who so far have managed science as best we can. To now at last coexist with her in full harmony, on two counts twice.

One, to remind ourselves, science is only part of our study range among all other subjects. Two, we the full species humanity are the only catalyst who can continue science to aid us as she must. By giving her leeway to add, in this case, my suggested open bracket, question mark, close bracket, (?) symbol for God.

To be added post and pre suggestion, to all definable formula ratios of whatever type or name. Which when done over and above even my suggestion. Allows for us all to speculate about the God is factor and his application, rather than for any to deny the concept of God, if scientifically led.

Which in not only being negative but could be damaging to the future welfare of all peoples, who while waiting. Begin to realise the pointlessness of all subjects and topics also.

Which is never to be an end statement, except if we/they or anyone, becomes disposed to lose contact with the wonderful reality of life and living in the positive. We all can reach our dreams. Which we have already began to realise from what has been written within these pages. By yours truly, which is us, we of the one species humanity.

To spite what politics or religions, even the negative spontaneity of how science has recently presented her own case. None of us, even if we do not believe in God politics or religion. Can use that image to promote our case of existence or nonexistence. To be a standard for all, in that others should follow our lead.

Don't believe by any means if you wish. But be warned without threat or condemnation. Your standards are yours along with all other creature species who we know of not to believe in God or politics or religion even science. For they are they and we are of the species humanity.

Without claim or denial, all we can do while we live in our 80 plus year time span. Is to set the positive situation whereby. Because of the order of events historically and refreshed in this meagre work, which is ours.

Irrespective of what the future might bring in any context. Alas often wrongly presented by some of our ablest scientific community. Who when projecting it in formula or expectation, fail to include the existence of their own charter in the rollout, which is we from the same species humanity?

In such instances when some scientists who may talk or sign about how our sun or planets will eventually disintegrate. Do not seem to realise they are talking to an empty room. For when their projections are ripe about wherever. No lifeform would have existed for a long time past.

Not least because the circumstances for non-existence are so far into the future, they overstep all scientific rationale. So, in point of fact, science would have no audience or checkers of her almost ridiculous projections. Unless she in real reality when accepting my (?) symbol for God.

Wakes to realise, there will still be a future, no matter what happens in the universe by projection. Because God never let go of the reins when he adopted the species humanity to fill him in on what he should and could do next.

To keep the ball rolling, when he gave all the God particles, three dimensionally dispersed. In their lattice field formation, in the room/space already there to accommodate them, in the coldness and darkness of absolute zero, in the grip of static gravity, motion, what next.

What was and is never to be known until, is how any order of events from any deep and dark past, occurred until they did. Which was a recent discovery from about four or five thousand years ago. When we first lodged to be now civilised, which alas was a nonstarter.

For that name calls for us to be able and draw the same conclusions about each other almost the same, not ten thousand different versions of the same subject. Which draws the real picture we have always failed to be civilised and still.

Sadly, expressed by myself, even after I had set if by my Dublin City Accord (UN) (R) (P) recommendation. All persons under and in any religious or political group, could now expect "Natural Body Death from old age" as an equal standard. Set for us to have found the Eldorado of all future expectations with regard of what we could expect in life.

Further endorsed by the adage to cover each person, none of us should have been enslaved, tortured, abused, bullied, intimidated or worse, even murdered. In any way to compromise my new Dublin City Accord or rational, leading to human species conduct from now on.

Even under such a fine light, we have to concede for a short period of time, perhaps in one generation only. It might be, political murder, in the name of to defend or protect a nation states integrity. Events could still include the murder of human beings by human beings in the false name of political nationality only.

But from now on, circa now, human murder can never be given a name religiously not even as martyrdom or suicide in God's name to kill God's enemies. For if God said yea, it was not the God who set all the God particles with motion who spoke.

For when the one and only God gave mind to set motion to work. He knew not what for but was already ready to wait and see what could occur in any time frame. So, he could eventually measure the stature of what chemical element. Over and above the 118 he was already made aware of by the same mix of creature species elements who were to form in a later time scale as little as 800 million years ago.

Though known to be different than the general structure of galaxy in their known of composition of those 118 elements, more pending. When a newish creature species while in the normal processes of evolving.

Suddenly out evolved how all other creature species had been operating under the evolved lines of following instinct. Into a newish state of being able to rationalise their surroundings in a different way than what seemed to have been done before by any other creature species.

Only at last to be able and assemble their own data into the new element of thought. In seeming a magic invisible form of not new but spent energy. Like how a star sun might expend its energy in the form of to create light, which works on the scale of movement only. Is that another word for motion?

For which in scientific terms, some of us have been given to believe or set to follow in style. What we sometime see in the night sky is not always there. Because the light from a star or sun, which might have ceased to exist millions of years ago. Is what we see and not the object.

In otherwards, in some cases, perhaps all over the universe translated as billions of galaxies. Fingers of light are pointing directly at us, Earth, which are not. Which could only honestly represent past or burnt energy. Which means they are nothing or light dark matter. Which means they could be God particles in motion to either resettle as per or rekindle to form different configurations of new matter plus 118, adding something like thought patterns to any connection they eventually remade.

All of which is theory or the new science of theory to cover what we do not know but might if we guess right, except about God, who was spontaneous or is he. Which is not a fair question if we include people who do not believe in God. For their input to be bias at best, also has to be obstructive.

On the basis that if actions good or bad are operated in God's name, then to the non-believer in God. There is no good or no bad, where then can we draw a line in the sand for no view. If no opinion can be offered about who is to murder or why murder.

Which cannot be given in condemnation of those who do not believe in God because of how or why some political and or religious groups who pretend God. Have no clue as to why or how about anything. Except our impartial God is on their side at the same time.

Without pointing fingers, but in good cause for those of us who stood with God and now stand with God under all circumstances. Never point your/our/my accusation in the direction of any person offering no God. For who knows their circumstances. But be prepared to listen, for if to change their opinion because of our new perspectives.

They might be able and better lead us in how we should mediate politically so in fair time we might shorten the allocation of time we must allow for all to pledge not to kill other human beings.

Without imagination, but through our unique ability of thought, which had to be our only key to be able and name our separation from other creature species forms. When we came to the idea of at first the Great Spirit in form. We lit all the stars in the sky. For it was then or thereabouts. We set the future to be. Not for the longevity of stars, but ourselves.

Which was the key to how and why we had to rationalise the factor of God into the future. Because when we came to the Great Spirit in mind we then also thought about the, our future. Refining the process as we have, already stated.

But in line to allow our imaged God, feed his image of us, to carry on with him, perhaps until we can exchange contracts.

Which has always meant. God associated with us all by image of too be from the one species, the only able to have formed the opinion we/they had a future. Which is a new real state of how to accept God is deeply involved with us alone. But in the collective, for in order to protect God is right and has not been fooled.

He must use his own force of energy to hold in record how each member of the species humanity behaved by action or reaction while we all lived. Crucially within our own generational life span.

Even if for no other reasons than his own, for if wait and see was his plan, how else could it be met, except by now and except by us all of the same species. Each able and operate on the same plane as the one as the whole. But specifically tied to how God would have set his own plan if he knew how until we came along.

Being the only species able to set an account of why God was prepared to wait and still, until his needs were met. Whereby he could share our view of thousands of years of history into a single lifespan era lasting no more than 80 plus years. But now crucially shared with God on his time scale which stretches us all into the future while the present is still represented by our own young who only still have our results to go by.

All of which needs this one last liner to set all thoughts in comfort. God knows our past because it happened, remember. God on our behalf alone, he who has kept his own records of our actions, because he can. Is now the only force who can make sense of what and why history occurred, which is not a riddle?

But justification for how and why God will take humanity on in partnership, to run some of our ideas front line. Not least because in species terms we have almost out thought God in the vector of the future. By realising the future and the present are not concurrent but chaotic when to realise we have left it for God to chastise some of us in death, even "Natural Body Death from old age". When in theory we have no right of reply.

Never to have been realised by God yet. But when in view, all to be seen, is for those to have suffered at the hands of their fellow men while we lived. Will be able and transmit to God our need for him to set the record straight now in heaven one or heaven two by his own code. Set by our generational young under species tenure.

Who can show God how they wish to change the rules of what is done in any heaven because they have learnt the proper lessons of what it means to be species aware for the benefit of all. Not because we are in Gods eyes. But because we brought God to the reality of himself in the full image of humanity for both our sakes.

So, to stand on the shoulders of God.

SECTION
THREE (A)

OUR CONCLUSIONS POST 14/04/2022, REAL TIME.

T O HAVE STOOD ON GOD's shoulders at any time over the past four or five thousand years. Can only translate to have been a wonderful experience, especially if to have come to a conclusion, God Is, even not to be a marker for everybody.

Though to be a well dressed version of to assume, I got it right. While at the same time of throwing sand in the face of others, some of us might think to be less than we are. Which alas is more a fact of reality than to suppose we are a truly united species in the one name of humanity.

So, in turn, let us examine why and how we can think differently about each other than we did in the past, if to suit our own ends under changing circumstances we could do nothing about.

From which in these next few pages. Pre or post to be read before I reach my term of to die naturally from old age, un-appointed. Whenever and however that event occurs, which can include for me to die naturally medically also. Not as an alternative, but just in case any of us die medically, beyond our control or input.

Which can be answered by anybody including yours truly. Who take the time to write down our ideas or thoughts in such a way to be built upon? Against any arguments that may be entered against what we wrote by intention when we lived.

Being a means to set standards for everybody, so we can be on the same wavelength, whether we understand it or not. All of which now begins in the positive, when to realise, I like so many others in the true belief of God or not. Set my/our plan, in the plural of humanity and the singular of species.

Shown directly by how I represent all, by using the singular context of the liberty of the individual in its true plural form. Allowing without argument of how and why we should all think from now on in the plural of we in the representation of the singular me.

For which I now illuminate or have already done so in our/my representation of what must be introduced post haste on or to alleviate the many self-made problems we suffer under. By not following these my/our simple rules. Which again are set so not to draw any representative arguments from those who do not agree with me or human expansion in particular. When it only means we continue to progress.

I rate no special treatment except for the fact of my presentation about the matters of human harmony. So, in consequence, to bring us all online without having to sign in to open doors. In regular monotony I put these ideas before us all without offering solutions to my understanding of the mix I make about any situation.

If God or the belief in God has been matched in any other way, then let it speak. Which can only resound if what is said is relevant to or above what I have indicated in my previous utterings.

In other words, don't question me, but my/our general philosophy. Which as stated really means I need to be tested. So, without further ado, gather all of your objections and fire them at me in malice, in harmony, in love, in disgust and anger, in fear and trepidation. But always as if you said them.

For my one line of defence ever, was always and only, me speaking for we. Always to bring us more or less to the same conclusions. Not least by insisting to the effect we are the only species among all lifeforms able to draw conclusions about what the future might bring.

Not laid against how other creature species have shown us how they preform, for in many cases, their standards are met mostly by us of humanity guessing. But in one range we can be sure of. None have shown signs, if only by our terms of reference, to follow any type of our God theory understanding. Historically set in 10.000 different picture frames.

Which from now again, allows us of humanity to be the prime movers in setting what the future is for and can deliver on our say so. Almost scientifically proved over and over, other than by general scientific means. Which is a reminder science, and all her tentacles have a limited reach range.

Unlike how we of humanity far outreach her finished products. Often expressed by how we alone have already prepared a case to prove our unique approach to cope with the real future to be. Based on how we can unravel some of our own conduct of the past to be representative of how the future will pan out.

A very good new start point for us of humanity to gather about, can be read if we realise. We like science carry more tentacles about our person in full reference to our individuality. To be able and inter-mix our ability to be naturally different in ways other than to be skin colour different.

Which when further examined, no microscope needed. Will better reveal how and why we are the only species ever to come to the idea of God let alone the proof of God in being. Delivered by or from our present thought patterns only and now. Because now we know where to look for God as the full form of all accumulated knowledge and understanding ever to be.

But only ever led by us of humanity, because we are the only group lifeform to have been able and rationalise the difference between the chemical and emotional forms of matter.

Which will become clearer when we better realise the role our mixed emotional spread is capable to deliver to the human psyche. Which by reality can be set to cover the full range of what some of us imagine are the full range of human emotions in any case.

Even if to clear the matter of our skin colour, which has no bearing in any way whatsoever upon the excellence of the one species we are. Not set to defuse any highlights but taken to offer the obvious. Our multi skin coloured species is alone and separate to all other creature species. Set by terms we may not yet fully understand. When to consider how we differ in any case, but only to our advantage.

Which might be very big stumbling blocks if we let our own forces, such as events like liberal autocracy or human rights or religious tolerance be maintained as per, however. Even if to have been general guides originally.

Which like to believe in God or not, were, are standards taken on by the same people differently, then why and how. Unless we in open harmony realise, apart to the obvious, we as species are different. But this time viewed from different angles while trying to keep the same emphasis for all in standard.

Meaning we are all the same but different. Which for now and perhaps for evermore translates to read why and how are we the same species of 10.000 different religions. Of thousands of different languages, of hundreds of different political systems, different, even if skin colour doesn't count from now on in our different range category.

We are different without necessarily being diverse, which is a cultural ploy often misused to explain why we act differently over different subjects and topics. Not to have realised how and why we came to different conclusions about the same topis and subjects. Not because of their structure, but ours?

Not to be ambiguous, but in line with that words reference. We of humanity, even when to discount our skin colour reference to have no real bearing on who we are except species.

We should and must follow the expert leads we have often been given from some scientific studies about the/our human character traits. Whereby in general some studies have indicated we can differ by titled references other than by skin colour alone. Like in our general emotional makeup. Which is not definitive. But needs further studies.

If some studies imply, we in general can be slotted into carrying many different traits with or without emotional backup. Perhaps as many as 16 people classifications or more about the type of person we are supposed to be.

Although very complicated, but easy for some of us in the individual. Who can belong to any group class, either self-claimed or designated by others. Sometimes sympathetically, sometimes not. Sometimes legally or medically, sometimes wrongly.

Not by intention, but because when others are asked to choose our menu, how do they know what we like. Unless to force feed us with what they think is good for us. When the reality often is, our taste buds differ, not necessarily by skin colour.

Apart to the usual people classifications of to be black, brown, yellow or white of skin colour. To be right left or centre politically or to revere or determine for God religiously. We hold other different personality traits. Which is not to indicate we are species different, for in all cases, except the unimagined.

We of Homo sapiens stock, are the only species representatively to have aspired, in such a way or ways to have cofounded our previous 800 million years of existence in the genre creature species. Which also references us to be unique among how flora and fauna undetermined, were mixed up in God particle interaction into new product forms of matter.

Hence to become the one species humanity, albeit with about 16 plus different character traits undefinable. Which is to be perhaps the crowning glory for us all to be who we are without limit, embarrassment or fear.

Unfortunately, if and when some of us try to define other character traits, often of people we do not know. To be schizophrenic, or paranoid or dangerous, extending to be shy or dogmatic or to hold other labelled conditions. Perhaps to be a logician or carry OCD as a backdrop. To be autistic, hyper, even dead pan, which might mean to be uninvolved or uninterested.

As well as to be or classed to be or claimed to be Gay in any form of mix, male or female. To be gender inclined other than to appearances, whatever that means without fear or favour. But if a person feels not to belong which is a situation as wide as it is long. If to have been considered to be other than they feel. How might we right the wrongs of any consideration if they occurred.

So not to be blameworthy or to insult blame on any human classification by others or upon self. We can use the wisdom of youth to demolish or dismantle old prejudices, but we must have the grounds to do so. Which are sourced from the very people we are if we are brave enough to grab the wisdom of age genuinely.

Combined in the very real time of now, while we live and are alive in our 80 plus year lifespan of time shared generationally. By which when we review any situation, we can leave the damage the past already caused, behind.

Especially now when we introduce my/our Dublin City Accords of to introduce through the UN. Our best consideration of setting "The Rights of Humanity" in full replacement for old bad habits. Which cures her of using old tools to plough new ground.

By now thinking in the plural, we can better round all the corners left sharp because of our inability to pick the right options at the right time. Which is a needed reform because when we set the past it was by using past remedies which only prolonged the pain.

Not least because we counted history to be our guide to the future not to have realised, history was only the needed foundations of how to progress by learning from it. And not the usual of not repeating the same mistakes by using old historical documents per se.

Having now at last realised we have better futures to look forward to than to try and remake the past. We should begin to make progress by counting the next two or one conduct marker shared twice by our religions first and politics second.

Whereby if not through any Dublin City Accord, but other headings, still through the United Nations. When we introduce for the first time the concept, we of humanity person per person Can now expect to die only under the conditions of "Natural Body Death from old age".

Plus, never to have suffered the blemish of slavery, intimidation, torture, torment, bullying or murder or worse delivered from our own hand of humanity. Who's only real job is to get the combined force of humanity to a position to be able and face the future post our 80 plus year lifespan.

All of which can be better achieved when at last to consider the newly reviewed state of our actual species. Whereby it has been given we per the single group we are, hold so many real and assumed, what are sometimes considered to be mental states of mind. Like from/in my short list of a few pages ago.

All of which are almost meaningless if we do not try and look into why such an unqualified person like me, dare make the statements I do. Which from without foundation, are set from the basis none of us know as much as some of us think we know.

Which can become an almost settled matter if we openly view the abstract of imagination. To determine how and why we might have already mislabelled some of our character traits, like to be paranoid or of to be schizophrenic. Which I now tackle in heart honesty carried with full emotional ceremony.

We of humanity, in this case me alone so far, apart to my obvious acceptance of God if by my own understanding, which stands that God is. Almost a standoff declaration, but again without fear or favour.

In general terms without argument but able to be held under discussion later if necessary. As stated by me many times, we of the species humanity are almost over unique. For in definition knowing we are the only to have come to the idea of God and his role to our future prospects in all cases, is real reality.

Which are standards for every single person alive and living today, plus to include our ancestral connections going back at least four or five thousand years. Not because of what they thought they knew. But because they thought they had found God in form. And were capable to condition our living to Gods expectations.

Which was always better than science, because through following our God concept precept. We were able and associate with God in our own way. Even if slow to realise by then we were beginning to lose the God plot in any case. Not because of what we realised then ago when ago. But because of what we have now become.

Which is exactly the same as before, but more sophisticated. Because now we have begun to realise wrongly, God might not exist, which is or has been force fed to us all over the past hundred years and still. By being allowed individually, to practice our human rights as our human right. Along with to be able and operate our religious tolerance as we see fit or not. Which delivers self-choice by operating self-choice with unwritten clauses in between.

All of which leads to the urgent matter of realising why we seem to have changed in many cases our opinion of God, when in theory we are closer to God than ever before. Not least because now that we can rationalise these 80 plus years of life in the form of how we presently live. As the best time ever to self-satisfy we are right, in so far as we can make a case for God not because of who we are, but more so we can better guide further thought to be of relevance to time in all of its ages.

Which is not yet an open wound unless when we draw our 16 plus personalities together, so we are all pulling in the same direction. Which is never a blame clause, except when we forget to realise. Now that we are about to introduce my crude clause of recreating our old maxim of human rights and religious tolerance singularities.

Into the combined of, "The Rights of Humanity", plus to underpin that with the single expectation. Every single person can now expect to meet death through the offices of reaching "Natural Body Death from old age" as a determined right.

Which in consequence ad hoc, brings us or the one stock range of humanity, to be the same insofar as we feel comfortable with. But now by codes of conduct we each contribute to by no more than sharing our 80 plus year lifespan on the one plane.

If only we can try to remember, perhaps one of our own creations of thought we set up for God. In that if and when we look into the mirror of life at the reflection of a person some of us rate to be Gay or paranoid or schizophrenic. All we can see is we, in our form of to be the same skin colour blind species.

If and when we look into the mirror of life at the desperation of worry of fear of to carry OCD or of to be set in mind to hate as the bigot might. If to be autistic or said to be of any other description in how we classify each other. Irrespective of previous stated expectations about how we used to define each other.

From now on the reality of the little we have to realise about each other will be met only by accepting the importance of accepting natural body death from old age as our equal expectation. Which is not a political or religious assertion. What said in open honesty without ticking any boxes.

Is, if any of our classed or otherwise group named people, who fall in any category or title name other than to be of our common ground species format, like most of us if we are. Then our lot is the same in the name of our final expectation.

Which is not a takeover clause of any type of human conduct. What we are to do under my insistence is realise when we move to force human unity. We use the same rules for all even if sometimes we have to tread on toes too slow to take the hint. Even if to have complained our rules are not their rules.

Which is never negative, because in leaving an open door for all to choose or reject is not the same as allowing personal and or individual choice run its own course. Which at its peak might give the impression, we by classifying people to be of type? No matter in whatever category.

Is all we can do to force human harmony by using our wiles to set one standard for all, free of will, but under control by the very terms that suit all. Whether we like it or not. But always contained within the framework of "The rights of humanity" and to the open prospect of setting the one standard for all, of "Natural Body Death from old age".

Although one liners, by saying such, we are to commit in verse of mind first. What we intend is the best so far of what we must deliver to each other in the one band of humanity we are. In the one band of species, we are.

But always under review, for in many cases, we sometimes forget the obvious in that if we feel we are African, Asian, Australasian, European, North American or South American, we can commit to be different because we act and feel different. Which is never a slight because that is who we are now, or who we feel we are now. Which can now be bridged if through our United Nations, when it offers our plan already described of how we can best come to the real standard of setting our human future into the future.

Which needs, although I offer unqualified suggestions about how or why among other things. We of humanity might follow at least 16 or more personality traits. That clause needs to be re-stimulated in order so we can drop some of the dead prejudices many of us carry.

By at least to leave the open wound of what I now suggest fester. Until we learn to apply the right treatment for any ailments some of us might have formed or feel imprisoned in. Which again is no slight on any person or group but might be on the rest of us who have far too often, been led to criticise rather than praise. Then at other times we keep our big mouths shut, when we should have spoken up.

Which is not to understand why some of us are classed to be different, but to try and set the reason or cause in some cases of why we differ. Often set from circumstances none of us understand. But in far too many cases some of us judge under the muddled confusion we know, when in fact we don't.

But at least some of us try which is why I attempt to prolong our study of self. So, even if some of us do not follow my trend. It will be there from now on as a guide to our real future prospects in all cases. Relative to the deserve of the one species humanity. We who named the night sky.

SECTION THREE (B)

THE SILENT ENEMY

T O HAVE STOOD ON GOD'S shoulders even by imagination, can only bring comfort on the grounds in respect. Whoever does so in honest pursuit, we, in the plural, are at last not only thinking of self, but now together. For to be near the concept of God, even in spirit. Is almost the culmination of what any form of wait and see could deliver over any time period of from 80 plus years to 13.8 billion years?

So, have we yet done enough to set the core standards of what human harmony needs in order to be able and continue in trend to follow what the future is for? Which I see to be part solvable when we try and honestly group humanity to be God's mentor for a while at least.

Which as a task already undertaken, needs the dull corners to be sharpened by the collective of humanity in form, which means in our present form. Which needs the inclusion of all of us however classified by whomsoever.

In good or true human style, we often overemphasise some of our differences which allows for some of us to be able and display our celebrity status, with armband on, so we are noticed. When taken literally this can become an amusing anecdote. Giving comfort to many people who sometimes feel less in themselves. But can rely on the aspects or conduct of celebrity to be their stimulus on the grounds of "there but for fortune go I.

At best the real form of celebrity is a display of people who think they know more than they do or think they are worth more than they are on both levels. Which is a human condition of no danger, when most celebrities are the same class of people, we all are, except some have better PR.

On the or our defined count of some of us to be different if ranged that we have over 16 personality traits, which can include any celebrity group type. Among other things, they all now as before are set to include our new expected additions soon to be set by our United Nations. Whereby we all will be set never to kill of the species humanity or our fellow human beings.

Plus, in like form and of similar force, we are all to consider in the plural about any forms of collective decision making providing it/they do not contravene our new standard of agreeing never to kill one another for any reason or cause. Which will remain religious first and political obligations next as far as we can politically in these present times.

With that said, not for the first time and without the need to reclassify some of our personality traits. We must take a broad view as to how some of our slight anomalies were formed. But with no set intension, except to limit any forms of distrust or harm or bigotry or hate to be directed at some people who may not conform to the supposed grand ideals some of us profess to live by or did at least historically at first.

Although linked, but not joined. In the past, some of us in good intention set to rid our situation of the devilment of witchcraft or sorcery. By the murder of such people assumed to have practiced such methods of deceit. Generally, on religious grounds first, but often intermixed with some political sentiments. Which can only be used to time mark some of our reactions of before.

Now, but not in sync, we almost do the same when some of us classify those elected to or classified by others to be different than some of us when following their own circumstances. Which must become a part study from us all, so we do not make the same mistakes as before. Which are drawn from the ignorance of not knowing but pretending some of us do.

Which I class to be a false economy on the grounds we do not know what currency to use to set the one standard. unless we should all stand on God's shoulders. And use the currency of the future to bring us all in line. Whereby we can see the mistakes the past made, all on its own account.

Because we did not read the small print of attempting to understand, when we came to the proper idea of God. That was almost it, until we were capable and able enough to present a united front to God about why we were who we were. And how we are who we are under our own acceptances. Which were only part realised until we looked over our own shoulders to notice we were not alone.

For among us were our contemporise if in the name to be Gay or to be cross gender inclined. Which if these our group personalities had primary sexual inclinations set not to propagate. They in us were as us in all cases, even when to be considered in God's good future with us also. which is not a myth but a study in the wonder of humanity in all and in general.

Sexual orientation is a true life form on the human scale only. For in our all examples of it, we are still the only species to consider the future on our own account which offers no problem to God in any case. He will be pleased enough to high five all who knock at his door ready for heaven one already.

Because in being Gay or sexually orientated, providing the limits of conduct to be self-set. Do not compromise the standards of what the rights of humanity or acquiring natural body death from old age deliver in harmony, are set to represent. Which is a key of not to be called to heaven two, where things might prove to be different than considered. For here at these gates the fee will already have been paid by our conduct pre natural body death.

To be controversial, there are no standards to be set about the choice of to follow self-sexual orientation as a clause. Except maybe when to examine the same but different lines of how and why some of us fill other of our personality classifications, self-acclaimed or medically appointed or socially appointed.

Which now gives me cause to attempt with partial success of how the unqualified in me, can try to set standards of reason and cause to some of our supposed mental conditions. Which although not always seen in the past, were always there in any case. But were often contained by some of the acceptances at hand. Even not to understand their influence.

Having previously used the interpretation of how I see my term of Liberal Autocracy to have been spread heavy handed to cover up some mainly wrongly directed political decisions. Whereby they support without declaration, often set by hidden agenda nobody really understands.

On the same lines but under different headings. I now take on again my previous remarks about the effects of foot-printing or of being foot-printed unknowingly. Which by term means we almost follow any so footprints wherever left or found. Even if not directed at a particular individual, the effect of the exercise can have far reaching outcomes.

Not in specifics, but if the class of people in we, I am now in mention of, carry any of our human held personality traits. Like to be paranoid as a loose example or the almost twin of paranoia, anxiety. Plus, other semi, what may have been wrongly grouped to only belong to our assumed mental capabilities already set on the wrong scale.

In terms of any fear factors, we may induce about what the/my/our term of what foot-printing is compared to any idea of how we are influenced. Like from hereditary traits often unread. At least worse so in modern times, for in most present-day instances. We have over categorised the same people we always were/are, wrongly.

Apart to some obvious exchanges we hold about our skin colour collection, which is standard. About our religions the same, about our politics the same. We need to clear ground about how it has been assumed some of us in name to be classed so are different when now we all can be settled to follow the same standards set by our UN under honest direction.

My study of now about how we must reconsider for all the achieved stations of our character. Must be directed to the neutral ground of how we manage our emotions, perhaps against how other creature species had and do if on the same plane. Which again is highly controversial on the same levels every time.

But first we must come to the idea of being able and set our proper human standards by the true and open study of how some other creature species expressed their standards of to be civilised if comparable to us. But only from how I represent them in my own crude way.

Which is never to be a standard, because when I attempt to represent the whole range of other creature species. Against the single species of humanity. I as any other person, cannot speak for any by representation, only imagination.

The two or three examples from their world I can offer, are merely to show how we might differ emotionally. Without offering a points system or an order of merit about any. Number one, refers to some birth rite ceremonies.

Like for example, many to be classed as reptile, including some egg laying mammals. Might clamber onto a beach or at least near a river basin and lay their clutch of eggs. In some cases, to then abandon their effort to the wiles of nature. Or in other cases some parents might protect the clutch until the young hatch and can then be left in a place of comparative safety to fend for themselves. Where are emotions, what is civilisation.

Other egg layers mainly in the bird class. Seem to offer better prospects for their clutch or hatchlings. Most birds generally build a nest to share the responsibility of parenthood in order to tend their young.

Although in seeming to follow a definable trend of good parental care for their young. As if by an unseen hand, if food becomes scarce. By some force of nature, some in the nest, generally the first hatchling. Will take by demand all the food available.

Alas this sometimes means it forces its siblings to the extremity of the nest, which takes it out of line in the food chain of being fed. Unfortunately, the parent birds seem to only respond to the wishes of the primary, now dominant hatchling. Offering no signs of concern to the fate of the nestling they once carefully nurtured. Where are emotions, what is civilisation.

Among the range of many other creature species who swarm or hive or school in collection. With some not involved with the act of procreation, for they only have a monarch to reproduce their season.

As with some fish of the sea, who if almost by chance in passing, the male and female even if not to make contact. Allow for their plethora of eggs fall and mix with thousands of other roe clutches. For random males to fertilise the ocean of eggs deposited. Where are emotions, what is civilisation.

If the examples above are the result of as long as 800 million years of creature species development. We can draw the uncomplicated conclusion. Species per species over time, simply footprinted each other as per the needs and desires of any species. To literally form their conduct of today.

To know some creature species, have a higher rating of care to their young, better expressed in numbers through the mammal range of species. It is still fair to assume they too have been footprinted. But their footprint is closer to carry means of to be emotional if not to be civilised.

Another notice about some species from the higher rating groups. Is many in pack or from herd or flock or group, even singly in comparison to other singles of the same genre. Can carry their characteristics apart to the normal conduct of group.

Which again can be a form of foot-printing which mixes on the same scale to be almost hereditary. But does indicate other creature species development is not on the same scale as it had been for us, humanity.

For our lines of development, even if to consider we were a natural follow on to how other species groups formed from how God particles eventually mixed. Can only be now challenged based on what next. But led by us the very people who still are the only group who can visualise the construct of the universe, galaxy, our solar system, our planet Earth and all its occupants.

Which in essence is every different type of mixed flora and fauna creature. But now on a different scale of development than the chemical mixture there was and is. Still running concurrently, but now after the past 3 million years or more so the past 60.000 years.

Or more so, the past timeline of when we came to the idea of the Great spirit leading to our concepts of God and purpose and reason and because. Leading to our better questioning of why of how and what for.

Leading to the true value of humanity in our species form, who may not be able and breathe underwater, but can live there. Who may not be able and fly as the birds, but do, in that we own the sky, because we applied the mechanics of science to allow us to do so?

Who may not be able and exist in the nothingness of the area we call space all around us, but can, again because of our scientific progress? Which has allowed us to use all the elements always there, just laying around. To be picked up and assembled by the only creature species to be able and do such tasks if necessary.

But in doing so, apart to mounting arguments about our skin colour at first. Then our tribalism or clannishness, leading to later forms of religious and political nationalism. Cross mixing to be international.

We seem to have become less capable of how we must improve in producing forms of unity over and above of how we strive to be apart. Which again are almost better signs shown than how any other living creature species has played their hand against our four aces.

Which are the three above, underwater, air flight and space occupation. Plus, the fourth to be the depth of our human species development. Insofar, now we can recognise if by imagination at first, our positive link with God in all shades. Was mounted by us all in all cases.

Alas, too many of us, have been whimsical by assuming we the individual in whatever coat we wear. Can form our opinion to be enough for all or not, because some of us can still use our human right in the singular to counter other human rights in the singular.

Which, if the key, needs to be put together to fit the lock of our surety in being the only species to have named the universe. Which will be better understood when we now take the plunge and study in open generosity. My or any other offering about what can be meant, when we refer to or about the new idea of how foot-printing should be managed. But in these next cases as far as humanity is involved.

When ambiguity and abstract meet, it must be like the clash of the titans. But in our case, we are not in conflict, nor plan to be. What I hope to deliver without accusation but pointed. Is my story of how and why we might be more responsible for the happy condition of humanity now? Than we ever could have known of or understood before.

SECTION THREE (C)

THE PENULTIMATE CORNER

HEREDITARY TRAITS OR FOOT PRINTING, how stands the odds on what is right or correct about each part of the same equation. Which when now laid down will carry us all into the future with better convictions than we may have held in the past.

All I will do in these next few pages is lay down a plan that was never set or never even occurred. Because the players in we never realised what we had in hand after picking up what was laying around. Unless it offered some of us advantages over and above how we should use them instead of how we did use them.

Though at various times recently I had indicated we of humanity might share 16 or more personality traits. Some to have been hereditary, which must remain unspecific. For no other reason than to consider we do not know. But must proceed in any case so we can tick boxes that are not there.

Hereditary in term, almost means to follow, but. Under the complexities, particularly concerning we of humanity, that feature is deeper than dark, but remains indicative. Because of our uniqueness to be the only species to have concluded the future has prospects set from our discovery of God in being. Which is our collective heritage whether we understand that fact or not.

Insofar as we are given to differ in character, my assertion in most cases, highly unqualified. Is almost supported by how we can or have foot-printed some of our offspring. Who essentially in self maturity, help make the same people we all are in species. But rightly now, classed if by me alone to be the same single species we always developed from into. When carrying our unique emotional range ability. Far and above all other contemporary creature species.

Which even now cannot be called or classed to be a dull emotional range if set to be inclined to how some other creature species are classed, but never self-classified. For other creature species unlike us, have shown no real sign they can think in our range about God.

Which I make clearer when I assert, much of how and why we in our species humanity, display 16 or more personality traits, is owed to past referencing. Whereby we in our teaching or training or controlling or influencing roles of to be parents or grandparents or leaders or teachers.

Have so far been unqualified to pass on in subject form what should be the best way forward for our/their young or offspring or charges to proceed. So, in unreal consequence, such follow- on participants, like for instance our younger generations, have to cut their own ground.

Which if when done because the cap fits, some might eventually form to be classed to not only belong too, but come from one of our, who's classifications of to be different than the normal difference of being different. Like the rest of us.

How so, might spin on two axis, set in the cause and reason areas of our human imagination. But further split into categories of their own making.

Alas proud parents might lend a hand more than seen in my following analogy, not for being wrong, but unsure. For when they/ we compare our young and their growth or age progress with others parent efforts, in the nicest possible way. Even when in comparison with their siblings of one or more in the same family group.

We can sometimes imprint over and above hereditary influences, which translate to us, foot- printing our young without our knowledge or understanding of or their intake of what just happened or is happening.

Without blame to either faction for our parents or guardians are only following on from what they knew or learnt. Often without proper direction or guidance. Plus, on a bigger negative, we their young have no guidelines except our guile, is that enough?

Which leads to darker areas of what needs to be done to put the record straight. When if to consider, some in the guidance of how our young should be led. Might not always get it right, not because we are incapable. But because we might have been led into the wrong standards or understanding of what was before us.

Plus on positive negative lines, it could be, no person has yet fully picked up on how best to prepare our young for maturity. Because from both camps nobody has yet realised the nature of how different and the same our young are. Ranged from to be very young of infant stock to the late teens. And our parents, teachers and guardians, ranged from the late teens. Can take on the full meaning of any answer if it needs self-defining.

Not to be how and when some of us can understand what two plus two equals. But more in the lines of how and why God chose us above all other tribes. Be they black, brown, white or yellow of skin.

Which when taken in the broad, under whatever pretext, can mean no matter how much we try to bring our children in our young under our wing. By not setting the right parameters, by oversimplifying their role of to follow my lead, no matter.

Often without direction, where is it to come from in some cases. We the guardians of the future unbeknown and unintentionally. Almost allow our young self-footprint from the bits and bobs we left lying around. Because when we taught, we thought we got it right.

Whereas in bit part style of assuming we got it right. When we come to realise some of our young seemed to have different personality traits. We looked elsewhere to account for what many thought was out of their hands or influence or concern.

When the case could be they/we are right, but still not to understand. Some personality traits often shown at younger or middle young ages. Are the product of what was not relayed at the right time to our young at the right time of their/our development. Which is never a blame clause. Especially for our young.

Who without the proper information and feeds at crucial times of their development? Might have almost suffered devastating experiences without cause or explanation. Creating feelings in them of needing more understanding, if not attention, if not comfort, if not other types of acknowledgement. If only to fill or cover the vital time of support all young and siblings need at various times of our development ongoing.

Times we cannot count, for generation by generation. As we of humanity grow, we sometimes forget or leave behind the care values we all need about each other even our young and offspring. Not least because in the hurry up of today we lose focus.

Never to have realised and still. Some human young personality traits in some cases need longer and better nurturing and understanding than some of us afford our offspring. Which is never to be a slight on any of us involved. Parent, guardian, teacher or young alike.

Except some of our young who are blameless in all cases. For when their development is at hand under all the same conditions of how other, even creature species are sometimes nurtured or not.

Whereas if in the vast cases of how other creature species development evolved, whereby all were subject to the hard and fast of natural instinct. Which automatically bestowed hereditary and foot-printed traits on all charges following the status quo.

Except us of humanity, for although we accept hereditary continuance in any case. We became cross wired about how we expected our young to qualify in some cases better than we, because they were a chip of the same block.

Therefore, what was, was going to be. Which was aided by the misnomer of how we still projected our foot-printing on to our young. Almost in the old-fashioned class of assuming the outcome was automatically to be like father like son.

But what if the son, child, had already been battered by the indifference of being fed the wrong care or influence at the wrong time or in the wrong dosage. Plus, as a double negative, what if our young were also bamboozled by sibling or classmate or friend, even in jest. They were silly or slow or under performers. To what effect?

Then worse, even without malice, they were intoned to be skin coloured different or of a different nationality or religion or none. Which in context such headings at such times almost exclusively could be made apply to our young particularly.

Which as an event or events were/are real? So, what of the target, who by other direct focus was most likely to be left to deal with such situations unaided. Who without any realisation might have been ostracised by their thought of friends?

Yet were prone to carry on as normal, only this time for some of us/them. Who might have developed the shadow mentality of getting by under our own ability to cope in any case but if now tied to some habits?

Which aided us in our ability to fit in now to situations as per, of getting older. Where in time, we can contribute in better ways than we might have gone through of how we can reduce the need for the same form of humanity. To not need to fixate to have to carry 16 or more personality traits just so we could grow up safely.

Which is nice to consider, we too, in all guises, are responsible for setting the two main accords of "The Rights of Humanity" and "Natural Body Death from old age" as new starting points for our young at any age.

Allowing time for us to absorb what hereditary clauses and foot-printing meant, even if some of us in being young missed the bus. Simply because we were not aware or made aware at such times as we should have been. We will have to grow into our responsibilities set under the rules of conduct by our parents or guardians or teachers on their terms.

Which as stated could have led to the fact of the matter, modern verse. Instead of humanity congealing as we should have historically, we left the doors open not to. That is until modern times just like now. When our young in group can be better involved for in all the best examples of humanity, they along with us can join in the future projects of how we can better begin to value each other. Starting at the early end of our 80 plus year lifespan expectancy.

Not least because we will have a clearer view of how we can change without alteration when we introduce across the board, my/our concept of applying "The Rights of Humanity" to stand for the plural of humanity.

Plus, to have written in religious stones first, our resolve to expect human death only under the conditions or reaching "Natural

Body Death from old age". Then to apply, sooner rather than later, the same maxim to cover all aspects of all political rationales.

Which is set by the same standing for all persons, people of the same species genre humanity. To be able and follow the simplicity of the reasoning. We of humanity have been all charged to find God. Not for our sake but his.

So, at last God might be able and understand why he gave God particles motion. To wait and see what the time of waiting could deliver on perhaps two fronts. But before he knew.

One. Relates to all the time he already waited for, but with huge and immense results. For from now on in heaven one and two, with the only species group to be interesting enough to God for both our sakes. He can follow our leads.

Two. Along with us now in tow, his wait and see prospect has been given substance. For although God is. For the whole time in his waiting. He now can envisage as we can of the new and extended reactive interface of how God particle interaction has brought new reasoning into the new sphere of heaven one and two, which might yet reach to be heaven only.

But in who's hands, except good hands, including ours the at peace and calm form of humanity anew. We if to be the only living creature in obvious style who were, are, the only form of counted intelligence, within range and reason.

Able to realise, there is more to the event of time by the new simple act of to understand.

The past was the first platform any lifeform could have used to set a meaning for the future.

Whether that was realised when to settle for procreation, we may never know. Whether to realise there was an open lead to the future. When we historically came to our understanding of God. Only now to be aware. It is from within our 80 plus year lifespan only. The real knowledge and understanding of the factor God is, can be made clear.

For now, we have realised, science is limited but the future is not. But in order not to undo such realisations. We must set to rationalise the importance of to follow our joined-up study of the future, can only now be set from within our 80 plus year lifespan and with our young.

So, is to stand on the shoulders of God in sincerity, humility and acclamation.

MY LEAD TO REVILATIONS

S UCH BOOKS LIKE THIS HAVE no real ending. For they are set in the future, even beyond the reaches of how some of us have travelled that road before.

Like if to have imagined in the past some of the real things to have occurred since they were offered as stories of fantasy. Space travel, or the ability to live under the sea or survive in the extremity of temperature zones. Either hear on Earth or in the far reaches of our own imaginations.

By the strangest of real fact. There is no other way than to envisage what the future might be or deliver. Except than to commit the human imagination to the task. Not least because we named the universe and gave it cause. For there it is in our night sky.

So not to disadvantage ourselves in any way, even imagined, even in counter to works such as this. Which have been liberal beyond intention. Not least to try and set the same result standard for all people.

When I have tried to make a better case for God, not particularly to always be on his side. Because that is not the real meaning of liberalism. So, in consequence and without tariff, by always offering the alternative of God or not. Was not generous on my part, when remembering my standard is, God is, in all cases.

Therefore, to cut to the quick. Even so for me to have always indicated to all people our mentor of free choice. Which is also wrapped up in the mire of liberalism applying to the individual on equal terms to all, except so, in full balance to much of my stand pro God. I offer all the anti-brigade without any classification, to convince me of their standard. Which for them is a lost cause for as far as I am concerned, I am a bigot about the reality of God.

Practically in all cases of opposition to God, most main arguments centre on the opinion of. When we die, we die. Which automatically exclude the other main opinion like mine of. When we die, we will then be open to God's judgement of us while we lived. How weird is that.

Except when to have realised, when we did live even as of today. We in our single species form at whatever level of maturity or age development. Have far outperformed all other lifeforms, even in the universe. How double weird is that.

Except when to have realised, our human minds in creature species terms, are so big and powerful relative to any other matter configuration. Not least because we so far, circa 2022. Are the only species to have filled the vast expanse of time owed to the universe.

In such a way to be now able and follow by our discovery of cause, of reason, of purpose, even how before the why. Our universe is as it is mechanically. Until two things happened without rhyme or reason.

One was to the matter of how matter got the idea of motion. Two was to how and why a new form of interactive matter in the different name of creature species, evolved separate to the standard of how galaxy formed.

Plus, in being able to extend their creature species capabilities, if in part by still evolving as per. Until perhaps a tangible break from all forms of previous methods to evolve were side stepped. Leaving open ground to be discovered of how the big picture was set and under who's terms.

Which could/can only ever be worked on, if and when any life form above the mechanics of when element and or elementary mixing was spent. But had left a trail of invisible vapour as a sign something else was afoot, but how or what.

Then leaving the ground clear, but unseen. Which is why humanity in we, picked up the remnants of the ten thousand world religions we found laying around. Which were exclusive to how we had developed to have different needs than other creature species.

Who had settled in seeming to only want to propagate as their only task and need?

Whereas yours truly, beyond invention. Knew, felt, even began to think there is more to the night sky than it being a pretty picture. Which at first was very hard to come by how to figure the whole story. Not least because at about the same time in years ago, our scientific awareness began to grow.

Reaching an apex about 100 short years ago. When science dressed in her Sunday best, began to give cause. She, more exclusive than the theory of our attempted understanding of God. Which was tangible, until she as a topic subject. Shot herself in the foot by assuming she had no cause of herself, except to have been spontaneous.

Unfortunately resetting the mould of how religions should be perceived. Not least because by speaking out of turn and to have been a figment of any imagination pre imagination. That consideration was the first nail in the coffin lid of many religions.

Some of which took up the challenge of to force endorse God's majesty. By allowing the encouragement of some pious religious members. Kill other religious brethren who were not deemed to be God worthy by the normal human standards of serving God religiously.

Never to have realised and still. The politics of life is not run for the benefit of our opinion, whomsoever. But God, our appointed medium of how we will eventually be able and follow his plan set by us.

For when God set God particles with motion, he forgot to fit them with sat nav capabilities. Only to wait and see what would happen or occur in his near future. Which it did over the past three million or more so the past two hundred and fifty thousand years. Or more so over the past sixty thousand years.

Then in reality, these past four or five thousand years, when we set God in his real domain of knowing all things. But in sequence to how we have learnt spiritually over the mundane of what science and other mediums can offer.

For their capabilities are limited, as per how when a given number of mixes are made between a given number of objects. A given number of results will be given.

Which almost allows my last page to be turned. Insofar as a single representative of the single, as it will be. Skin coloured blind mass of the one human species, who give substance to the matter of the universe. So, we can be led into the future proper which is not an ending.

MY BOOK OF REVILATIONS

WITHOUT FORM, FEAR OR FAVOUR, all to do now at any level, is set this part of my thesis to become a standard realisation of what the future will bring or is intended for.

I in we do not have to lay down any topical experimental format to achieve at first my then our ends. For the future is untenable, unless we are able, and rubber stamp its very existence. Which can be forced on the very real grounds of what happened yesterday.

Being a story told many times but often in the wrong context. Simply because some of us are too pedantic about how we should measure the length of a piece of string in inches or centimetres. When in fact all lengths of string are in length from end to end.

Never to close doors by the insult of not listening. But in small cases, we must at last set the plan of the future to involve all of humanity. For no other reason than we can envisage it as a form of time in general, but relative to us exclusively because we are the species humanity. Even when to carry 16 or more highly defined personality traits.

We on the same terms, are the only lifeform breed worthy and able to have forecast the future so far. Which is, we have one.

Although found under the very complicated investigation about how the future can be maintained other than by formula projections. When we rounded on the idea of God, we got it near right, except to realise it is down to us to end God's story in continuance.

Which can only ever be done in the reality of what we have designed to be Heaven or paradise. Which as a reality clause, we can now come to call the future to belong in Heaven one or Heaven two.

Not now or ever to have been hell, the assumed place of retribution for all wrong doers. For in that adoption, at the same time of accepting God, we denied him.

Nor so to be a place called paradise. For in essence that offering could mislead on the pretext we would be selected to go there or end up there on God's say so. Because we followed God's direction as told by others not to be God but claimed representatives.

Therefore, as paradise could be usurped, I find the need to reinstate it to be heaven in all future cases. Which as a condemnation has no bearing, for in my case I set the one decision of who goes to heaven, plus now heaven two also. To be a matter of God's discretion in all of our futures.

Which is a reminder from within our 80 plus year lifespan ongoing, we are and will always be mixed generationally. So not to down grade or disrespect our younger following generations. Our instructions to God in good faith for when we die our "Natural Body Death from old age". Is to deal with us as we now are.

Never to reveal our fate to our up-and-coming younger generations, for we all know the consequence of that. Which would be to destroy their ability to further create our human species status of holding God's interest. Not for what we assume, but for what we are prepared to forgo so God has his own opportunity to eventually call time when he is satisfied all his criteria of clean time have been met, if on that basis and not much more perhaps. What I give to the idea of the future, which was set by the one species humanity. Plus, to incorporate the fact of our future generations in being, are better placed than we ever were. To set an understanding between God and us whereby we all might join in harmony.

Because it is/was only we of humanity who were able to set by our understanding for God's sake. Of how and where he can deal with us while at the same time ongoing, be interested in what our next generations will or can deliver about the future as it gets closer.

Not that we have to prove anything to God. But in the name of scepticism. I now offer this fable of when we die and go to heaven in all cases. Not least to quell the alarm of what losing the concept of hell might be.

We are not alone, irrespective of how we feel even if to have been cursed or blessed with one or other of our human personality traits. For when God first showed interest in us which could have been as far back as when we first came to our Great Spirit imaginings. He then had more to work with than before. But still lacked guidance.

Which over time could only manifest from the plural of humanity, who in time managed to congeal to be the singular form of presenting one face intermixed with different personalities. Which leave no trails as to who what or why? Except to cause us doubt, which had to be passed on to God on our terms.

Which is why God had to take an interest in us individually. One, because he was capable. Two, for good record keeping in any case. From which standards could be set in scale to compare what might impair our human ability to progressively progress.

Although God was always in full power. He only ever could release his ability to exercise that phenomenon when items of interest were before him. Which is almost the human story in full.

Therefore, in real time, but in God's domain of heaven one and two. Encased in the true reality of moral fortitude human style. Our intention of to steer God to pass our judgement on some of our compatriots who fell to be in cruelty, intimidation or murder or worse. Under our direction if led by our emotional range, must be a let.

For if we condemn those who claim they can kill in God's name. We cannot expect God to deliver retribution or punishment in our name. which is not a let. For we are the one people, even in 16 or more personality guises. Who came to set God free one way or another?

Providing he followed a standard found suitable for him, so the time mark was not wasted but met. By whomsoever, whensoever. But now run on such lines so not to compromise any plan we might have devised to promote the excellence of progressive human harmony.

Set to allow our up and coming young to be able and fix God's future plan, inclusive of when they arrive. So, their next generation has less to deliver to God when they arrive.

Perhaps to eventually blow the gates of heaven off their hinges and allow all comers entry, for who will have anything to hide in the hope of the future among heaven one and heaven two, with God our host.

www.ingramcontent.com/pod-product-compliance
Lightning Source LLC
Chambersburg PA
CBHW021609120626
46545CB00001B/146